£6-50

D1135604

is to see that we grow
Nearer the sky.

—*Lizette Woodworth Reese*

A POUND OF PAPER

A POUND OF PAPER
CONFESSIONS OF A BOOK ADDICT

John Baxter

TED SMART

TRANSWORLD PUBLISHERS
61-63 Uxbridge Road, London W5 5SA
a division of The Random House Group Ltd

RANDOM HOUSE AUSTRALIA (PTY) LTD
20 Alfred Street, Milsons Point, Sydney
New South Wales 2061, Australia

RANDOM HOUSE NEW ZEALAND LTD
18 Poland Road, Glenfield, Auckland 10, New Zealand

RANDOM HOUSE SOUTH AFRICA (PTY) LTD
Endulini, 5a Jubilee Road, Parktown 2193, South Africa

Published 2002 by Doubleday
a division of Transworld Publishers

A catalogue record for this book is available from the British Library.
ISBN 0385 603681

Typeset in 12/14pt Granjon by
Falcon Oast Graphic Art Ltd.

Printed in Great Britain by
Clays Ltd, Bungay, Suffolk

3 5 7 9 10 8 6 4

For Martin Stone, without whom . . .

CONTENTS

'Outside a dog, a book is a man's best friend.
Inside a dog, it's too dark to read.'

Groucho Marx

PART ONE

PART ONE

CHAPTER ONE

Collecting Graham

The value of a collection to the collector lies less in its
importance, surely, than in the excitement of the hunt, and the
strange places to which the hunt sometimes leads.

Graham Greene, in his introduction to With All Faults *by David Low*

IN 1951, ROBERT BLOCH, NOT YET THE AUTHOR OF
Psycho, published a short story in the pulp magazine
Famous Fantastic Mysteries called 'The Man Who
Collected Poe'. In a pastiche of Poe's own doom-laden
style, it tells of an enthusiast for the author of 'The
Raven' and 'The Pit and the Pendulum' who meets a
fellow fanatic, Launcelot Canning, and is invited to
a lonely Maryland estate.

Canning's collection dazzles the narrator. 'Copies
of the *Philadelphia Saturday Courier* during the period

3

of Poe's editorship, *Graham's Magazine*, editions of the *New York Sun* and the *Evening Mirror* boasting, respectively, 'The Balloon Hoax' and 'The Raven', and files of *The Gentleman's Magazine*. Lee and Blanchard's edition of *Tales of the Grotesque and Arabesque, The Conchologist's First Book*, the Putnam *Eureka*, and finally the little paper booklet, published in 1843 and sold for twelve and a half cents, entitled *The Prose Romances of Edgar A. Poe*: an insignificant trifle containing two tales which is valued by present-day collectors at fifty thousand dollars.'*

More garrulous with a bottle of wine inside him, Canning displays further treasures: unknown and unpublished horror stories such as 'The Worm of Midnight' and 'The Crypt'; and 'The Narrative of A. Gordon Pym', thought to have been left unfinished at Poe's death. Many other writers had taken it upon themselves to complete this story, but Canning's version is in Poe's own distinctive hand, and accompanied, what's more, by a sequel, 'The Further Adventures of A. Gordon Pym'.

Then Canning reveals the secret – he has managed to raise the writer from the dead, and put him to work in his cellar, churning out new creations. He has literally collected Poe.

There is a germ of truth in Bloch's conceit. Collecting

* For today's price, just add another zero, or perhaps two.

a writer's work is a way of owning the artist you admire, and each step in the collection of a title takes you closer to the author. First a copy of the book, perhaps a paperback, just to read. Then, once you decide you like it, a more durable edition. After that, the first edition, followed by a first with the author's signature. Then the proof copy, which precedes the first printing. Then the manuscript. But after that? Bloch exaggerates when he has Canning crow of 'the end-all and the be-all of my planning, of my studies, of my work, of my life! To raise, by sorcery, the veritable spirit of Edgar Poe from the grave – reclothed and animate in flesh.' But to meet the writer, to sit down with him and talk about his work: that surely is within one's grasp.

Let me tell you about me and Graham Greene . . .

I caught the Graham Greene bug in the winter of 1978, when I lived in north London. In those days, I ritually cruised the weekly flea market at Swiss Cottage which materialized every Saturday morning on a triangle of hard-stamped ground behind Basil Spence's abattoir-like sports complex.

That morning, someone new had erected a couple of trestle tables and was selling books. A pale, crushed-looking young woman sat behind the tables, well wrapped up against the insistent wind and the damp chill that, if you stood still long enough, would numb you to the knees.

The stock looked a cut above standard market fare, but since one most often found the bargains with those amateurs who, like unseasonal picnickers, had spread their blankets on the sodden ground and scattered them with their gleanings from jumble sales and charity shops, I headed for them first. The books on the tables could wait.

Almost immediately I struck it lucky: a copy of Greene's children's book *The Little Horse Bus*. Tossed in a basket of exhausted felt animals, it was mine for five pence. It was illustrated by Dorothy Craigie; not very *well* illustrated, but Craigie, as I later discovered, was another of Greene's mistresses, so he made allowances. Once the relationship ended, he let the more talented Edward Ardizzone illustrate not only this book but his other two stories for children.

Carrying my find, I headed for the trestle tables, where the woman had been joined by a very thin man in a black beret who had the air of a minor-league pickpocket.

I reached for a book I'd noticed earlier, a collection of pieces about Edwardian writers, illustrated with murky sepia photos by E. O. Hoppé. Fumbling for money, I put *The Little Horse Bus* on the table. The man's eyes assumed a sleepy expression I came to know well. He tilted his head like an inquisitive bird.

'D'you mind?' He held out a skinny and trembling hand; between two stained fingers a mangled fag guttered in the moist morning air.

'I just found it,' I said, nodding behind me. 'Over there.'

'Want to sell it?'

I didn't even need to think. 'Not really.'

It was a defining moment. A dealer mostly meets people who want to sell him books, when his most pressing need is for people who want to buy. In two words, I had ranked myself with the buyers, and the man in the beret wasn't slow to recognize the fact.

Darting along the lines of spine-upwards books, he grabbed a couple and laid them in front of me. One was the first British edition of *Our Man in Havana*, my favourite among Greene's newer novels. The other, in plain brown boards, I hadn't seen before, though I got to know it well as *In Search of a Character: Two African Journals*, an uncommon item that reprinted passages from the diary Greene kept in a Congo leprosarium while researching *A Burnt-Out Case*.*

'Five pounds each,' the man in the beret said.

I looked down at the three books. It took little

---

* Years later, Philippe Lechat, the hospital director to whom Greene dedicated the novel, confided to me that he and Greene rewrote some of the journal to save the face of a local bureaucrat and protect the hospital's funding.

imagination to visualize them next to my copies of Greene's more recent novels. In an instant, an accumulation became a collection, and my life would never be quite the same.

Chatting with the man later, while his friend piled the unsold books into a succession of battered suitcases and staggered with them to the tube station, I had no idea I was in the presence of a legend.

Martin Stone is one of those people who found in bookselling the same spacious environment and unfettered morality that drew loners to the American west at the start of the nineteenth century. Not for him the formalities that define our lives. At various times cokehead, pothead, alcoholic, resident of a Muslim enclave, international fugitive from justice, and a professional rock musician rated by historian Brian Hinton as 'one of the two great guitarists of the era' who 'makes Clapton look boring and provincial', he has never owned a house or learned to drive, hates bank accounts, won't write letters, and scorns computers. He did get married twice – once to Ruth, the woman behind the table, with whom he would even produce a daughter – but family life was not for him. His past is littered with abandoned, but still – generally – affectionate ex-partners, most of them even now hoarding a carton or ten of his books in their basements.

Martin became, and has remained, my mentor,

teacher and friend, but as he wandered off into that Saturday lunchtime crowd, at peace with the world, to join Ruth at the tube station, perspiring next to her Globite Stonehenge, he was, to me, just a peculiar bloke who knew a lot about books. Maybe I'd run into him again but, as a collector, I thought of myself as being out on my own.

I could not have been more wrong.

In his second volume of autobiography, *Ways of Escape*, Graham Greene recalled lounging in a Saigon opium den named Chez Pola in 1955. Noticing a shelf of books beside the bed and taking one down, he discovered that he'd written it. 'It was odd,' he mused, 'to find two of my own novels in a *fumerie* – *Le Ministère de la Peur* and *Rocher de Brighton*. I wrote a *dédicace* in each of them.'

Reading this, most collectors of Greene probably felt, as I did, a quickening of the pulse. Imagine finding those books. Imagine *owning* them. But the thrill didn't last. This had been twenty-five years before, after all. And the big Greene collectors would already have scoured Saigon, ferreted out whatever books he left behind, and carried them back to the climate-controlled Armed Response-guarded Floridian or Bahamian bunkers that housed their treasures.

All this was assuming the story was true, and not

another of the fables created by Greene for the benefit of those of us who so loyally and . . . all right, *fanatically* collected his books.

Because, make no mistake, it was personal between us and Greene. A lifelong collector himself, he knew what made us tick. In their teens, he and his brother Hugh had put together a major library of Victorian detective fiction, from which, in the Seventies, Hugh, by then director-general of the BBC, compiled a couple of anthologies and a successful TV series under the title *The Rivals of Sherlock Holmes*.

Greene continued to collect until his death in 1991, even when his world had contracted to an apartment just off the waterfront in Antibes. Clearing the place, his nephew and literary executor Nick Dennys, himself a book dealer, found rare Henry James first editions, a major collection of Ezra Pound, and almost every book Evelyn Waugh ever wrote, each with a long and affectionate inscription. Not to mention numerous less significant books of which Greene had recorded his opinions in meticulous and often sarcastic marginalia. Rumours that Nick was to sell the collection through his South Kensington shop enormously increased his popularity for a while, but finally Boston College swallowed the library whole.

One can imagine Greene's relish at our collective disappointment. Though, more than many writers, he understood and tolerated collectors, this didn't mean he liked us, or gave us much help. You'd never find him behind a table at Hatchard's in Piccadilly, adding that minute, spidery signature to hundreds of copies of his latest work. Nor did he respond to letters begging him to sign one or more of his books – always supposing these requests reached him, since his whereabouts in those days were obscure.

One was aware that he occasionally visited London. It became a standing joke – behind the counter of Any Amount of Books in Charing Cross Road, someone stuck his picture clipped from a newspaper, and scrawled under it: 'Give this man a discount'. But who, spotting him wandering around his old stamping grounds of St James's and St Martin's Lane, would have been lucky enough to have one of his books to hand? Or, even having the book, would be brave enough to sidle up to him and, clearing his throat, murmur diffidently, 'Er, Mr Greene, I wonder if you . . .'?

There were legends, naturally. They usually involved – and this alone made them dubious – some timid kid, or, occasionally, a barber or shop assistant, who proffered his Penguin reprint of *The Third Man* and scored a long and informative inscription. Unfortunately these stories were near enough to Greene's ways of behaviour to be credible. Maybe he didn't do signing sessions but he *did* sign books for all sorts of people, and in all sorts of places – that Saigon

11

fumerie, for instance, but also for friends, or the children of friends, and occasionally for charity. One *never knew* . . . and that, of course, was the fun of the game.

If you could call it a game, that is, when the items you hunted were worth hundreds, sometimes thousands, of pounds on the open market, and acquiring them meant midnight assignations in seedy corners of London, white-knuckle bidding at auctions, speculative drives across England to cities you'd never seen, and nervous knocking on the doors of strangers that, in all probability, would leave you, a minute later, humiliated and empty-handed on the doorstep a hundred miles from home.

But at such moments you might look up and, at the end of that grey street, see a tall, stooped figure just disappearing round the corner, perhaps even glimpse the half-smile on that creased face. *You bastard, Greene*, you would think, before returning to the hunt in which he was the most dangerous quarry of all.

I once asked film director Josef von Sternberg, Svengali of Marlene Dietrich and creator of *Shanghai Express* and *The Blue Angel*, whether he had a hobby.

'Yes,' grated the toneless voice, which still retained a whiff of the Vienna of Mahler and Freud. 'Chinese philately.'

It wasn't what I expected to hear. 'Why that?'

'I wanted a subject I could not exhaust.'

No collector could ask for a less exhaustible subject than Graham Greene. For a start, there was the sheer quantity of his output. In fifty years of writing, beginning with the traditional Slim Volume of Verse, in his case called *Babbling April*, published in 1925, he'd never put out less than one new book a year.

Unlike most writers, however, he hadn't confined himself to regular publishers. He wrote an introduction to the memoirs of a Cambodian warlord which appeared only in a tiny printing from a soon-defunct press in Vientiane, and another for *With All Faults*, the reminiscences of London book dealer David Low, published in Tehran. He contributed a preface to a cookbook of supposedly aphrodisiac recipes assembled on Capri by his old crony, the novelist Norman Douglas. Ten years later, Australian restaurateur Gai Bilson would trade me dinner for four at her Berowra Waters Inn, then the most exclusive and expensive eatery south of the equator, for a first edition of *Venus in the Kitchen*. As we ate goose neck stuffed with forcemeat and pig's ear with *sauce ravigote*, a party of six who had arrived by private seaplane without reservations was turned away at the dock – a sight from which Greene would have derived as much malicious enjoyment as we did.

Most Christmases, Greene's intimates received a

little booklet containing a chapter from his next novel, illustrated with the delicate sketches of Edward Ardizzone. Produced in printings of two hundred at most, these were always personally inscribed, and none was ever for sale. Then there were the simple obscurities, like books where the true first edition was not the British or American printing but the German, French, or even Swedish. And always under a different title, of course.

Since Greene kept both a *pied-à-terre* and a mistress in Paris, it wasn't surprising that some of these rarities emerged from his French publisher, Robert Laffont, himself not above playing games with the literary establishment. In the Sixties he established the Laffont Prize for Literature, the first recipient of which was his old friend Greene. Laffont had an enormous cake prepared, opened a few dozen bottles of Laurent-Perrier champagne and toasted Greene at a press reception. Greene accepted the medal, after which Laffont retired the award; it was never presented again.

Nor was signing his books the extent of Greene's involvement in the game. So much did he loathe *Babbling April* that he told people he bought up any copies that appeared on the market and burned them. If true, this was extraordinary, since the printing was tiny, probably no more than three hundred, and copies, when they appeared at all, sold for a fortune.* The rumour, true or not, turned the search for this flimsy book from a matter of acquisition to one of preservation.

Preservation also came into the collecting of even his famous works. Greene had gone from obscurity with *The Man Within*, *It's a Battlefield* and *Rumour at Nightfall* to best-sellerdom with *Stamboul Train*, *A Gun for Sale* and *The Confidential Agent*. As a result, his earliest books appeared in tiny printings while the later ones almost instantly went into second and later impressions. This made first editions of both almost equally rare.

But the fact that many of his novels appeared during the Second World War, under paper rationing, made them even rarer. Fragile objects on grey stock only one step up from newsprint, with wrappers that dissolved in your hands as if not made of paper at all but a sort of compressed dust, the books that did get published, and weren't subsequently destroyed when the Luftwaffe levelled the warehouses, had a shelf life measurable in weeks. Worse, from the collector's point of view, many found their way into circulating libraries like the one run, improbably, by Boots the chemists. Boots rebound all its books, gummed their shield-shaped label on the front and, in all but a few cases, threw the wrappers

* The going rate in 2002 is £3,250.

away. Serious collectors woke up in a cold sweat just *thinking* about that.

By the Sixties, a copy of *Brighton Rock* even without its wrapper was worth about £500 but with the wrapper more like £2,000 – if you could find one.* *Brighton Rock* was a high-point, but first editions of other early Greene books weren't much less valuable. And then there were signed copies, or those foreign printings, and the books for which Greene had written introductions, or contributed an essay. Not to mention a few limited editions, numbered and signed, or those Christmas booklets . . .

Oh yes, it was a lot of fun.

* It costs a little more today. The last copy with a perfect wrapper changed hands at £50,000.

CHAPTER TWO

Left-handed Guns

Corso was a mercenary of the book world, hunting down
books for other people. That meant talking fast and getting his
hands dirty.

Arturo Pérez-Reverte, The Dumas Club

UNTIL THE MID-NINETEENTH CENTURY, ONLY RICH
individuals and institutions collected books. Value lay
not in how they looked but in the information they
contained; a second edition, updated and corrected,
was normally worth more than the first, and when
owners annotated books, corrected errors in the
margin, or added new information, it increased
rather than diminished the value. Some books were
intended to be added to. British publisher James
Granger's 1769 *Biographical History of England*
contained blank leaves for owners to paste their own

illustrations – an encouragement to break up valuable antique histories for the engravings. The practice of slipping clippings and letters into books is still known as 'Grangerizing'.

By the 1880s, however, books had become cheaper and widely available. The 'personal library' evolved into a collection. And collectors of books, like those of stamps, coins or engravings, valued items according to condition and uniqueness, not content. Mostly, they wanted first or limited editions, and in the most pristine state possible.

For many bibliophiles, this was the golden age of collecting, but by World War II it had run its course. Authors like John Galsworthy, Arnold Bennett and Somerset Maugham, whose first editions had traded in the hundreds of pounds, were now unsaleable. The bottom had fallen out of the market in sets of collected works, often issued in high-priced bindings, with one or more volumes signed by the author.

By the early Seventies, anyone asked to evoke a second-hand bookshop would have described a musty establishment on a back street ruled by a Dickensian curmudgeon in a moth-eaten cardigan who snorted snuff and mumbled to himself. The books he sold, bound uniformly in brown leather, were obviously destined for some oak-panelled library. And almost certainly he had something to hide.

Second-hand bookshops became a thriller cliché. Dusty, ill-lit premises, open at odd hours and run by eccentrics – what better front for a spy ring?* Graham Greene put into the mouth of the ageing Soho bookseller and traitor of his novel *The Human Factor* all the prejudices of someone who recognizes he's part of a dying breed. Overcome with nostalgia, the shopkeeper reminisces about the days when people would queue to buy the latest Penguin classic reissue the day it came out. Greene's hero, a mole in the British secret service, uses a code based on just such antique novels, like *Clarissa Harlowe*, to communicate with his KGB 'minder'.

And yet, by the late Sixties, book collecting had transformed itself from the obscure pursuit of a few ageing specialists to the hobby of rock stars, movie actors and best-selling authors who casually wrote cheques for thousands of pounds for books that once cost a few pence.

Why the change? Wealth came into it, obviously. The new élite had money to spend, but a limited number of things on which to spend it. 'We only stay in five-star hotels,' said one Sixties British rocker belligerently, 'because there ain't no *six*-star hotels.' Once they'd sated their taste for cars, houses, dope

* In 1961, Peter and Helen Kroeger, well-known London book dealers, were convicted of spying for the Soviet Union. Real life could imitate fiction.

and girls, they often began to dabble in art, or what were vaguely called 'first editions'.

But first editions of what? If they had heard of *Clarissa Harlowe*, they thought she was that foxy blonde who sang back-up on Mike Oldfield's *Tubular Bells*.*

Instead, they bought the books they knew, or on subjects that interested them. Overnight, there was an abrupt and, to the business, puzzling new interest in drug novels and the occult. Everyone wanted William Burroughs's first novel *Junkie*, written pseudonymously as 'William Lee' for Ace Books, a *déclassé* American crime and science-fiction paperback house. The ramblings of Aleister Crowley, devil-worshipper and so-called 'Great Beast', flew off the shelves. So did copies of *The Strand* magazine from the turn of the nineteenth century containing the Sherlock Holmes stories illustrated by Sidney Paget, and Mervyn Peake's Gothic *Gormenghast* trilogy, hardly known except to a few connoisseurs of Peake's convoluted prose and even more intricate drawings. *Fin-de-siècle* 'decadent' writers on sodomy, flagellation and 'Uranian' pursuits, i.e., paedophilia, long exiled 'under the counter', enjoyed a new and lively sale. Above all, American hard-boiled crime novels zoomed in value – not simply Raymond

*Actually, that was Mundy Ellis.

20

Chandler and Dashiell Hammett, but obscure talents such as Jim Thompson, Horace McCoy, Cornell Woolrich and David Goodis.

Just as a different kind of tailor had sprung up in the Sixties to provide the new élite with the clothes they wanted, we began to see a different style of bookseller. John Bell and Chris Radmall, who ran Bell, Book and Radmall in London's Long Acre, near the transforming Covent Garden, were both in their twenties, and would have looked at home selling high-priced *schmutter* in Carnaby Street. Even the name, a pun on John van Druten's play *Bell, Book and Candle*, suggested rag trade more than book trade. Chris, who, technically, owned BB&R, was an Old Harrovian and friend of Beatle George Harrison, with whom he launched the fashionable disco Annabel's. He'd been a collector when he heard that the ailing Covent Garden Bookshop was bankrupt and the owner, a notoriously fly dealer named Arnold Nothman, was about to 'shoot the moon', as the Victorians put it, to escape a regiment of creditors. Impulsively, he bought it, and transformed it into the avatar of an emerging bibliophilic *chic*.

The new bookshops became more like boutiques, the books in their windows bright with coloured dust wrappers which were often objects of beauty in themselves. Dust wrappers, in fact, became *the* key issue in collecting. First introduced around 1810, dust jackets almost overnight put the designers of lavish embossed colour bindings out of existence. Yet as late as World War II, collectors still often discarded them, preferring shelves filled with uniform green, grey and brown cloth. Soon, however, a copy of the first James Bond novel, *Casino Royale*, would be worth ten times more with its jacket than without, and *The Great Gatsby* or *Tender is the Night* fifty times.

Science-fiction writer William Gibson noticed the same impulse towards style and flourish in the work of new clothing-makers who transformed London into a fashion mecca in the mid-Sixties. What he says about designers like Paul Smith could equally apply to the new breed of collectors and dealers who surged into the world of books, finding beauty and value where nobody had imagined it existed.

In the hands of these gimlet-eyed, detail-crazed obsessives, elements of a self-consciously Anglo-inflected Americana were sent out on a cultural mission that my schoolmates and I could never have comprehended. In the context of mid-60s London, these clothes meant something 'else', something entirely and brilliantly new. They became a crucial gesture of a very genuine sort of independence . . .

Though it's absurd to apply the term 'cutting edge' to so battered a blade, Martin Stone was at the forefront of this change. Typical of the new book people, he started out doing something else entirely: he was a rock guitarist. His best work was done with a group called Mighty Baby, formed in 1968. Their first album attracted much attention, particularly for Martin's imaginative improvisations. After a second album, *A Jug of Love*, the group seemed to be heading for the big time, but three members abruptly converted to the Sufi faith and left to become Habibiyya. Martin formed Chilli Willi and the Red Hot Peppers, but never really got back into the groove. His likeness stares out from album covers of the early Seventies, an apparition with more hair than one would have thought possible on a head that, all the time I've known him, has been, except for a ragged fringe, gleamingly bald.

Martin began by selling books to fellow musicians like Steve Nieve, keyboard player for Elvis Costello, who only collected first editions of Anthony Burgess's *A Clockwork Orange*, one of the books the new collectors most valued. It took an insider to understand the kind of collecting rockers favoured – a style not noted in classic texts like John Carter's *ABC for Book Collectors*.

But the rest of the trade soon caught on. Wandering into an expensive rare book store, one rocker explained to the owner that he had a new house and wanted some books for it. His eye had been caught by the uniformly-bound sets of Dickens, Trollope and Hardy, but he was surprised at the prices, which ran into the thousands of dollars.

'Do you mind if the sets aren't complete?' asked the bookseller, hardly daring to hope.

'No,' said the star. 'I just like the way they look.'

Every dealer harbours a few incomplete sets, hoping one day that the missing volumes will turn up. Once a year, the trade magazine *The Bookdealer* devotes an entire issue to lists of the so-called 'odd volumes' needed by subscribers to fill a set. Buying quantities of these for peanuts, the dealer sold them at caviar prices to his client, who might never open any of them.

Sets also drew Rick Gekoski to the book business. As a student at Oxford in the Sixties, American-born Gekoski was attracted by a set of Dickens owned by a friend, and bought his own set for £10. A month later, wanting to give his wife a sheepskin coat, he sold the books to Blackwell's bookshop for £20. Over the next fifteen years, while teaching at Warwick University and writing books on Joseph Conrad and other enthusiasms, he became a successful book scout, then opened his own London shop.

Some of the new dealers wrote poetry or fiction, like Iain Sinclair, later the author of *Downriver* and *Radon's Daughters* but at the time an obscure poet, or Joseph Connolly, thickly bearded and glowering with stifled creativity from his kennel-like shop in Flask Walk, Hampstead. Others came from more practical backgrounds. Maurice Neville, perched in a book-lined converted chapel above the Pacific in Santa Barbara, made millions in property before he got into the book business. Sydney dealer Nicholas Pounder emigrated from London as a boy, became a hippie (and, having lived for a time on a commune, is one of the few dealers competent to slaughter and butcher a goat). Louella Kerr, his neighbour in Sydney's smart Paddington district, had been an air hostess, while David Spode, just down the road in Double Bay, was a designer who won the lottery and decided to open a bookshop. Harvey Jason of Los Angeles's Sunset Strip was, and remains, a movie actor who leaves the shop in the hands of his actress wife, Pamela Franklin, when Steven Spielberg calls him to appear in films like *The Lost World*.

These booksellers developed a fresh style to suit their clientele. At book fairs, a newly popular phenomenon, everyone gravitated to the stand of Santa Barbara dealer Ralph Sipper. Trading as 'Joseph the Provider', after the novel by Thomas Mann, 'Joe the Pro' was legendary for the quality of his stock. Not for him the pine shelves and cardboard cartons of other dealers. Sipper's carpeted stand comprised a table, a chair and a single brass-mounted display case. Casual punters could gawp through the glass; serious clients were handed white gauze gloves and permitted to leaf reverently through a first edition of *The Wasteland and Other Poems* inscribed by T. S. Eliot to Ezra Pound, or the copy of *The Great Gatsby* that Fitzgerald gave Ernest Hemingway. '*The rich are very different to you and I, Ernest.*' Yes, they don't throw away dust wrappers.

The dean of these new dealers was Larry McMurtry, author of *The Last Picture Show*, *Horseman, Pass By*, and *Cadillac Jack*, one of the few novels about the art of dealing that professionals respect. In 1971, McMurtry, a lifelong collector, opened Booked Up in Washington DC's fashionable Georgetown. As discreet and well-furnished as the waiting room in the better class of brothel, it boasted a miscellany of print collectables that would have given any traditional bookseller a stroke. A manual on trout fly fishing sat next to a first edition of Jean Cocteau's *Opium* and Hemingway's *To Have and Have Not*, not far from *The Postman Always Rings Twice*, inscribed by James M. Cain to Lana Turner, who starred in the movie version, and rebound to her order in lipstick-red morocco leather, with a slipcase to match.

That this was the future of bookselling became clear when, in 1999, McMurtry bought up most of Archer City, Texas, setting for the film of *The Last Picture Show*, and turned it into America's first 'book town', where every third shop sells second-hand books. He took the opportunity to announce that he would no longer stock his own books nor sign copies brought by literary pilgrims. 'It's become a tourist thing,' he said dismissively. And so McMurtry-autographed copies moved onto the 'preferred' list for collectors, and their price began to rise. The game goes on.

McMurtry was unusual in actively hunting stock for his shop. He regularly scouted the main book markets and book sales, pitting himself in *mano a mano* contests with other dealers to find the best books in the shortest time. Most bookshop owners around the world had long since given this up. Like antique dealers, they knew that, when they ambled into their shops at 11 a.m., one or more ragged men would be loitering around their door or in the café opposite, battered airline bags sagging with treasures found by diving in dumpsters – 'skips' in Britain, '*bennes*' in France – combing charity shops – 'thrift stores' in the USA, '*l'Emmaüs*' in France – and attending the midnight-to-dawn flea markets.

Those markets were the treasure trove of the business, the mother lode of junk. All over Britain, in squares, streets and areas of open ground, hundreds of people would drive up once or twice a week and unload their stock. Local councils and police maintained a casual control, but mostly fees were collected, rentals paid and order maintained through the same genial anarchy that had prevailed under George III, and, indeed, Alfred the Great.

As late as the Eighties, a handful remained 'open markets', not subject to Common Law. Even if the goods you bought turned out to be stolen, they remained yours. Of these markets, the richest was 'The Stones' at Bermondsey, a vast flagged square that filled like a tidal pool every Friday night with dealers from around the British Isles. Around 4 a.m., that hour of lowest ebb in the energy of mankind, when babies are born and people die, a few dozen ragged men began to drift down the lanes of makeshift tables and yawning car boots. Converging like tattered moths on the hissing blue light of a pressure lamp, they squatted to ferret in nests of crumpled newspaper that might hide Georgian silver, Regency porcelain, art deco glass – or books. By sunrise, anything of value was already inching sluggishly through the network of capillaries that kept a community of dealers, scholars and museum curators alive.

'Running' books has always been the last refuge of a particular brand of antisocial eccentric. A century ago, you'd have found their like on the goldfields of the Yukon or southern Australia, or in Tombstone or Dodge City. (Of Martin Stone, Iain Sinclair wrote, 'He had to be a thousand years old. I pictured him bagging Oscar Wilde's library, punting Chatterton's forgeries.') Too unassertive to have been revolutionaries like Peter Lalor or gunfighters like 'Doc' Holliday, they'd have been closer to the ragged figure of Moultrie in Gore Vidal's *The Left-Handed Gun* who trails Billy the Kid, snatching relics for his box of souvenirs.

Many, like their present-day equivalents, were educated men who found no place in the academic world. In 1843, poet Matthew Arnold wrote in *The Scholar Gypsy* of:

> the Oxford scholar poor,
> Of pregnant parts and quick inventive brain,
> Who, tired of knocking at Preferment's door,
> One summer-morn forsook
> His friends, and went to learn the gypsy-lore,
> And roamed the world with that wild brotherhood,
> And came, as most men deemed, to little good.

If ever there was a potential runner, it's this man, down to the 'outlandish garb [. . .] figure spare, [. . .] dark vague eyes, and soft abstracted air'. As for thirsty shepherds finding him already seated with a mug of the local brew in some 'lone alehouse in the Berkshire moors', if anyone can get into a pub before opening time, it's a runner.

Nor is 'outlandish garb' an exaggeration. Most

runners wear rags as a matter of course – the more prosperous-looking, the higher the prices – but Martin Stone's mouldy beret and up-curling winkle-pickers were legendary. A lack of precision when lighting a fag also resulted in some *ad hoc* ventilations to his *tailleur*. 'Excuse me,' novelist Anne Billson warned me once during dinner at our home, 'but Martin is setting fire to his trousers.'

Another prominent London runner of the Seventies and Eighties, 'Driff' Field – true Christian name unknown – claimed to dress exclusively at Oxfam. He affected a Thirties retro-chic, the most extreme manifestation of which was a yellowing Evelyn Waugh-ish three-piece suit, the trousers a billowing pair of plus-fours. I never saw him in his kilt,* but did once glimpse him in bulky tweeds. With his brick-outhouse frame and spiky crewcut, he looked like Abel Magwitch gone grouse shooting. He was also capable of turning out in a white dinner jacket and bow tie, though the tie appeared to be manufactured from white tissue paper.

Physical infirmities add to the bizarre impression of many runners. Canadian Don Bell limped and

---

* The sight of Driff in his kilt inspired Martin Stone to compose the following limerick: 'Mister Driff Field in kilt – what a sight!
  When the wind blew, we got such a fright.
  There were pamphlets up there, incredibly rare,
  That we'd had on our shelves just last night.'

puffed around Paris, his cheerfully beaming satyr's head perched on a cruelly twisted and foreshortened body. Another, known around London's auction rooms for his distinctive military bearing, turned out to walk that way because the pack that held his shoulders back was jammed with stolen books, as was his artificial leg.

As Matthew Arnold's scholar tells his friends, he's wandering with the Romanies in order to research some secret power that gave gypsies 'arts to rule as they desired / The workings of men's brains / And they can bind them to what thoughts they will'.

Such paranoia isn't uncommon among runners. Some people will even tell you that most are dangerously insane. This is clearly an exaggeration. I've only met one book person convicted of killing with his bare hands (he strangled his mistress, cut up the corpse and buried the bits on Leatherhead golf-course). Most are simply strange. Gustav Hasford, author of *The Short Timers*, on which Stanley Kubrick based his film *Full Metal Jacket*, stole books from libraries all over the world, squirrelling them away in Californian warehouses and ending up in jail for it, where he died. Stephen Blumberg looted American libraries for years, removing labels and bookplates by licking them until his saliva dissolved the glue – a repellent method that hints at an almost necrophile fascination with books.

For many years, Driff Field was preoccupied with suicide. He collected only books about suicide or by writers who had killed themselves, and announced that he proposed to commit suicide himself at an appropriate time, and have his corpse cremated on a pyre of his collection. He'd already worked out the Order of Service, including the music to be played, and would even sell you a ticket to the event.

'Driff's a bit . . . strange, isn't he?' I asked another dealer.

'A bit,' he conceded cautiously.

'This suicide thing . . .'

'Oh, *that*,' he said dismissively. 'No, that's fairly new. He's become quite lucid since he got into suicide. Before that, he was *seriously* weird.'

The obsessions harboured by most runners are less homicidal. One became besotted with a pre-pubescent girl, took her on expensive trips to Paris for the opera and, once she reached puberty, maintained her as a mistress, stealing from other dealers to finance his lifestyle. Others, like Don Bell, or George Locke of Ferret Fantasy, one of the leading dealers in and bibliographers of nineteenth-century fantastic fiction, have written a book, though their efforts are normally so riddled with collecting lore as to be impenetrable to anyone but another insider and, like those by Don and George, have to be published at the writer's expense.

Many runners dream of owning a little bookshop, coming in at noon and spending the rest of the day chatting with old colleagues who drop by to sell them rarities at bargain prices. The reality is more like the conversation between bookseller Hugh Grant and a customer in the film *Notting Hill*.

CUSTOMER: Any books by Dickens?

GRANT: This is a travel book shop. We only sell books on travel.

CUSTOMER: Right. Do you have the new John Grisham thriller?

GRANT: That's not a travel book.

CUSTOMER: How about *Winnie the Pooh*?

I once walked through a London bookstore with my old friend Brian Troath, who used to own a shop in a quiet street near Euston station. Our conversation, about where to eat lunch, began before we entered, continued uninterrupted as we glanced over the stock, finding nothing of interest, and didn't end until we were back in the street.

Brian looked back at the phlegmatic proprietor, who hadn't looked up the whole time we were in his establishment.

'How often I've heard conversations like that,' he sighed.

Martin Stone did briefly own a shop near King's

Cross station in London, but, as Iain Sinclair says, it 'opened only in the middle of the night so that he could call in and exchange suitcases'. For a while, Driff Field also had a shop at the end of Portobello Road. From there, he compiled and published *Driff's Guide*, a tendentious handbook listing as many of Britain's second-hand bookshops as he had been able to visit, which was hundreds, and summing each up in such sulphurous terms that the owners seldom allowed him through the door again.

Driff went everywhere, even into outlying suburbs of London, by bicycle, since he can't drive. Neither can Martin Stone, nor most other runners and scouts. This isn't entirely an affectation. The brute bulk of books plays a part too. They weigh almost as much as bricks, but bricks, once stacked, sit comfortably, while books slide and topple, with resultant damage not only to the books themselves – a disaster, in a field so preoccupied with condition – but to the person carrying them. Any runner who hasn't at least one major back injury, not to mention cumulative damage to his knees, doesn't deserve the title.

Most, however, would rather risk a herniated disc than get behind a wheel. A book-loaded car displays the sullen inertia of a water buffalo in heat, as Australian dealer Nicholas Pounder found out when he rented a truck to collect the library of painter Russell Drysdale from his rural retreat:

On top of a mountain, the view was gawpingly good, but the atmosphere (on that 37-degree day especially) was suffocating. I chose and packed the books, abandoned calculations because I thought I should get moving as the weather might change.

Then the sky went black and I decided to make a dash for town, risking the books on the back of the truck without a tarpaulin. Large truck, large load, steep mountain, and then the splats started hitting the windshield, backed by the LOUDEST thunder I have ever heard. I pulled over and tied other boxes over the top of the boxes of books. Then the wind came. I flattened the accelerator and slipped and skidded down the mountain road. The whole vehicle went from side to side with weight, speed and wind. By now I was really anxious as it was pissing down, and the boxes on top of the boxes were either falling in shreds or being torn off by the wind. Then a sheet of roofing iron cartwheeled across the road in front of me and I stood on the brakes. I smelt rubber, saw smoke, felt every box cannon into the seat behind me, but nothing would slow the truck. I was now hurtling straight into a major intersection over wet road. I was going to die. I could see lorries and cars travelling at motorway speeds without a thought for the steep minor road from which I was about to enter.

The truck did a half turn into the first lane at a point where there was a sizeable break in the traffic, and faced me back up the mountain broadside to two lanes of traffic.

I don't know how I did it, but I straightened that Toyota and had it moving as a school bus screeched to within a hair of my laden tray. The horn noise was deafening.

I had given death the slip but now risked financial ruin. I did a bit more stunt driving across a road divider and found an exit opposite near which I could see a sign for a nursery. I covered the load with black plastic seconds before the water went through the boxes.

Given such risks, it's not surprising that most runners, few of them as young or as agile as Pounder, prefer to be driven. Iain Sinclair, who could drive, described his adventures with Driff Field and Martin Stone in his novel *White Chappell, Scarlet Tracings*, and also in a profile of Martin for *The Independent* in 1995:

Once, Martin talked me into writing off a distressed motor in a madcap dash to Bordeaux. He'd had a preview of a catalogue, first editions of Virginia Woolf, unimpeachable rarities. We had to beat the pack; away from Camden Passage and on to the road, toothpicks propping up our eyelids. The phone calls from sawdust bars were all bad lines. But we made it, steam hissing from a punctured radiator. One sad table of Book Club editions of Iris Murdoch. 'No problem,' Martin said. 'We'll hit the Channel Islands.'

Give him his due, it worked out pretty well – after the

strip search (Martin had mislaid some energy-giving medicinal compounds) and the Prevention of Terrorism forms, Jersey was a time warp; shopping malls of apartheid tat, brandy and cigars and perfume, backed up by miraculous books, sacks of them. Pre-First World War Ford Madox Ford in pristine jackets. Take away the expenses and the terminated hatchback and we almost broke even.

It was only a matter of time before showbiz discovered the runner. When Roman Polanski filmed Arturo Pérez-Reverte's *The Dumas Club* as *The Ninth Gate* in 2000, Johnny Depp played its book-finder protagonist Lucas Corso as a figure of glamour. Pérez-Reverte's Corso wears scuffed Oxfords, an old overcoat and worn corduroys, and carries his finds in a canvas satchel. Depp, name changed from 'Lucas' to 'Dean', is as handsome as a Kenzo model, with a neat goatee and moustache. Clothing and satchel subtly upgraded to resemble the best Parisian *couture*, and on first-name terms with the concierges of Paris's smartest hotels, he resembles a book runner as much as Paul Newman does Billy the Kid.

One of Depp's brushes with the Parisian book world, as a junior staff member at the American Library in Paris gleefully recounted to me, was less glamorous. Visiting the Library to research his role in the film *Chocolat*, Depp enquired at the

Information Desk if they had any books on gypsies.

The librarian on duty saw only an unkempt young man in opaque coin-sized dark glasses.

'Are you a member?'

'No.'

She pushed a card at him. 'Fill this in. A day reader's card is fifty francs. And take off those glasses. They annoy me.'

Depp's characterization of the runner in *The Ninth Gate* owes much to the burgeoning fashion for antiques that has swept the world over the last ten years, from the BBC's *Antiques Roadshow*, which transformed the public image of what used to be called dismissively 'dealers in old wares', to the 'bibliomysteries' of John Dunning and Lawrence Block, and the Lovejoy novels of Jonathan Gash, successfully filmed by the BBC, featuring Ian McShane as an East Anglian antiques dealer forever involved in glamorous scams.

In a market that increasingly puts a price tag on everything, the trade in rare items can only flourish. Exhaustible commodities like salt, sugar, wheat, even power and water, fluctuate in worth. But books – which, having been sold once, survive to be sold over and over again – simply increase in value.

This is also true of furniture and paintings, but, while restoring a canvas or reupholstering a chair can as easily diminish the value as increase it, a book gains value with each transaction, particularly if it passes through the hands of a celebrity. Some improvements go far beyond the signatures Graham Greene scribbled into those paperbacks in the *fumerie*. When Luis Buñuel told the Surrealist Roland Tual over lunch in 1928 that he'd never read the Marquis de Sade's forbidden classic *120 Days of Sodom*, Tual (with a generosity at which one can only marvel) lent him his copy of the 1904 first printing, which had belonged to both Marcel Proust and André Gide. Once Buñuel read it, that copy became more valuable still, since he used an episode of the book to conclude *L'Age d'or*, the film he made with Salvador Dali.

Sylvia Beach at Shakespeare and Company in Paris provided another classic example of exponential improvement when she produced 750 numbered copies of James Joyce's *Ulysses* on linen paper in February 1922. They sold for 150 francs each. Publisher Robert McAlmon bought copy no. 540 and glued his bookplate to the front pastedown, giving the copy extra value by association, since he'd helped Joyce by typing the last fifty pages of his manuscript, making some small editorial changes. Further value was added when McAlmon had the book bound in full black morocco leather, and Joyce himself multiplied its worth by inscribing the copy to him. An item that began simply as rare was now unique.

As 'The Robert McAlmon Copy', it sold in 1996 for $55,000.

And had Ernest Hemingway or Wallace Stevens or Marilyn Monroe or Charles Manson or Andy Warhol or Madonna later bought it and added their signature or bookplate . . . ? Such items sell into the millions. The sale of Marilyn Monroe's effects at Christie's in 1999 included a group of paperbacks. The estimate of $700–900 was high, even for two titles from the erotic Olympia Press and a couple more with covers by the fashionable designer Edward Gorey, but, on the day, they sold for $4,020 – and this without her signature, or any sign that she'd owned them. Diamonds may be a girl's best friend, as Marilyn (and Anita Loos before her) suggested, but she can do a lot worse than books.

CHAPTER THREE

The Rules of the Game

Not a soul in this district knows who I am or what I mean to
do here. Odd to think that of all the plainsfolk lying asleep (in
sprawling houses of white weatherboard with red iron roofs
and great arid gardens dominated by pepper-trees and
kurrajongs and rows of tamarisks) not one has seen the view of
the plains that I am soon to disclose.

Gerald Murnane, The Plains

THE FIRST BOOK I EVER COLLECTED WAS *THE POEMS
of Rupert Brooke*. I was eleven. That was in 1951, the
year my father, a pastrycook with a minimal flair for
business, moved us – mother, younger brother and
baby sister – from the relative worldliness of Sydney
to a tiny town called Junee, not far from Wagga
Wagga, in the hinterland of New South Wales.

For me, the shift was seismic. When we used to

swim at Manly Beach, near Sydney, we'd pass a red brick building on the ocean front – the Far West Children's Home, set up to give children from the remotest corners of the state their first look at the ocean. I imagined such children – pale, probably, and thin, with Chesty Bond singlets clinging to their bony ribcages and khaki Hard Yakka shorts hooked on angular hips – recoiling in fear from the thud of the surf. And now I was to be part of that deprived pariah group? No Lucifer ever felt a more despairing fall from grace.

The reality was all I'd feared. Willa Cather, Isak Dinesen and Doris Lessing found poetry and drama in the sun-baked grasslands of America and Africa, but Australia would have severely tested their enthusiasm. Considering D. H. Lawrence's description of rural perfection in *Women in Love* – 'uninterrupted grass, and just a rabbit, sitting up' – it's not surprising that *he* liked it, and spent some time there writing *Kangaroo*, though prudently beside the ocean, where he could be reminded of the dramatic South Wales coast after which that part of the country was named.

Drama was conspicuously absent from our area. The tallest thing for a hundred kilometres was a grazing merino – as Barry Humphries once said, 'You only had to travel a thousand kilometres in any direction to find something *really* interesting.'

In fact, like the American West, which begins not at any geographical point but where, in any given year, the average annual rainfall drops below twenty inches, or in Iran, where journeys are measured in *farsangs*, the distance which, in that terrain, a camel can cover in a day, the true distance between Junee and civilization stretched and contracted. When the temperature topped 40°C or dropped below freezing, one thought only of hunkering down, and the cities seemed far away. But in spring or autumn, as my brother and I, with half the other kids in the neighbourhood, loitered on the railway embankment at the bottom of our street, ready to scavenge the boulders of coal that fell from overloaded tenders and lug them back to feed the kitchen stove, the hump-backed 57-class locomotives labouring towards Sydney dragged at me like a magnet.

I began to accumulate derogatory quotes about my native land and scatter them through conversation like sixpences in a Christmas pudding. I particularly liked John Collier's story, 'The Devil, George and Rosie', where Satan offers a prospective victim a look at Hell.

> They sank into the bowels of the earth, and came out in a suburb of Sydney, New South Wales.
> 'Here we are, then!' cried George.
> 'No, no,' said the Devil. 'Just a little further on.'

Oh, and there was Eric Newby's description of farmers perched on combine harvesters, monotonously ranging their equally monotonous landscape and cursing, no less monotonously, 'Fuck, fuck, fuck.'

But Junee was no more distinctive in its isolation than in anything else. Many years later, visiting Modesto in northern California, home town of George Lucas, creator of *Star Wars*, I recognized its twin, down to the interminable freight trains clanking through level crossings, severing one side of town from the other. Mimosa Avenue, where Lucas was born, wasn't too different from Lillian Street, Junee, and my own teenage resentment was reflected in Luke Skywalker's moan about his home planet of Tatooine: 'If there is a bright centre to the universe, this is the place that's furthest from it.'

There were worse places to be raised than Junee, and we weren't poor. Had I not been so prejudiced, I might even have found as much fantasy there as Ray Bradbury did in equivalent towns in middle America. In retrospect, it had enough oddities, 'characters' and tragedies to spare. There was 'Brum', a greasy derelict who slouched around town, and could occasionally be encountered, stinking of old piss, sleeping it off under the 'Tree of Wisdom', a giant pepper tree by the station where old railway sleepers had been arranged in a kind of bench, supposedly as a place for the town elders to congregate. Stories also circulated of the pharmacist, a lowering Nordic built like Boris Karloff, who merchandised a patent cure for diseases of turkeys from his gloomy shop, and was rumoured to be a nudist, with a cement pool in his back garden where he could immerse his large white limbs in private – a disturbing transgression against the egalitarianism that ruled not only Junee but Australian culture in general. And nobody ever fathomed why a reserved, apparently untroubled young woman of a good Catholic family – someone we saw at church on Sunday and glimpsed occasionally around town, demure and dreamy – should have walked out of her home one night, crossed the road to the railway line, climbed through the fence, put her head on the track and waited for a train to sever it – a train of which her father was the driver.

More than twenty years later, I took my French wife-to-be Marie-Dominique on what I thought of as a nose-thumbing triumphal return to the town. As I'd so often visualized, our car topped the same hill where we kids had waited to scavenge coal. For a thousand kilometres – indeed for every kilometre of the trip from Paris, and long before – Marie-Dominique had endured my scornful references. But the reality surprised her. '*Mais . . . c'est mignon*,' she said.

And, as we drove down the long avenue towards the centre of town, some part of me had to agree. It was, indeed, cute. Abandoned by the railways that once pumped life into it, Junee had fallen off the freight train of history. In one of these bungalows, shaded by a pepper tree that, in the hot breeze, brushed the corrugated-iron roof with a sound like lightly scampering claws, a freckled Sleeping Beauty in khaki shorts and T-shirt might lie breathing softly under a mosquito net, awaiting the kiss of a rugby-playing Prince Charming . . .

I put my foot down, and we accelerated out of there, heading for Wagga Wagga and a motel with a swimming pool. Any longer, and I might have got to like it.

The featurelessness of Junee's landscape was nothing compared to its intellectual flatness. There was an Olympic-sized swimming pool, and both a cricket and football field, but no public library and no bookshop. The local newsagent sold me the Rupert Brooke, a grey-covered Sidgwick & Jackson edition with a photogravure portrait of the poet, looking peeved, as well he might, having died of a mosquito bite before millions of post-war admirers had a chance to lionize him.

Of course the Brooke wasn't the first book I owned. Like all kids, I trailed a small library of school prizes and Christmas presents. In some cases – a glossy but largely unused set of encyclopaedias, for example – I'd been influential in the purchase. But the Brooke was the first book I *collected* – bought for myself, not because it was recommended by parents or teachers.

In acquiring it, I exercised a personal taste. Like the appearance of the first pubic hair, at once alarming and exciting, it marked one's passage into a new state of existence. Nor was it bought to be read. I knew these poems already, and had even memorized a few. The book was of no practical use – it existed solely as a treasurable object.

Almost all collectors are male. A few women collect, but in an entirely different way from men. The difference would be brought home to me in the late Nineties, after Marie-Dominique and I had married and moved to Paris. She had never collected anything in her life, but an artist named André Pécoud had illustrated some of the books that were her favourites as a child, and, in looking for copies to give our eleven-year-old daughter, she decided to make a collection of his work.

Her approach was systematic. She compiled a list of dealers, then made the rounds of their shops. If they were out of Paris, she caught up with them in summer, or when they came to the weekly book market in the old abattoir on Rue Brancion. She advertised on the Internet, and began researching Pécoud's life, finally tracking down his will and, from that, locating relatives who filled in his biography. Her search brought her into contact with other collectors of Pécoud, with one of whom she launched *L'Association Pécoud*, correctly registered under *le loi de 1901*. By concentrating on Pécoud alone, she accumulated, within a few months, multiple editions of almost all the three hundred books he illustrated, not to mention some original paintings and a wealth of background information.

Her single-mindedness confounded me. Far from compiling one collection, I have several, and add fresh ones regularly, like an investor 'taking a position' in a stock. The closer it is to completion, the less a collection interests a collector, until, when he has everything, often he will sell it and turn to some other writer. The whole point of collecting is the thrill of acquisition, which must be maximized, and maintained at all costs.

Male collectors seek, as Jo von Sternberg put it, a subject they can't exhaust. To me, Marie-Dominique's method was like a game of poker where one was dealt five cards face up, and the best hand took the pot. With no tension, no bluff, no guile, where was the fun?

For most male collectors, the urge appears in puberty. Forrest J. Ackerman's collection of fantasy and science fiction, the world's most complete, began with a few pulp magazines in the Twenties. When he'd accumulated thirty, his mother, alarmed, made him sell them to the boy next door. 'But I pined and I moaned, and I wouldn't eat,' recalls Ackerman, 'so after a few days my mother bought them back again.' At last count, Forry's collection numbered fifty thousand items, and he had to buy a second house to live in. For some years, he's been trying to will it to some city that will put it on permanent show. All have refused – they simply don't have the room.

Michael Neal, the pre-eminent scholar and collector of anti-Semitica, bought his first book when he was nine, but decided to start collecting when he was eleven, in the early Sixties. Collecting who? 'For a start, George Orwell,' he says. 'Because he was the writer I admired most.' But that impulse passed. 'I could have bought almost all of Orwell. You could find most of his first editions in those days for relatively little money. But that would have only taken a couple of months.' Instead, he sent away one and sixpence, with twopence postage, for a twenty-page booklet, *The BBC and the Learned Elders*, by one A. K. Chesterton, the cornerstone of a collection of anti-Jewish propaganda that not only fills his large house outside Paris but most of a nearby barn too. Naturally, it isn't complete. It never could be – which, for a collector, is the whole point of the thing.

But I was an unlikely candidate to become a collector. We were not book-owning people.

Australia, in those days at least, was a country where the old joke: 'Let's buy them a book' – 'No, they already have one,' actually had some social basis. Of the twenty or so volumes on the family bookshelf, ten had a practical use: a *Webster's Dictionary* in red leatherette, a *Home Doctor*, *Household Hints*, a *Good Housekeeping* cookbook, some tomes about pastrycooking, those encyclopaedias I'd hectored my father into buying.

The others had lodged there the way dust bunnies reproduce under a bed or wire coat hangers accumulate in a wardrobe. Nobody sees them arrive, but every time you lift the bedspread or open the cupboard door, there are more. The oddest was a copy of *Kirstin Lavransdaater* by Sigrid Undset, who won the Nobel Prize in 1928, mainly on account of this door-stop novel about moral choices in fourteenth-century Norway. Nobody could re-member where our copy came from and certainly we'd never read it, but, too thick and imposing to throw out, it travelled with us, useful as an *ad hoc* book-end to stop the others from falling over.

We were Catholics. Or at least my mother had been, and my father promised, when they married, that any children would be 'raised in the faith'. In practice, this meant sending us to a Catholic school and urging us every Sunday with empty stomachs to cycle three kilometres to the red-brick church on the hill while they stayed in bed, eating buttered toast and reading the papers.

Catholicism is a creed of hot countries. In the world's remoter corners, where the blood of belief flows sluggishly, it has a tendency to fester. Rome would hardly have recognized Australian Catholicism. Presided over by a fiercely Fenian cardinal named Gilroy, its roots ran directly to Dublin, which sent us quantities of beery 'priests with a past', unchristian Christian Brothers given to paedophilia and flagellation, and Sisters of Mercy neither sisterly nor merciful.

When the occasional pastoral visits of our local bishop earned us an afternoon off school, most boys raced off, raving, to play cricket or footy. I headed downtown to the Victorian red-brick Railway Institute and, with the building vibrating to the pounding thud of the typing class upstairs, raided its members-only lending library.

Collectors abominate lending libraries. They are graveyards of good books. Everything a librarian does to prepare a book for lending disqualifies it as a collectable. Stamps are slammed on the title page, label pockets gummed to the rear pastedown, dust wrappers discarded, covers vulcanized in plastic – or, in those days, a toffee-brown buckram tough enough to withstand acid. Restoring a library book to collectable condition is like trying to return a Kentucky Fried

Chicken to the state of health where it can lay an egg.

I'd already been introduced to such places. My father's shop and the apartment where I was born in the Sydney suburb of Randwick were part of a building that also housed the Randwick Literary Institute. A heavy metal door in the bakehouse could, with some judicious thumping, be coaxed open, admitting me to its large lending library. The hours I spent wandering in the empty library after hours instilled my lifetime fascination with books. By the time I was nine, I'd read all the titles nearest to the door, which happened to be the mythology section, and was working my way into biography when my father sold that shop and, moving to Junee, inaugurated the seven lean years of my childhood.

Fat with heavy reading, cocked by poor shelving, spotted with dubious stains, the Junee Railway Institute stock ran mostly to whodunnits by Agatha Christie and Ngaio Marsh, with the distinctive orange boards of William Collins' Crime Club peeping round the edges of the rebind, or historical novels by people like Frank Yerby, king of the bayou bodice-ripper (and, as I later discovered, an African/American, something his publishers kept very quiet indeed). Australia's own Ion L. Idriess contributed stories of cannibals in New Guinea or murderous aborigines in the Kimberleys that held back better race relations by half a century.

I'd started at the 'A's, borrowing everything even halfway promising, even if I brought it back the next day only half-read. As the youngest library member, and the most active, I excited the suspicion of the matrons browsing for a nice Barbara Cartland, not to mention the gorgon behind the desk. For the first few weeks, she scrutinized each book I returned, for fear I'd drawn on the endpapers or left something disgusting between the pages.

Most librarians don't like books any more than butchers like lamb chops. Few read, and almost none collect the objects that they work with, which they seem to view merely as commodities. The most famous literary librarian, Philip Larkin, preferred porn magazines. The Junee librarians read *The Australian Woman's Weekly* – not much different.

The Railway Institute library usefully introduced me to the mediocrity of most literature. Reading ten Leslie Charteris novels in succession cruelly high-lighted his weaknesses. Likewise Agatha Christie, and even Conan Doyle. 'Sherlock Holmes after all is mostly an attitude and a few dozen lines of unforgettable dialogue,' wrote Raymond Chandler. And once you'd grasped the attitude and heard the lines, why read on?

I got to know the games writers play. Titles told you nothing. What a disappointment to find only a well-bred detective novel within the covers of

Margery Allingham's memorably named *Tiger in the Smoke*. Settings were just as misleading. Java or Valparaiso could feel as fake as the painted backdrop of a carnival sideshow. It came as no surprise to find, years later, that Dennis Wheatley, whose occult thrillers such as *To the Devil a Daughter* and *The Haunting of Toby Jugg* were library staples, recreated Constantinople and Crete from tourist brochures. His books reeked of photogravure.

But now and then, reading even half a page of a book produced a shock like the metallic tingle when, chewing a toffee, your tooth strikes a bit of tinfoil. Eric Ambler's *The Mask of Dimitrios* had that effect. When Colonel Haki, chief of the Turkish secret police, looks up at the crime-writer narrator and asks, 'I wonder if you are interested in *real* murderers, Mr Latimer,' I felt a throb that made me want never to be parted from this book.*

Likewise with Raymond Chandler's *The Big Sleep*. In this case, it wasn't the story but the details that gripped: General Sternwood exhibiting 'the outward-turning earlobes of approaching dissolution', the ill-chosen ivory curtains and white carpet in his daughter's room ('the white made the ivory look dirty and the ivory made the white look bled out'), the rage

* Others agreed. Of Ambler's many novels, it's the most valued. A dust-wrappered copy of the 1939 Hodder & Stoughton first edition will cost $15,000 – in part because most of the stock burned in a Luftwaffe air raid.

Marlowe feels at finding Carmen Sternwood naked in his bed, and the way he tears it apart after she's left, removing the impression of her 'corrupt little body'.

Chandler, of course, knew as little about ivory curtains and corrupt little bodies as Wheatley did about Constantinople. All earlobes don't turn outwards with increasing age, while a body, corrupt or otherwise, leaves little mark on even the softest mattress. And, as Chandler himself would later admit, the typical private detective was not, as he imagined Philip Marlowe, an intellectual whose idea of a good time was a quiet night at home with a bottle of rye and a book of chess problems, but an ex-cop with the brains of a turtle who spends his time finding out where people have moved to. Yet his details *felt* right. They furnished a real world, and, like millions of other readers, I happily took refuge in it.

Chandler was not so much urban wolf as metropolitan mole. What he knew of crime came mostly from books. Not surprisingly, then, the theme of bibliophily runs through *The Big Sleep*. One of the subsidiary villains, Arthur Gwynn Geiger, runs a lending library of erotica. He photographs Carmen Sternwood naked, presumably to illustrate such books, and is killed for his trouble. Investigating this racket, Marlowe poses as a book collector, and finds the girl behind the desk at Geiger's bookshop woefully ignorant of variant printings of General Lew Wallace's *Ben-Hur*. 'You do sell books?' he asks querulously, and she, waving at the shelves, says, 'What do they look like – grapefruit?'

By the late summer of 1956, despite repeated returns to Ambler, John Buchan, Raymond Chandler, and others, I had worked my way through the Railway Institute's stock to the 'G's.

The first Graham Greene I read was *Brighton Rock*. It was probably the Heinemann first edition, though its brick-red cloth had been swamped by the habitual brown bombazine. After a couple of chapters, it was clear I wouldn't be able to discuss this book with Sister Mary Dolores, who liked to know what I was reading. The set books that year were two stories by Conrad, 'Youth' and 'Gaspar Ruiz', and a collection of stories about eskimos, Alan Sullivan's *Under the Northern Lights*. All bracing stuff, heavy on manly action. She wasn't going to care for Greene's world of cheap journalists, racecourse touts (whatever they were) and the razor gang led by Greene's hero Pinkie.

And yet Pinkie was Catholic, and serious about it. Scrunched up on my creaking bed on the half-enclosed veranda of our bungalow, with the *rush-rush* of the cicadas in my head and the smell of red dust from the unsurfaced street outside, I navigated the twisting inlets of belief and doubt leading to the interior of what literary journalists glibly called 'Greeneland'. It was a landscape I instinctively recognized. When it was finished, I itched to find others by him: *A Gun for Sale*, the wonderfully titled *Stamboul Train*. But every few weeks I'd re-borrow *Brighton Rock*, and keep it beside the bed. In intent, I had already become a Greene collector. All I lacked was the books.

CHAPTER FOUR

Surly Bonds

In an age when the idea of heroism seems likely to quit the army, since manly virtues may play no part in those future wars whose horrors are foreshadowed by our scientists, does not aviation provide the most admirable and worthy field for the display of prowess?

André Gid, Introduction to Night Flight *by Antoine de Saint-Exupéry*

WHEN I WAS SIX, A DEHAVILLAND MOSQUITO disintegrated above our part of suburban Sydney. Every kid in the street sprinted to Number 17, where we hauled ourselves up the fence of splintery palings to gape at the chunk of battleship-grey fuselage, big as a sofa, embedded in Mr Giannini's lawn.

Once I was allowed to touch it, my wonder increased. It wasn't made of metal but painted plywood. And not only was it the size of a sofa – it weighed about the same as well. Until then, I'd imagined aircraft to be empty and feather-light, like balloons. How could something as solid as this take flight?

That fallen Mosquito launched my fascination with flying. Over the next four years, I read dozens of *Biggles* novels, harrying my parents into acquiring the latest from the apparently tireless Captain W. E. Johns. Most were the Oxford University Press's reprints, in a generic dust wrapper that showed Wing Commander Bigglesworth in fleecy-lined flying jacket, goggles and leather helmet against a sky of synthetic blue. The gritty colours evoked wartime austerity – intentionally, no doubt, since the books, with Biggles and his pals battling the Hunnish duplicity of Erich Von Stalhein, celebrated a gentlemanly air war that crashed and burned with the first thousand-bomber raid over Germany. Most kids disliked the dust wrappers as much as I did, and discarded them – which explains why a first edition of the 1953 *Biggles in the Gobi* in a good dust wrapper will cost you $70 and any from the Thirties in similar condition more like $1,000.

Like hothouse plants in a foreign land, distorted by inbreeding, the values of Tunbridge Wells flourished with unhealthy vigour in Australia. Rupert Brooke, not to mention Sapper, Dornford Yates and P. G. Wodehouse, would have been perfectly at home with my relatives. 'He Won Through,' my aunt Betty would say, meaning that someone had gained a scholarship. 'Going back home' meant visiting a Britain not even your grandparents had seen. And of *course* we stood for 'God Save the Queen' after every film; not to do so was probably a criminal offence, though I never had the nerve to find out.

Aviation stories, fact or fiction, celebrated the same values. 'Pomp and Circumstance' emanated from every page of Paul Brickhill's *The Dam Busters* and his biography of Douglas Bader, *Reach for the Sky*, from *Enemy Coast Ahead,* the memoirs of the Dam Busters' commander, Guy Gibson, and even from *I Flew for the Fuehrer* by that archetypal 'good German' Adolf Galland. For writers such as Nevil Shute and Hammond Innes, two staples of the Railway Institute library, a couple of guys running a one-plane charter company in some corner of the old Empire provided, like Biggles' continued skirmishing with Von Stalhein (now working for 'the other side', i.e., East Germany), a metaphor for Britain's place in the New World Order. Whatever happened in Moscow or Washington DC, the old values of 'knuckling down' and 'doing the right thing', not to mention the ability to repair an oil pump with a hairpin and some chewing gum, would keep jumped-up fuzzy-wuzzies and oily Levantines in their place.

Moving to Junee accelerated my interest in flying.

My parents also gave me a subscription to *Flight*, the sober monthly review of Britain's faltering aviation industry, in which, like thousands of adolescents around the world, I found sensual pleasure in tracing the hydraulic schematics of the Comet.

But the Comet, in illustration of the dictum 'Brilliant British design, lousy British craftsmanship', was shortly to start falling out of the skies, victim of a fundamental engineering flaw. At the same time, even the British were starting to suspect that wartime principles no longer applied. Britain echoed with the clatter of Royals and Imperials (ironic names for instruments of revolution) as the Angry Young Men got started on their first novels or plays. A furious correspondent to *Films and Filming* magazine spluttered, 'Sir, Last night at my local Odeon, I stood at the end of the screening for the National Anthem. When I turned to leave, the cinema was empty, and I had been locked in!'

The wizard-prang-good-show-chaps heroics of Brickhill and Gibson began to wear on me too. My new enthusiasms among flying books were Antoine de Saint-Exupéry's *Wind, Sand and Stars* and *The Big Show* by Pierre Clostermann, one of the youngest French pilots to fly with the RAF. Saint-Ex's description of sweeping south across France with the African mail, or Clostermann's of climbing to intercept a Messerschmitt Me109, its underside painted sky blue, glinting like a fresh-minted penny on a perfect day over the Pas de Calais, stopped my breath.

Dreaming of a career in aviation, I organized friends into building two-metre box kites from calico and dowelling, which we launched into the hot wind off the bare hills behind our house. I wrote to the flying club in nearby Wagga Wagga, asking about lessons. What sort of aerial bus driver might I have become had my parents not, for my sixteenth birthday, given me *The Flying Omnibus*? It changed my life.

Since aviation alternates long periods of boredom with brief episodes of terrifying activity, any writing about flying is usually quite short. All the same, the *Omnibus* editor, Paul Jensen, stirred up some prime pieces. They ranged from the description of 'a front porch in flight' (as Guy Gilpatrick remembered the Wright Brothers' first aircraft) to James Thurber's 'The Greatest Man in the World', about what might have happened if Charles Lindbergh or some other heroic aerial pioneer had been, not modest and well-bred, but a bum who did it for the money. The blue cloth binding of my copy of *The Big Show* was rubbed shiny with use, but *The Flying Omnibus* literally fell apart.

Some writers, such as Clostermann and Saint-Exupéry, I already knew. Others were new to me. Among these was John Gillespie Magee Jr, author of the sonnet 'High Flight', which opened the book.

This is the one that begins, 'Oh! I have slipped the surly bonds of earth' and ends:

> And while with silent, lifting mind I've trod
> The high untrespassed sanctity of space
> Put out my hand and touched the face of God.

Not Ezra Pound or Auden; more like Robert Bridges on a bad day, but impressive enough for me to memorize – a compliment I'd so far paid only to Rupert Brooke and Dylan Thomas – and startle friends and family by declaiming its choicest lines.

Magee, half British, half American, and the son of a missionary to China (as had been Mervyn Peake), enlisted in the RAF during the Second World War, and, like Rupert Brooke, became another poet/serviceman who never saw combat, dying in a collision over Lincolnshire in 1941. He was only nineteen.

His death gave to 'High Flight', his only published poem, an unearned poignancy. Copies, soberly framed, hang on the walls of many an aviation museum and flying school. Two of its lines are engraved on Magee's headstone; Ronald Reagan lifted some phrases (without credit) in January 1986, as he eulogized the seven victims of the Challenger shuttle disaster.

But 'High Flight' was eclipsed by the last item in

The Flying Omnibus, a science-fiction story called 'First Contact', introduced with the tentative, indeed dubious, claim that such fiction 'has always been a part of aviation literature'. Magazine writers are mostly paid by the word, and Murray Leinster, the author of 'First Contact' which was originally written for *Astounding Science Fiction* magazine, was enough of a pro to inflate his five-hundred-word anecdote to five thousand. Briefly, ships from earth and an alien planet encounter each other in deep space. The crews make friends, yet neither trusts the other not to track them back to their home system and perhaps launch a pre-emptive attack. Eventually, they swap ships, each race disabling its own tracking equipment: the guarantee of a comprehensive job. As they part, having agreed to rendezvous in a year, one earthman is confident the two races will become friendly, since he and his opposite number spent the last hour exchanging dirty jokes.

With 'First Contact', I slipped the surly bonds of earth, or at least of Junee. Though I'd read H. G. Wells and Jules Verne, neither had the snappiness of Leinster, the casual sense of enormous distances and vast spaces.

A visit to Wagga Wagga established that *Astounding Science Fiction* was still being produced, albeit in a thinner, paler 'Australian reprint edition', a relic of wartime currency restrictions. I read half the latest issue on the station, and the rest on the trip back. By then, I was hooked. I never thought again about going into aviation. Instead, I started to collect science fiction.

To anyone who knows books, that last phrase will have produced a chorus of groans. It's not a question of quality but of quantity, because a science-fiction collection, by its very nature, takes up a lot of room. From its earliest days, when Hugo Gernsback first inserted stories in the monthly *Electrical Experimenter*, the primary outlet and market for science fiction was magazines. The *Experimenter* was the size of *Life*. So was *Amazing Stories*, the all-fiction magazine Gernsback launched in 1926. In the Thirties, the pulp magazines shrank to standard quarto, but doubled in thickness as publishers used the cheapest paper around. (After all, who the hell would want to hang on to such crap?) Shipping lines bought unsold pulps by the bale and used them to ballast their freighters, dumping the magazines on the dock at Portsmouth, Durban or Sydney to load up with iron, wheat, wool or coal. Enterprising jobbers retrieved them and sold the magazines to chain stores, where more than one science-fiction career was launched when a kid, attracted by the sign 'Yank magazines, twopence each' in Woolworth's, discovered *Astounding*, *Unknown Worlds* and *Planet Stories*.

Few pulps survived the Second World War paper restrictions. Some, including the best, *Astounding Science Fiction*, remade themselves in 'digest' format. They were soon joined by *Galaxy*, *The Magazine of Fantasy and Science Fiction*, *Fantastic* and the revived *Amazing Stories*. And then, in the Fifties, Britain weighed in with *New Worlds*, *Science Fantasy* and *Authentic*. Even Australia had a few.

So if you collected science fiction, you collected magazines. But twelve issues of a single pulp like *Startling Stories* filled a foot of shelf space and weighed two kilos. *Astounding* weighed more, particularly its 'broadsheet' issues of the early Forties, when it swelled to the dimensions of the old *Electrical Experimenter*. A year's worth of the major pulps from the mid-Thirties would jam the standard library bookshelf, and if you added *Black Mask*, *Air Aces*, *Weird Tales* or *Spicy Detective*, which sometimes published fantasy stories . . .

When I got interested in science fiction in the late Fifties, the pulps were little more than a memory. More than a year after reading 'First Contact', I had never actually seen one, but when I did, the effect was, once again, seismic. I owe it to *The Creature from the Black Lagoon*.

This is no place to analyse that extraordinary film, or the others, like *The Incredible Shrinking Man*, made by the same talented director.* It's enough that it turned up at the Junee cinema some time in 1955 and, even mutilated by a censor paranoid about anything approaching 'horror', impressed me so much that I returned the following night.

As usual on a week night in winter, so few people occupied this draughty barn of a cinema that the projectionist, a guy in his thirties, came out to chat in the interval.

'Weren't you here last night?'

'Yes. It's a terrific film.'

'It's all right.' He went into the bio box and came out with a sheet of paper. 'Take a look at these. If you enjoy this sort of stuff, I can book some of them.' He looked around the empty cinema. 'Might as well at least get one paying customer in the place.'

I stared at the twenty or so names: *The Conquest of Space*, *It Came from Outer Space*, *When Worlds Collide*, *The War of the Worlds*, *Riders to the Stars*, *The Day the Earth Stood Still* ... I had no idea of their relative worth (from inspired to insipid, as it turned out), but the titles were enough.

'Can you get them all?'

'I suppose.' This interested him. 'You really like science fiction, then?'

* Anybody who wants to know more could read the chapter 'Lucifer: The Films of Jack Arnold' in my book *Science Fiction in the Cinema*.

'Yes!'

'So does my boy Rodney. He's at your school. Get him to bring you home some afternoon.'

A few days later, I did just that.

Rodney's father was reading the *Sun* on the front veranda. 'Take your friend out the back,' he said.

Rodney led me across the yard and opened the side door to a wooden garage. There was no car inside. Just drifts of science-fiction magazines, disappearing into the warm spider-infested dark, which they scented with the faintly lactic smell of newsprint. They appeared to have been heaved there, basket by basket, over years. There were thousands.

I picked up the magazine nearest my foot. It was a pulp, the first I'd seen: *Super Science Stories* Volume 1, Number 1, dated March 1940. On the cover, apparently illustrating the lead story, 'World Reborn' by Thornton Ayre, two spacemen and a heavy-breasted girl in a low-cut dress bombarded what looked like a giant teacup with blazing projectiles.

Is it unreasonable to talk about *pity* for books? I don't think so. Books in quantity and disorder induce in collectors a sort of compassion. When the novelist Hugh Walpole, visiting William Randolph Hearst at San Simeon in the Thirties, wrote of his library that it was 'crying out from neglect', I understood him instantly. Dozens of times in my collecting life, I have been faced with such a mass of books, and always with the same reaction: *I have to sort these out*. As a cook will look at a packet of cheese crackers, a can of tomato juice, a lemon, some grapes and an egg, and see a three-course meal, a bibliophile looks at a chaos of printed paper and sees a library.

I held up *Super Science Stories*. 'Can I borrow this?'

'Yair, help yourself,' Rodney said. 'We've read 'em. Take all you like. I'll get you a bag.'

I filled up an old Gladstone bag. When I had wobbled home on my bike (reminder: buy a wire shopping basket to hook on the handlebars), I dumped it beside my bed, opened *Super Science Stories* and started to read 'World Reborn'. It was rubbish.

So was 'Trans-Plutonian Trap' by Ross Rocklynne, 'The Lotus Engine' by Raymond Z. Gallun and 'Phantom from Space' by John Russell Fearn. The plots were stupid. The writing made W. E. Johns look like Hemingway.

The second magazine, a late issue of *Amazing Stories*, was no better. I'd stumbled on the great rule of science fiction: ninety per cent of it is crap.

And yet, every few days for the next year, I returned to the garage and exchanged one bagful of magazines for another. Those I'd read I stacked to the right of the door, while a widening space of earth floor on the left side indicated how far I'd progressed.

The breakthrough came in the eighth or ninth week. That day's haul included the August 1953 copy of the Australian reprint edition of *Astounding*, with the opening episode of a novel by a writer new to me, Hal Clement.

The first line of *Mission of Gravity* put a chill up my spine: 'The wind came across the bay like something living.' And even now the ghost of that *frisson* returns. Like the minister in Richard Llewellyn's *How Green Was My Valley* who gives *Treasure Island* to the invalid Huw, I want to say, 'Imagine, to have the pleasure again of reading it for the first time.'

Hal Clement – actually Harry Clement Stubbs, a working physicist – was no Herman Melville, but the story! A planet with gravity six hundred times that of earth; a lone earthman collaborating with the locals, a race of armoured millipedes, to retrieve a stranded ship . . .

It took a day of rummaging in the garage to excavate the other three episodes, but I didn't begrudge the time. In the process, I made a decision. What I liked were alien environments, and the more detailed the better. Since they seemed to appear mainly in novels, I should be collecting books, not magazines. *Mission of Gravity* saved me from a life enslaved to pulps.

Super Science Stories Number One did confer one other gift; probably the most important of all. Towards the end, it allocated three pages to a department called 'The Science Fictioneer'. It began:

Wherever you live, you are not alone. In New York City or London, the greatest metropolises on the earth, in a small town in the United States, in Africa or Australia, wherever – you are not alone. Not if you read science fiction, not if you are a fan. For science fiction readers live in every corner of the globe. And where a fan lives, very soon two fans live – for science fiction is more contagious than any disease.

Readers were invited to clip a coupon and send for membership in the Science Fictioneers. The magazine also gave addresses of clubs in various American cities, in Liverpool and, incredibly, in Australia: something called the Futurian Society had an address in downtown Sydney. I was fifteen years too late to clip the coupon, but the knowledge that there had once been – and perhaps still was? – a science-fiction club only a thousand kilometres away, instilled an itch which, it was already clear, would need one day to be scratched. *Super Science Stories* was right: the science-fiction disease was contagious – and, as it turned out, incurable.

CHAPTER FIVE

Star Begotten

EV: Don't even suggest it's science fiction.

JB: It's only a label, Ed.

EV: So is 'Leprosy'.

Conversation between the author and literary agent Ed Victor

SHUDDERING INTERMITTENTLY, THE LIFT INCHED UP to the sixth floor of the ancient building on Pitt Street, Sydney.

From the couple next to me drifted the scent of talcum powder and old age. I watched their reflections in the glass covering the IN CASE OF EMERGENCY sign. Decades of brushing had worn the wool of his double-breasted tuxedo almost as shiny as its satin lapels, while the body to which it was tailored some time during the reign of George V had shrunk like a nut in its shell, until a good inch gaped between the starched collar of his dress shirt and his Adam's apple.

Dusty pink, ankle-length, her dress belonged, like the white fur tippet around her shoulders, on Dame Mae Whitty, the lady who vanishes in Hitchcock's film. Her stare into the middle distance never wavered as we ascended past floors of secretarial services, accountants and fabricators of false teeth, their offices dark behind doors of pebbled glass. Occasionally, over the clatter of the lift equipment, the echoing slap of feet on cement suggested that less patient people were using the stairs that spiralled round the shaft.

Between the fourth and fifth floors, the ancient motor faltered like a tired heart, jolting the cage. In silent unison, my companions swayed towards me, but returned inexorably to the vertical. A single hair detached itself from her moulting pelt and corkscrewed to the dusty floor.

These were the science-fiction fans of Sydney? Custodians of a rational scientific future? The people who, borrowing an H. G. Wells title, thought of themselves as 'star begotten'? If so, my time in science-fiction fandom would be brief.

I owed the fact that, at seventeen, I was living again in Sydney to the New South Wales Government Railways. Two years earlier, I'd taken charge of my life and left school to become a clerk with Junee's main employer. This had nothing to do with an affection for locomotives, but a great deal with the NSWGR policy that anybody with two years' service could transfer out. Two years and six weeks later, I was back where I belonged, in Sydney. Subsequently, my parents moved to a town within a two-hour train ride of the city, but effectively I was on my own.

At the sixth floor, the couple in the lift, to my relief, veered to the left, passing under the sign SYDNEY BRIDGE CLUB and into a room where other people of similar vintage and wardrobe clustered round a dozen folding card tables.

At the same moment, four men, anything but formally dressed, arrived noisily via the stairs. 'You for the science-fiction group?' one asked amiably. 'It's through here.'

I followed them into a room that, in memory, seems vast. The floor was bare boards, the pressed tin ceiling brown with cigarette smoke and dust. Fizzing fluorescents of minimal wattage cast a yellow light. Large uncurtained windows looked out on the grimy brick walls of the building next door, zigzagged with contrastingly painted downpipes, as if to boast, 'Look – indoor plumbing!'

People rented rooms in these buildings by the night, week, month or year, for anything from a wedding reception to a sweat shop. You furnished them with what you needed – which, in the case of the Bridge Club Science Fiction Group, was one large trestle table and half a dozen folding card tables and chairs. For a few pence a mug, the Bridge Club shared its coffee and tea.

The resulting sense of the tentative, even illicit, not only typified the group but was almost sought by it. In all the Thursday evenings I spent at the Bridge Club, I never lost the sense that someone would arrive in a minute or two and turn us out.

The four who entered ahead of me were debating over by the windows, ignoring, and being ignored by, a stocky man in his forties with a heavy moustache who was methodically laying out paperback books on the table.

Waiting until he was at the other end, I started browsing. Some names I knew: Robert Heinlein, Cyril Kornbluth, Ray Bradbury. Others meant nothing to me: Philip K. Dick, Cordwainer Smith, Robert Silverberg. One series of thin booklets with attractively drawn covers appeared to be Australian. Most, however, exhibited that confident gloss unique to American publishers. All carried a small rubber stamp: 'Blue Centaur Book Co.'

'I don't think I've seen you here before,' said someone at my elbow. It was the man with the moustache. He held out a hand. 'Dave Cohen.'

He had an unexpectedly horny palm; Dave, it transpired, earned his living as an office messenger, and spent the day hauling string-wrapped parcels around the city.

'Hello, Dave. John Baxter.'

If Cohen smiled, it was lost in his bushy mo. 'Ah,' he said, 'the boy from the bush.'

This was the first time we'd met, but Dave and I had been corresponding for almost a year. He advertised in *New Worlds*, offering a postal lending library of sf, and I joined, mainly to find the copies of *Astounding* and *Galaxy* missing from Rodney's garage. This developed into a full-blown correspondence, my raves about the newest Arthur Clarke or Ray Bradbury story answered by ten-page letters from Dave, closely typed in blue ink and inveighing against the Forces of Evil who plotted to destroy his livelihood by prejudicing the landlords of potential clubrooms against him and sending anonymous letters to the Customs department claiming the sf magazines he imported were Communist propaganda.

Over the next year, various people explained Australia's science-fiction wars to me in not-always-consistent detail. All agreed, however, that the Bridge Club and Dave, its central figure, were lone survivors of the cosmic calamity that was the disbanding of the group I'd seen mentioned in that issue of *Super Science Stories*, the Futurian Society of Australia.

The first Futurians were New Yorkers who'd caught the bug of science fiction from the pulps. Seldom more than a dozen strong, they lived, mostly communally, in various bedbug-infested tenement apartments, and schemed to impose their philosophy on the world. Their crest featured a large flat-headed screw and the motto '*Omnes qui non Futurianes sunt*' – '*Thus* to all who are not Futurians'.

The group preached the overthrow of capitalism, though since none was older than twenty-one, few had even graduated from high school and almost all were severely dysfunctional, either physically or emotionally, or sometimes both, their political philosophy wasn't, to say the least, well thought-out. Mostly they visualized a universal version of the testy anarchy with which they ran their private lives. As part of this policy, they had inserted, as 'The Science Fictioneers', that piece I'd read in *Super Science Stories*, and persuaded other science-fiction clubs around the world, including the Sydney one, to adopt the 'Futurian' label.

Oddly for communists, every Futurian wanted desperately to sell science-fiction stories or edit a magazine. Since all were prepared to work day and night, and for almost nothing, many succeeded, notably Fred Pohl, James Blish, Cyril Kornbluth, Judith Merrill and Damon Knight. Donald Wollheim, whom Damon Knight calls 'the group's natural leader' (and who, therefore, in the natural law that rules radical groups, was instrumental in destroying it), co-founded the paperback house Ace, and, later, Daw.

Super Science Stories had been edited by Fred Pohl, then nineteen years old. He earned $10 a week – a derisory sum even in 1940 – though his assistant had to work for three months without salary *before* he received even $10. Pohl paid half a cent a word – 50 per cent of the going pulp rate; which explains why the stories were so bad – just as his association with the Futurians explains why he gave them three pages to plug science-fiction fandom.

The Australian Futurians began to expire explosively in the Fifties. First, Dave Cohen split off to found the Bridge Club Group. Although the Futurians continued to exist, they eventually shattered into even more fragments, and everyone at the Bridge Club agreed that the reasons for the break-up were best not discussed – particularly in Dave's hearing – and that I must never *ever* mention the name of the Australian Futurians' president and now, apparently, sole member, Graham E. Stone.

'Who is Graham E. Sto—?' I began.

'Sshh!'

From George Melly's account in his memoir *Rum, Bum and Concertina* of Edouard Mesens' Surrealist group in Forties London, and Lenin and his fellow exiles in Zurich as described by Tom Stoppard in *Travesties* ('Remember the time they had a meeting? Social Democrats for Civil War in Europe. Total attendance: four. Ulyanov, Mrs Ulyanov, Zinoviev and a police spy'), it's clear that all fringe groups share the same dynamics. Even the Australian Futurians' hara-kiri followed tradition, since the New York group also self-destructed. In 1945, Wollheim, offended by a letter circulated by some of the others, sued his fellow visionaries for libel. Another fan, Ed Saha, dropped into the Futurian hangout on the pretext of having a cup of coffee but distributed subpoenas instead. This was thought a particularly low tactic, though the battles that followed eclipsed it.

Over the next few years, Thursday night at the Bridge Club became a fixture of my week. Of the twenty or thirty fans who eddied in and out, I made friends with a few, in particular Doug Nicholson, an amiable dreamer with sufficient belief in science fiction to have launched a semi-professional magazine, *Forerunner*, but not enough to keep it going: it died with the third issue still half-finished. Australian science fiction was littered with these monuments to a spasmodic sense of futurity. In an earlier generation, some had been produced by the improbably named Vol (for Voltaire) Molesworth, another legend whose name couldn't be mentioned around Dave Cohen, since he had been aligned with the loathed Futurians.

Having left school early, I'd leapt large areas of formative experience, social and intellectual, but Doug and other older members of the group behaved generously towards someone whose brashness served to conceal the fact that he knew almost nothing about anything. In fact it was at one of the first 'adult' parties I ever attended that Doug carefully explained the mechanism of evolution to me – something the nuns in Junee clearly believed flew in the face of holy writ, since they had never mentioned it. Until then, I'd thought that Man just . . . well, *happened*.

Since what I liked was science fiction itself, it was a surprise to discover that most of the people who came to the Bridge Club didn't read it any more, since nothing was ever likely to rival Stanley G. Weinbaum's *A Martian Odyssey*, published in 1934. An American fan, Redd Boggs, so loathed the modern stuff that he wrote: 'The best thing one can do for science fiction today is to go round all the news-stands and put the sf magazines at the back.'

For one of Australia's periodic sf conventions, Robert Bloch penned a long verse that concluded, 'Tell me now, you folks down under / Do you have a sense of wonder?' It was a fair question, to which nobody had an answer. Thinking about the future was just too much trouble. But if the fans weren't interested in science fiction, I certainly was, and, moreover, in collecting it. This put me in a minority, though it made an instant friend of Dave Cohen, who smelled a new client.

I still own books bought from Dave, among them first editions of Alfred Bester's *The Demolished Man* and *Tiger, Tiger!*, aka *The Stars My Destination*, the precursors of modern 'cyberpunk'. Both carry dust wrappers so rare that I don't know anybody who has ever seen them, let alone owned them. And both have been signed, in, of all places, Dublin, by a scowling, bearded and, by then, irredeemably alcoholic Bester, who stopped pacing the conference room at a convention of sf writers long enough to inscribe *Tiger, Tiger!* 'In the Royal Marine Hotel, waiting for a *drink*!'

Dave also sold me Jim Blish's *Earthman, Come Home*, with its concept of entire cities lifting off from Earth and wandering the galaxy in search of work – the 'Okies' of Steinbeck's *The Grapes of Wrath* scaled up to cosmic proportions. When New York mayor John Amalfi proclaims at the end, 'Earth isn't a place; it's an idea,' my heart lurched as it had when I read the first lines of *Mission of Gravity*. Years later, I lifted Jim's image for a screenplay. He was dead by then, of smoking-induced cancer of the tongue, a cruelly ironic death for someone who spent years as a publicist for the tobacco lobby, but I expect he would have greeted this ambiguous *hommage* with his usual shrug and smile, to which his beanpole height gave a quality of Olympian remoteness.

Fandom, though I remained within it for years – and in which in fact I became more active, publishing amateur 'fanzines', corresponding with fans in other cities and around the world, attending conventions, and even meeting the notorious but, in real life, mild and ineffectual Graham E. Stone (shhhhh!) – was always a transitional enthusiasm, something to be passed through *en route* to ... what? That wasn't clear.

CHAPTER SIX

The Loneliness of the
Long-Distance Reader

Now I find that once more I have shrunk
To an interloper, robber of dead men's dreams.
I had read in books that art is not easy
But no one warned me that the mind repeats
In its ignorance the vision of others. I am still
The black swan of trespass on alien waters.

'Ern Malley' (Harold Stewart and James McCauley),
Dürer, Innsbruck, 1495

SINCE IT MIRRORED EVERY INTRICACY AND
eccentricity of the larger world of bibliophily, but on
a reduced scale, collecting science-fiction books
offered a good opportunity to learn. It was still
relatively rare for a British hardback publisher to
dabble in genre books. Science fiction, fantasy,

westerns, even crime were regarded with suspicion. In addition, Australia had only one other serious collector, a Melbourne industrialist named Ron Graham, so, if something interesting turned up, you'd likely be the only person in the market.

Answers to almost any bibliophilic question could usually be found in *The Checklist of Science Fiction and Supernatural Fiction* by the American Everett Bleiler and in Don Tuck's two-volume *Handbook of Science Fiction and Fantasy*. Bleiler's book was unimaginably rare; I never even saw a copy until long after I became a serious collector. Even so, the phrase 'Not in Bleiler' after a catalogue listing would get one twitching like a birdwatcher told that a Lesser Crested Crimson Sapsucker had just been spotted in a swamp where it hadn't nested since 1876.

The *Handbook* was more accessible, since the compiler, a monument to anal retention named Don Tuck, lived in Hobart, Tasmania, appropriately as close as one could get to the end of the world without leaving the planet. His two blue-covered foolscap volumes, reproduced by Roneo on insubstantial paper, became my bible. Don and I carried on a vigorous nit-picking correspondence over many years but never met. I had uncles and aunts in Hobart to stay with, and could even have travelled there free on my railway pass. But, like most fans, both Don and I shied away from personal contact – he even more than I, since he seldom entertained visitors, and, after agreeing to be guest of honour at Australia's first World Science Fiction convention in 1975, didn't show up.

In building libraries, Don and I were really erecting walls of books against the world. 'And nothing wrong with that,' I would have insisted at the time. Compared with America as depicted by Fred Astaire or Marlene Dietrich, or the outer planets of the solar system as described by Robert Heinlein or James Blish, the real world, as represented by Sydney, showed up in no good light.

Collecting books became my life – or, if you like, a substitute for one. Saturday mornings, I'd take the train across the Sydney Harbour Bridge and, battling the tide of beach-bound tanned families, head towards the Central Railway station. In the gapped grin of brick buildings running up to the red-sandstone pile of the station itself, a dozen second-hand shops were snagged like scraps of gristle. I combed them all.

Difficult to explain the pleasure of the Saturdays spent, often on hands and knees, ferreting in those dusty shops, in the cavernous Edwardian brick barn of Paddy's Market, or in Ashwood's, a book and record shop with a turnover so torrential that its stock seemed to renew itself every day.

Most of us, when we first learn chess, see

everything in terms of the game; the man in front of us in the post-office queue is safe, but those diagonally to left and right in the flanking queues are under threat from our pawns, just as we stand in a knight relation to that woman addressing a parcel at the counter to our left. It was the same with short-hand – another largely useless skill I had acquired as part of my railway training; for years, Isaac Pitman's spidery hieroglyphs would unroll as subtitles to one's subvocalized thoughts.

Like all collectors, I created a similar mental geography to model my search for books. With me, as with most other bibliophiles, it was an analogue of some other activity, often rural and bucolic. We might talk of 'harvesting' a particular shop or market once or twice a year. My wife calls the bookshop opposite our home in Paris my 'cabbage patch', which I visit every day to do a little light spadework. The term, borrowed from hunting, 'to go round the traps', is common too.

To me, bookshops have always seemed as rivers do to a fisherman; maybe it's a reflection of Melville's comment in *Moby Dick* that all thinking people will find their way, sooner or later, to running water. A big flea market is a delta where merchandise flows sluggishly through scores of channels over which the collector must dart and hop. Ashwood's and its fast-changing stock evoked rapids where hundreds of salmon leapt in the sluicing water. Other shops mimicked still pools. You could safely let a book remain on the shelf for years, lurking like a crafty old pike in the cool depths.

In Australia, nature and the book existed in a state of war. Summer damp and heat reacted with the bleach in paper to produce 'foxing'; an apparently pristine book could be marred on every page by its rusty blotches. A few of Sydney's arrogant varnish-brown cockroaches were likely to scuttle out of any carton you started to excavate, but other bugs were more insidious. Some could drill a perfect millimetre-wide tunnel through the heftiest tome. Others confined themselves to the surface. When a publisher coated his covers with the wrong sort of 'size', bugs headed for them in the millions, slithering under the dust wrapper to browse until the boards were covered with winding white tracks. Certain books were notorious for this fault. In a shelf devoted to works by Randolph Stow, insects always singled out his collection of poems, *A Counterfeit Silence*. 'It was bound in a turquoise cloth that was sized with gelatine,' remembers Sydney bookseller Nicholas Pounder. 'Once a critical humidity was achieved, it was like aniseed to a hound; the silverfish and cockies would scamper, slavering.'

But people could do far worse damage than any insect. Annotations, underlinings and marginalia were common, the reader carrying on an exasperated conversation with the writer. A scribbled 'Fool!' in the margin was common, as was 'Yes!' or 'No!', with the occasional 'So true!' Obviously they never expected anybody else to read these books, since, even when they wrote 'False', they never explained *why* it was false.

Many people, it seems, are convinced that the front endpaper – the blank page at the beginning of a book – exists to be written on. Ladies and gentlemen, the free endpaper is *not* there to scribble on, or otherwise, as it used to say on computer cards when computers used cards, 'tear, fold, spindle or mutilate'. The endpaper has the same significance in a book as the silences in a Pinter play, the gaps between movements in a Beethoven quartet or the unpainted canvas of one of Bacon's screaming popes. Between the gaudiness of the dust wrapper and the solemnity of the text, it provides a beat.

Anything written on it should at least equal the binding in beauty or the text in intelligence. In the case of most books, admittedly, this isn't a challenge. When Michel Houellebecq's hero in *Atomised* masturbates on a Metro train and catches his ejaculation – though hopefully *just* his ejaculation – in a hastily-slammed geography text, the book undoubtedly gains in the process. However, in scrawling 'Dear Clive, thought this would remind you of our happy school days ha ha ha' on the flyleaf of *Lord of the Flies*, 'Your old pal Clary' does nobody a favour.

But there are worse sins. Once, in a London bookshop, a discussion I was having with a bookseller about an early printing of Nigel Kneale's *Tomato Cain* was interrupted by a customer asking if we knew a book by Hemingway with a name 'to do with bells'.

'You mean *For Whom the Bell Tolls*,' the bookseller said.

'*That's* the one!' Taking out a pen, he reached over to the Kneale book, tore out the endpaper, and started to write on it.

Both of us squealed – there's no other word for it. From £30, the value of the book dropped to 10p.

'It's OK,' the man said, alarmed but certain he could reassure us. He showed us both sides of the paper. 'There's no words on it.'

It took a long time to convince him that this wasn't the point, and a longer time to extract £30. He probably still tells this story at dinner parties. 'One time, I was in a bookshop and met these two *crazies* . . .'

Book 'exchanges', which offered one second-hand book for every two you brought in, further depreciated their stock by slamming giant rubber stamps on the flyleaves – a bad habit that I didn't encounter again until I moved to Paris and met

George Whitman at his so-called Shakespeare and Company bookshop.

Occasionally, however, I found a book which, even in terrible condition, was too desirable to discard. Truman Capote's first short-story collection, for example, was something I simply had to have, even though the catalogue entry of the copy I ferreted out of a rural junk shop would have read:

CAPOTE, Truman. A TREE OF NIGHT AND OTHER STORIES, William Heinemann, London, 1950. First British printing. Lacks dust wrapper. Original green cloth bumped at all corners. Cloth faded to a blotched rust colour around all margins of front and back boards, and along spine, which is also sunned. Large stamps on front pastedown and front free endpaper ('SECOND-HAND BOOKS, STAMPS AND MAGIC, City Centre Arcade, Penrith. Bought, Sold, Exchange'). Small bookseller's label on front pastedown. Figure '$2' in ballpoint on front pastedown. Illegible signature and date on front free endpaper. Fore-edges, prelims, and first pages of text foxed . . .

Everything, in short, but a used condom for a bookmark.

Dealers got to know I would buy science fiction, and kept interesting items under the counter. Not that there was much. Sf magazines were failing, but only a few publishers maintained a book list, and, of those, most soon wearied of this fickle market. A dozen small American presses like Gnome, Prime and Fantasy intermittently issued minuscule printings of obscure titles. But since Australian distributors shunned them, they could normally only be bought by sending large sums in almost unobtainable US dollars to places like Sauk City, Wisconsin, where August Derleth of Arkham House cackled over crumbling files of *Weird Tales* and guarded the wan flame that was the literary reputation of H. P. Lovecraft.

Occasionally something from one of the specialist presses came to rest in Sydney, like a gorgeous butterfly blown impossibly far off course. One could hardly miss them, since they often had covers commissioned from artists like Hannes Bok, Edd Cartier or Virgil Finlay who had learned in the pulps how to catch the eye. Bok's cover for L. Ron Hubbard's *Slaves of Sleep*, with its cutlass-carrying pirate and simpering harem girl, looks Disney-ish today, and the vivid baroque of the artwork created for Robert E. Howard's *Skullface and Others* owes too much to Maxfield Parrish, but I wouldn't part with either of them. They convey an indelible memory of those rummaging years.

Otherwise, in the Anglophile Australia of the early

Sixties, the book market belonged to British publishers with names like firms of solicitors: Hodder & Stoughton, Routledge & Kegan Paul, Eyre & Spottiswoode, MacGibbon & Kee, and particularly Faber & Faber.

Many of the British science-fiction books I collected in those days were produced during World War II, and mustily evoked that world of recycling and rationing, of dried egg, margarine, utility furniture, demob suits, and making do. One could tell from the grey, speckled paper that other books had been pulped to make them, and that any unsold copies went back in the stew. Sometimes even the wrappers were recycled, covers for new novels printed on the verso of the old.

The Festival of Britain in 1951 – 'that gaudy flyleaf', as George Melly called it in a not very accurate bibliophilic metaphor, 'dividing wartime austerity from the excess to come' – revived British typography and book production. Paper became creamier, boards stouter, dust-wrapper design more inventive. Pen-and-wash artists such as Edward Ardizzone, John Piper and John Verney gave way to men who worshipped foreign gods. Michael Ayrton loosed a Picasso-esque monster on Ray Bradbury's first collection of stories, *Dark Carnival*, but almost everyone designing for a fantasy book fell back on Surrealism. Some – Paul Nash, Bip Pares, and the

American E. McKnight Kauffer, for example – borrowed with imagination, but, as T. S. Eliot said of poets, the mature plagiarize while the immature imitate, and plenty of second-rate artists appear just to have taken down their album of Yves Tanguy reproductions and reached for the tracing paper.

The narrator of John Updike's story 'The Astronomer' succumbs to the writings of Kierkegaard by reading him in the Princeton University Press editions:

> Beautiful books, sometimes very thick, sometimes very thin, always typographically exhilarating, with their welter of title pages, subheads, epigraphs, emphatic italics, italicized catchwords taken from German philosophy and too subtle for translation, translator's prefaces and footnotes, and Kierkegaard's own endless footnotes, blanketing pages at a time as, crippled, agonized by distinctions, he scribbled on and on, heaping irony on irony, curse on curse, gnashing, sneering, praising Jehovah in the privacy of his empty home in Copenhagen.

What seduced me was the gloomy reticence of Faber & Faber's *The Death of Grass*, its design and presentation soberly appropriate both to John Christopher's story and to a house with T. S. Eliot among its directors; and to John Wyndham's *The Day of the Triffids*, *The Kraken Wakes* and *The Midwich*

Cuckoos; William Golding's *The Inheritors* and *Lord of the Flies*; John Bowen's *After the Rain* – any novel, really, where English men and women battled menaces from outer space or from undisciplined technology as they ravished the home counties.

Above all, I treasured the Eyre & Spottiswoode first editions of Mervyn Peake's trilogy *Titus Groan*, *Gormenghast* and *Titus Alone*. Bound in cloth of the same dried-blood red as Mark Rothko's *Dance of Death* paintings, and with dust wrappers drawn with all Peake's mastery of the pen and ink line, they were printed on a slightly yellow half-transparent paper that (intentionally?) suggested parchment. The blurb copy alone was enough to win me. 'Candles gutter. Towers of black ivy drip. Festooned in old ritual, figures move by, loom and impend along the half-lit corridors of Gormenghast . . .'

One day I'd become friendly with Peake's widow, Maeve, and hear stories of life with the mercurial Mervyn, and of his death too, as he sank into a pit of disease and madness deeper than anything he imagined for the Castle of Groan. I'd also walk the lanes of Kent with John Wyndham's widow as she remembered how, strolling on a windy night, she and her husband passed a bank of blackberries, and he, staring at thorny brambles thrashing in the wind, had murmured, 'My God, if they could walk and think, how terrible they would be' – the germ of *The Day of the Triffids*. But, paging through Michael Joseph's discreet editions of Wyndham in the heat of an Australian summer, both the books and their locations seemed impossibly remote, and, therefore, ascetically seductive. Not only this corner of a foreign field but large portions of the future as well were 'for ever England'.

By comparison, Australia felt to me like the country Tennyson wrote about in 'The Lotos-Eaters' – 'a land / In which it seemed always afternoon'. Enthusiasms evaporated in the hot dry air. It was as if, because of some genetic abnormality, Australians lacked the ability to communicate on any but the most concrete level. One could discuss facts incessantly, but passions induced an embarrassment that rendered them literally speechless. It would be decades before this intellectual lockjaw passed.

Meanwhile, a few people desperate to communicate searched for an audience. Every Sunday, dozens gathered in The Domain, Sydney's version of London's Speakers' Corner, hectoring crowds who wandered among them in the sun, eating ice cream, like people inspecting the animals in Taronga Park Zoo. Most were quickly classified, in the pungent local taxonomy, as 'ratbags'.

Among them, three cultural revolutionaries chose words as their weapons. The first, Bea Miles, smelly, dumpy but charismatic, the black sheep daughter of a wealthy family of clothing merchandisers, roamed Sydney, wearing a hand-lettered cardboard sign offering to recite Shakespeare for a shilling a time. Once paid, she would gabble half a minute from *Hamlet* before leaping into the back seat of a cab and demanding to be taken to some outlying suburb – trips for which she was never known to cough up. Priests in a Catholic church near Central Railway let her sleep under the table in their kitchen, from where she ranged the city in her quest for an ear.

The second was Arthur Stace. Illiterate, an alcoholic and son of alcoholics, Arthur spent his youth in the family brothel business, until, one night in 1932, he wandered into the Burton Street Baptist Tabernacle in the heart of Sydney's red light district, and heard evangelist John G. Ridley preaching. This is how Stace recalled it:

He kept shouting 'Eternity, Eternity', and his words were ringing through my brain as I left the church. Suddenly I began crying and I felt a powerful call from the Lord to write 'Eternity'. I had a piece of chalk in my pocket and I bent down there and wrote it. The funny thing is that before I wrote I could hardly have spelt my own name. I had no schooling and I couldn't have spelt 'Eternity' for a hundred quid. But it came out smoothly in beautiful copperplate script. I couldn't understand it and I still can't.

For thirty years, Stace pursued his solitary ministry, writing 'Eternity' on footpaths and walls, first in yellow chalk, then in more permanent yellow crayon. Only five feet three and a hundred pounds, habitually dressed in a grey felt hat and double-breasted blue suit, he passed unnoticed until 1956, when the minister at the church where he worked as a cleaner caught him.

'Are *you* Mr Eternity?' he asked.

'Guilty, Your Honour,' Stace said shyly.

Discovery just added to the legend. When the clock tower of the General Post Office in Martin Place, dismantled during World War II, was re-erected in 1960, 'Eternity' was found written inside the bell that had been crated and stored for twenty years. 'Eternity' in solid brass was embedded in the footpath when the area in front of the Sydney Town Hall and St Andrew's Cathedral was redeveloped in the 1970s. And when fireworks lit up Sydney Harbour on New Year's Day 2000, people round the world watching the first visual celebration of the millennium were puzzled to see, as its climax, 'Eternity' blazing hundreds of metres long across the Harbour Bridge in Stace's fine Australian hand.

Through Dave Cohen, whose Blue Centaur Book Company was named for one of his drawings, I also came to admire the work of the third and most eminent of this trio, that archetypal rebel (and, in the eyes of many Australians, ratbag *sans pareil*), Norman Lindsay. Painter, sculptor, print-maker and pen-and-ink artist of enormous gifts, ship-modeller, novelist, essayist and all-round scourge of the establishment, he was still alive and working when I came to Sydney. His last painting is dated September 1969, just a few days before his death at ninety.

It's tantalizing to think I could have met him, but my contact was confined to cruising periodically down a gum-tree-lined red dirt road in the Blue Mountains near the town of Springwood, and staring through high untrimmed hedges at his austere colonial bungalow on the hill. What went on there was the stuff of legend. Locals whispered of naked men and women cavorting under the gums, of parties where . . . well, best not even to *suggest* what might have taken place.

After his death the legend, if anything, grew more florid. John Duigan's film *Sirens* embodied much of it, showing an English curate and his wife tempted to paganism by their encounter with Lindsay and his family of hangers-on. The curate, a joke figure Lindsay employed often in his work, usually as a horrified onlooker to some debauch, falls for one of the models, while his wife succumbs to Sapphic love in the billabong with three of them.

However, one visit to Lindsay's house, now a museum, and a look at the cement-and-chicken-wire nudes that dot the gumtree-shaded hilltop, puts him into perspective as a Georgian bohemian who should, like his son Jack, have moved to England and pursued his calling in the more congenial atmosphere of Bloomsbury and Garsington. Instead, Lindsay stayed in Australia, writing his libertarian novels, producing his provocative paintings, both of which the censors periodically banned, and keeping Jack's Fanfrolico Press afloat with scores of sexy illustrations for high-priced editions of *The Satyricon*, *Lysistrata*, *Catullus* and *The Memoirs of Casanova*.

Lindsay produced so many anti-German cartoons for *The Bulletin* and other magazines that, as World War II spread into the Pacific, it was widely assumed, as one friend warned him, that he would be 'the first person the Germans will shoot when they invade' – a disaster regarded as a foregone conclusion by most Australians. Lindsay was so virulently anti-Jew and anti-black that he and Albert Speer would probably have become mates. All the same, his wife Rose decided all his original drawings and paintings should be shipped to America for safe-keeping. Loaded into freight cars, they got as far as New Jersey, where the first truck caught fire, having been attached, with conspicuous lack of intelligence, just behind the locomotive. The train stopped at a rural station and the guard dragged the smouldering boxes onto the platform. Locals, coming to watch the show, first examined Lindsay's pictures of heavy-breasted women pursued by horny satyrs, then righteously heaped the filthy things together and fanned the flames. Almost nothing of his pre-war work survived.

Lindsay bewitched me, particularly when, on a trip to Melbourne, I stumbled across a show of his etchings in one of the city's Edwardian arcades. They hung on bare walls in an empty shop that had sold shoes the previous week and would be selling towels the week after. All were for sale, at prices ranging from £20 to £50. What desperately broke or terminally bored collector decided on this bleak means of raising money? I never knew. Scraping to the bottom of my bank account, I bought two of them, a large scene of a witches' coven called *She Arrives*, with a voluptuously naked witch rejoicing in the adoration of her acolytes, including an imp who's fastened his mouth on her doughy thigh, and the smaller and more restrained *Bargains*, in which a demon kisses a girl's hand with the appraising look of a money lender who knows the borrower has no hope of repaying the loan.

She Arrives wore out its welcome after a while, but *Bargains* has followed me around the world, having become the cornerstone of what is now a large Lindsay collection. I even have one of his rare pre-war pen-and-ink drawings, found via the Internet auction site eBay in, of all places, Wisconsin. A sketch for a page heading for some classic translation, with centaurs parading through a wood, it's been partly torn and carefully repaired. Did some secret connoisseur snatch it from the flames on that New Jersey station platform? It would be nice to think so, if only as evidence that the collecting instinct can appear anywhere and in anyone.

CHAPTER SEVEN

Haunted Screens

Other people, so I have read, treasure memorable moments in their lives: the time one climbed the Parthenon at sunrise, the summer night one met a lonely girl in Central Park and achieved with her a sweet and natural relationship, as they say in books. I too once met a girl in Central Park, but it was not much to remember. What I remember is the time John Wayne killed three men with a carbine as he was falling to the dusty street in *Stagecoach*, and the time the kitten found Orson Welles in the doorway in *The Third Man*.

Walker Percy, The Moviegoer

UNTIL MY EARLY TWENTIES, SCIENCE FICTION, BOOK hunting and the railways occupied all my days. Mine was the social life of the loner – which is to say no social life at all; just a succession of meetings with fellow obsessives on neutral ground, for the playing of chess, the exchange of books, the reinforcement of our treasured detachment. We lived with parents, or alone, and took satisfaction in the way others perceived us as outlandish.

But then, around 1965, whatever it was that made the Sixties such a distinctive decade began to work its liberating magic on Australia. Hints of other lifestyles and different points of view drifted across our skies like UFOs. Some saw them in the literature of the Beat Generation, others in rock music, but for me the vehicle of revelation was the movies.

Most Saturdays, I'd stop book hunting around noon, buy a slab of roast pork-belly at the Chinese takeaway on Campbell Street, watch the owner hack it into slices with his cleaver, then carry it with a bottle of Coke across the road to the Capitol Cinema. There I would pay, in those pre-decimal days, 2s 6d for a ticket and search the empty circle for a seat without protruding springs to spike my backside, and where I could munch the deliciously greasy spiced meat with no risk of being rousted by some officious usher.

A few moments usually remained before the start of the first film in the day's double bill to contemplate John Eberson's flaking midnight-blue ceiling, and wonder how it would look with its tiny stars illuminated – a feature rusted up long before I discovered the place. Since then, the Capitol has been restored and even its stars shine once more, but in those days its greatest appeal resided in its shabbiness, offering as it did both cheapness and anonymity. One could lose oneself in the warm dark – 'lie low,' as Leonard Cohen said, 'and let the hunt go by'.

But what drew me back every week was the films. Mostly black and white and Italian or French, invariably dubbed into English, cut down to a jerky ninety minutes, and further hacked by the film censor, they reflected lives utterly alien to someone who'd never eaten an olive, seen a subtitled film, spoken to a Frenchman or kissed a girl, let alone slept with one.

Occasionally, during my adolescence, a foreign film had reflected back some flashes of my own experience – a 1954 movie called *The Game of Love*, for instance (a title attached by British distributors to almost anything French where the heroine removed a garment more intimate than a cardigan). Two teenagers, friends since infancy, meet at the same resort every year. They're too shy to do anything about their mutual attraction until an older woman seduces the boy. The experience frees him to see his childhood friend for the first time, but undermines their uncomplicated love. An adaptation, in short, of Colette's *Le Blé en herbe – Ripening Seed*. But its world of the beach and holidays was familiar enough to hint at lessons I might put into practice, some time, with some woman, if I ever got to know any.

Anybody in Australia hoping to learn about life from the cinema faced an uphill struggle in the Sixties. Nudity, violence, horror, obscenity, blasphemy and sedition – the censors cut them all. In the film of John O'Hara's *Butterfield 8*, Liz Taylor, explaining to Eddie Fisher how she came to be a 'party girl' – i.e., part-time prostitute – traces it back to childhood, when a boyfriend of her mother's, whom she regarded as a sort of uncle, took her on his knee and 'interfered with' her. Liz goes on, 'But the worst thing was . . .' At which point the film hiccuped, the sure sign of a cut. The next shot was of Fisher, looking bemused. Only much later did we discover that Liz said, 'But the worse thing was, I *enjoyed* it.' Enjoying *sex*? Obviously that had to go.

Interesting as I found the occasional flashes of eroticism in foreign films, the one that got me thinking most had no sex at all. The version presented at the Capitol was known as *The Bandit's Revenge*, though it was actually called *Salvatore Giuliano*. Set in the rocky landscape of Sicily, it was a half documentary / half drama about a young man – face never seen – who, dressed in an incongruous grey dustcoat and with a World War II machine gun over his shoulder, led his gang against . . . who exactly? I couldn't make that out. It would be years before I decoded the film, but Francesco Rosi's darting direction remade my sense of how a story is told, as did the near-operatic behaviour of the characters – the old man who walks to a hilltop, for instance, and apostrophizes his native land like a character from Greek tragedy. Above all, the ink black and lime white of Gianni di Venanzo's photography prepared me for Antonioni and the French new wave, just as the content lured me to history, politics, and, above all, to Europe.

It's not surprising that my first reaction to this new stimulus was to start a collection of books about the cinema. When each month these days brings countless new movie books, it's hard to believe that, in the early Sixties, the total was numbered in dozens. The 'classics', dating from the Thirties, were long out of print. When anything about film turned up in my scouring of the shops, I grabbed it even if, as was often the case, it was in French or, occasionally, German. Ashwood's, for instance, disgorged a battered French paperback of Lotte Eisner's study of German expressionist cinema, *L'Écran démoniaque*. I puzzled out the title as 'The Demonic Screen' (the later English publisher preferred 'Haunted') and also some of her text, but German terms such as *Kammerspiele* and *Stimmung* hovered tantalizingly out of reach.

But even if I couldn't read it, there were the pictures! White-faced men and women, eyes rolled like bolting horses', stumbling down shadowed corridors or twisting staircases as if fleeing from invisible demons. Some stills I already knew from *The Film Till Now* or other books I'd accumulated: Siegfried Kracauer's *From Caligari to Hitler*; *The Rise of the American Film* by Lewis Jacobs – soon to teach film history to George Lucas and John Milius at USC; *A History of the Film* by Maurice Bardeche and Robert Brasillach; Sergei Eisenstein's *The Film Form* and *The Film Sense*; and Robert Florey's *Hollywood, d'hier et d'aujourd'hui*.

If the images were familiar, so were many of the ideas. All these books tended to regard movies through a very narrow window, as film study in the Thirties was mainly the playground of the intellectual left, in particular a London group called the Film Society. Belying the staid title, its members enjoyed melodramatic private lives. Ivor Montagu, one of its senior members, ended up in Hollywood, holding open house to Sergei Eisenstein, Charlie Chaplin and other left-wingers. The equally socialist Iris Barry ran the Society between bouts with the bottle and disastrous love affairs, including one with the writer Wyndham Lewis. She ended up running the Museum of Modern Art film library in New York, with a staff that included Luis Buñuel and Jay Leyda, who translated the Eisenstein books and who, like Buñuel, would be driven out of America by the anti-Communists. Barry translated Maurice Bardeche and

Robert Brasillach – an odd choice, since Brasillach was a Fascist and almost the only French author executed for collaboration. The irascible Paul Rotha, another Film Society member, would also have his day in the headlines when his wife stabbed him. And so on. Contemporary film critics are nowhere near as interesting.

The film books I couldn't buy, I borrowed from Sydney's central public library, working my way through the entire 791.43 Dewey designation. The library squatted at one end of the block-long Queen Victoria Building, just opposite the town hall. These days a chic shopping precinct of marble, stained glass and polished brass, the QVB in 1961 was a Gormenghast-like pile, dilapidated and dingy, the haunt of cheap tailors and cut-rate radio stores, and permeated end to end with a yeasty tang from the wooden kegs of beer that filled its basement. Subdivided into chaos over the years, the building drew developers as surely as dead meat. They circled it like tiger sharks, eager to erect a nice Miesian office block on the site.

Having access to the library was all well and good, but as a collector you had to *own* the book. This wasn't simply a matter of mindless acquisition. To have an object under your control is halfway to improving on it. Painters learn their craft by repainting works they admire, and some writers have educated themselves by copying out, by hand, the entire text of other books. Once they learned the rhythm of another's words, they could put their own words in their place. And it was no less so with movies. While I was paging through the Sydney library's much-repaired copy of the Jonathan Cape first edition of Paul Rotha's cranky *The Film Till Now* ('now' in his case being 1930), Martin Scorsese in his local library in New York was falling under the spell of Deems Taylor's 1946 *A Pictorial History of the Cinema*, snipping out some of the illustrations I just salivated over. At the same time, François Truffaut, as he remembered in a dream sequence for *La Nuit Américaine* (*Day for Night*), cruised Paris by night, using a walking stick to hook cinema display panels close enough to the grille to steal stills from *Citizen Kane*. 'I am eaten up with the image,' Ken Russell would tell me years later, 'with the way things *look*.' Scorsese, Truffaut and a whole generation of film-makers echoed him.

In the autumn of 1961, NSW Railways had assigned me to the relief staff who filled in for people on sick leave or holidays. Railway offices dot the outback of New South Wales, and every few weeks I arrived at one of these forlorn little towns, the kind of archetypal whistle-stop that Edward Abbey, author of the classic *The Monkey Wrench Gang*, evoked with unsentimental clarity.

> William Creek looks like a showdown town out of some classic Hollywood western. *High Noon*. A couple of trees. Windmill and water tank. A couple of buildings. One is the depot of the Central Australian Railway, where five of the seven William Creekers live. They work for the railroad. The other building, a single-storey structure with tin roof and rambling white wings, is the William Creek Hotel with its pub, the only beer joint and watering hole within 100 miles, in any direction. This tiny outlier of what is called the modern world sits alone at the centre of an enormous flat, red, empty circle of sand, dust, meandering dry streambeds and open space. No hills, no woods, no chimneys, no towers of any kind break the line of the clean, bleak horizon.

I got to see plenty of places like William Creek. Squinting against the sunlight, I'd climb off the train at a station that was yet another blurred carbon copy of one built in India or South Africa when Victoria was still on the throne, and lug my suitcase down the wide main street, keeping to the shade of the verandas in front of the few shops. All but a handful would be empty behind the glass, their floorboards littered with FINAL DEMAND envelopes gone yellow with age. Occasionally, a window cataracted with

Dulux paint showed where a shop had become someone's home.

As Abbey noted, the largest and most prosperous building in these towns was invariably the pub. Most were single-storey, but some boasted a second floor, with a wide balcony supported by four-square veranda posts, studded with hitching rings for the occasional patron who arrived by horse rather than the ubiquitous Holden utility truck or 'ute'.

Like the railway stations, the pubs were a little more imposing than the towns they served, and occasionally exhaled a breath of frustrated grandeur. Had Australia not been so culturally marginalized in the nineteenth century, had the Republican movement born on the goldfields in 1854 not died there at the Eureka Stockade, had the country been less eager to live on selling off wheat, wool, meat and iron to Europe and instead developed industries of its own, pubs like this might have rivalled the Palmer Houses and Cattlemen's Associations of the American West, where cigar-smoking beef barons met amid mahogany, brass and baize to parcel out the frontier.

Gerald Murnane described such an alternative Australia in one of my favourite books of speculative fiction, *The Plains*, but no Australian pub ever equalled his vision. The glass in their swinging front doors was frosted rather than leaded, the carpets, where any existed, threadbare, and the wood plain varnished pine. Upstairs, narrow corridors with a strip of cheap carpet down the centre led to utilitarian bedrooms, with a single bathroom and toilet at the end of the hall. In *Rio Bravo*, *Call Northside 777*, *Double Indemnity* and *To Have and Have Not*, James Stewart, John Wayne, Fred MacMurray, Edward G. Robinson, Angie Dickinson, Bogie and Bacall paced or prowled such corridors, plotting murder, hunting villains or nervously circling the idea of sex. Nothing so glamorous was ever going to happen here. In Australia, a cheap hotel was just a cheap hotel.

Few people penetrated further into the hotel than the public bar. In khaki shorts, blue singlets, heavy black boots with short socks, and the occasional felt hat, they spilled onto the footpath, giant 'middies' of gullet-numbing iced lager in their hands, while, in the stuffy purdah of the lounge, their women sipped tiny waisted 'ponies' of shandy – lager and lemonade.

Drinking took priority over eating, but if you did venture towards food, you could choose between vulcanized steak, celluloid fried eggs and greasy chips at the milk bar, or dine in the hotel dining room off grey lamb with gravy, tinned peas and two kinds of potatoes, plus trifle or canned peaches, doused with cream from a can; rather than trust anything from a bottle, it was safer to 'milk the cow with a spanner'.

Most people contented themselves with a meat pie

from the pub's warming cabinet. As the son of a pastrycook, raised on the profit from meat pies, I knew the intricacies of their manufacture, and would not have eaten one at gunpoint. My father once explained his system. On Monday, you took ten kilos of minced meat and ten kilos of pastry and made twenty kilos of pies. On Tuesday, you diced the three kilos of unsold pies, combined these with seven kilos of mince, made another ten kilos of pastry and produced twenty kilos of pies. You continued in this way until Saturday, the week's big pie-selling day, when pubs and sports clubs in the area ordered them by the hundreds. By then, recycled pies made up most of the filling, and the pie as a whole was about 85 per cent pastry. 'But do you know,' my father said in some awe, 'they like those Saturday pies best.'

Knowing that time would weigh heavy on my hands in such places, I never arrived in an outback town with less than a dozen books in my bag – usually the largest library in town. How little people read was underlined by the size and design of hotel bed-lamps. Invariably tiny, with opaque parchment shades, they illuminated only a saucer-sized circle on the bedside table, leaving the rest of the room dark, while the unshaded overhead bulb cast a yellow light too weak to read by.

In this hostile environment, a paperback, its binding shrunk in the dry heat, would gradually arch open in a rictus like death, pages agape and curling. If you left the window closed, you stifled but, open, it admitted every insect, some of them the size of small helicopters, not to mention the barely muted roar from the bar downstairs, where drinking, 6 p.m. closing time or not, continued into the small hours.

When the town was large enough, I would go out in search of a cinema and occasionally strike it lucky. But what cinemas! They were a catalogue of filmic eccentricity. The single-storey white stucco building that still defiantly flashed a blue neon sign saying 'Talkies'; the State or Kings or Hoyts in Gunning or Culcairn or The Rock where I was the only person waiting as the manager, arriving fifteen minutes after the announced starting time for John Ford's *The Searchers*, said over his shoulder to the projectionist, 'We're a bit late tonight, Sid. Better begin with reel three.' Then there was the fenced field with a screen at one end and rows of seats constructed from lengths of canvas suspended from poles, like a continuous deckchair. So unless you were the same weight, you slid inexorably out of your marked zone towards your heaviest neighbour. In another, the entrance was under the screen, so that you stepped right into the blinding projector beam, groped two steps before crashing into the front row of seats, then fumbled your way along the aisle, ruffling the hair of other patrons or trying to sit in their laps. Another town had no real cinema – just a hall with folding wooden chairs, a piano in the corner and dusty paper streamers permanently nailed to the rafters. The film arrived in the sidecar of the projectionist's motorbike. There was only one 35mm projector, so, every ten minutes, he stopped, the lights went up, a blue-rinsed lady struck up *Marchetta* at the piano, and everyone danced until the projectionist stuck his head out of the hatch, said 'Right' and we sat down to the next reel.

One got used to films shown with reels out of order, the image out of focus, or the frame line halfway down the picture; with deafening sound, or none at all. Often, the reel ended and the cinema lapsed into darkness and silence. In such cases, one stormed to the projection box, usually to find it empty, with the projectionist in the lobby chatting up the girl who sold the tickets. Or sometimes he was there, but snoring by the view port, oblivious to the slap slap slap of the film.

If the cinemas were wildly varied, railway offices were as much the same as were the pubs and the menus. Clapboard wooden bungalows, they perched on piers of red brick, with corrugated-iron roofs and a wide veranda along two sides. A grey burlap water bag, beaded with moisture, always hung by the fly-screened front door, its water, with the faint jute after-taste, rendered, by the magic of evaporation, deliciously cool. You needed it, since the buildings themselves were furnaces, particularly when, if pilings didn't offer enough protection from termites, snakes and bull ants, a despairing local engineer had lined the floor with sheet metal which also ran up the first three inches of the walls.

I struck one of these buildings in the far west during a summer when the temperature regularly climbed into the high thirties centigrade. Even wearing nothing but a singlet and shorts, the heat was barely tolerable, until I thought to flood the floor. Paddling around ankle-deep in tepid water helped, but then an engine driver stuck his head around the door, shoved a burlap bag at me and said, 'Look after this for me, willya? I'll get it on the way back.'

When the bag wriggled, I was incautious enough to undo the string. A small kangaroo, the mother of which the driver had run down along the line, stared out. Before I could decide what to do, he wriggled free and bounded round the office, wild-eyed, looking for escape. Each landing drenched the desks and the files on them. It also made the joey wetter, and more difficult to grab.

Giggling hysterically, I pursued it around the increasingly sodden office until the screen door swung open, dramatically framing the local District Engineer, who was making one of his periodical inspections. Seeing its chance, the 'roo bolted by him to freedom, leaving the DE's beige gabardines comprehensively soaked.

None of my postings seemed quite so remote as the one to Newcastle, a city north of Sydney, where the NSW Railways maintained an inspection office in the works of Industrial Iron and Steel, which made most of its axles and wheels.

I arrived by train on Thursday, and took a cab through a no-man's-land of link-fenced vacant lots piled with rusted scrap iron that surrounded the works, marked from miles away by columns of gritty and no doubt noxious smoke rising sluggishly from its chimneys.

To reach the office, I had to cross the enormous casting floor, where they were cracking an open hearth furnace. Molten steel poured into a bucket the size of a house and thence into a maze of moulds, the noise, heat and smell recalling a factory system one imagined dead with Isambard Kingdom Brunel.

The other four men in the office were shrugging into their coats as I arrived. Clive, the boss, said, 'G'day. We'll take you down to the caravan site. Then we'll have a beer.'

'What caravan site? I don't have a caravan.'

'No pubs around here with rooms, mate. We've got you into a caravan. She'll be apples.'

The site, anything but 'apples', was an empty lot

beside the main road, with a brick toilet block and a couple of tyre-less plywood caravans propped on bricks. I stuck my head inside the one assigned to me. A platform with two slabs of plastic foam upholstered in slime-green Naughahyde served as a bed. Every drawer and cupboard, except for the odd silverfish, was empty.

'How am I supposed to eat? And what about bedding?'

Clive said thoughtfully, 'They said they supplied bedding.'

'Is there a manager?'

'On site? No. Look, I'll send someone down with some blankets and a pillow.' He checked his watch. 'Let's get to the pub. It'll be closing time soon.'

I declined. A brief tour showed that I was alone in the park. I sat in the caravan while light faded and the cold evening wind started to gust. Any stronger and the whole thing would blow away, I decided.

I walked back along the main road until I came to a milk bar and opposite – thank God! – a cinema. Relief faded when I saw the title of that night's film. *Scream of Fear*. Almost alone, and with the greasy hamburger I'd eaten for dinner making periodic attempts to be reunited with the rest of the very tough cow that produced it, I watched Susan Strasberg, confined to a wheelchair, screaming and fainting as the villain hid the corpse of her father in places around their Riviera villa; cupboards, the deep-freeze, the swimming pool.

After a ten-minute walk back along the dark road, I let myself into the caravan. Nobody had brought bedding or anything else so, wrapped in three layers of clothing with my underwear as a pillow, I crawled onto one vinyl slab, balanced the other on top, forming a human sandwich, and tried to sleep. At about 3 a.m., the wind freshened and shook the door loose. It slammed against the outside wall. At the same moment, the hatch in the ceiling sprang open with a crash. Any hair not already standing on end turned white.

The next morning, some arm-waving and shouting produced bedding, utensils and some groceries, but as I returned to Sydney that afternoon, it was obvious that I'd need to find a major distraction if I were to stay sane. I arrived back in Newcastle on Sunday night with a dozen books and my portable typewriter.

For a year, I'd been corresponding with E. J. Carnell, editor of *New Worlds Science Fiction* in London. 'John' on the masthead but 'Ted' to his friends, Carnell printed a few of my letters, and even a 'Guest Editorial' in which I fulminated against the declining state of my favourite literature. Now I carried the criticism further by writing a story. This took me a couple of hours, and the following day I mailed it off with a covering letter taunting Ted that if even *I*, a mere fan, could turn out a fair approximation of a *New Worlds* story, then surely his *real* writers, the pros . . .

Two weeks later, back in Sydney and clearing my mail box before embarking on another Saturday of book hunting and Continental movies, I was astonished to receive a blue air-letter from Ted in which he announced he was buying the story, and would shortly send me a cheque for £30.

I stood dazed in front of the old Victorian King Street post office. It never occurred to me that my publishable work would go beyond letters and polemical pieces. I was a *fan*, not a writer. Writers were . . .

Well, *what* were they?

Grown-ups, for a start; at twenty-four, I still regarded myself as an innocent and a naïf. Secondly, professional. They earned their living from writing – or so, erroneously, I imagined. And third, they were foreign. The idea of Australian writers, particularly Australian writers of science fiction, seemed laughable. As well to imagine, well, *women* writing it.

I went home, sat down at the typewriter, and wrote another story. It wasn't that hard. Ideas bubbled up. For the rest of the day, I hardly thought about books at all.

After a year of sending me around the remotest corners of the state, NSW Railways relented and gave me a permanent job in Sydney. About a year later, early in 1966, a colleague from the Staff Department visited my office behind Central Station. As plenty of writers before me had found, the civil service demanded so little from its employees that I could finish my work by lunchtime and spend the rest of the day, hemmed in behind a wall of files, hammering out short stories for *New Worlds*.

'Your long-service leave is coming up,' the staff man told me. 'How do you want it? Days or cash payment?'

I tore myself away from outer space. 'How do you mean, "long-service leave"?' This was something I associated with doddering oldsters who spoke longingly of the fishing trips they'd take or the afternoons they'd spend digging the garden.

He consulted his file. 'Ten years in the job,' he said. 'You're entitled to a month of full pay. Or you can keep working, and just take the cash.'

There floated into my brain the image of a balding, stooped Baxter in the grey cardigan of the ageing railway clerk, receiving his gold watch for forty years' service. For the first time, I understood William Holman Hunt's painting *The Awakening Conscience*, where the young mistress starts up from

121

the lap of her lover in a sudden realization of What She Has Become. To the astonishment of the staff man, I walked into my boss's office and said, 'I want to resign.'

In those days of cradle-to-grave employment, it proved surprisingly hard to quit. The first reaction of my bosses was deep suspicion. What was the hurry? If I'd been in the paymaster's section, they'd have suspected I'd fiddled the books. As it was, a series of increasingly senior executives invited me in 'for a chat'. Finally, two of them arrived unannounced at my home, ready to counsel me on financial or emotional problems. But, eventually, they decided I had simply lost my wits, and let me go.

It took a few weeks to get used to the idea of freedom. Not until I left the railways did I realize how much I'd come to loathe office life. To do nothing but write! The idea was intoxicating, and sitting down each morning to the keyboard would remain one of my greatest joys in life. Still, the change in lifestyle did demand some intellectual adjustments. How did writers live? What did they do? I had no idea, since the few I'd met were, like me, spare-timers.

Fortunately, Hollywood was ready to advise me. Authors in movies rose at about nine, breakfasted lightly in their dressing gowns, read the papers and their mail, bathed and dressed in time to lunch with friends in town, and returned home about 3 p.m. for a little light scribbling before dining with some ravishing companion.

My career as Australia's answer to Noël Coward didn't last. One of the first people to whom I turned for advice was Ron Smith, another science-fiction fan. A native New Yorker, Ron had woken up one morning in October 1962 to news that American warships were intercepting Russian freighters off Cuba. Bundling his wife and son into a cab, he headed for Idlewild and took the first plane to Australia – where, as everyone knew from the film of Nevil Shute's *On the Beach*, the cloud of atomic fall-out took longest to arrive.

Hearing he was in Sydney, I tracked him down in the middle of an electricity blackout to a tiny rented flat. A harassed, pop-eyed, balding figure, he paced the darkness trying to pacify a squalling baby, while his burly wife Cindy lowered in the gloom. I was disappointed. This scene of domestic misery hardly squared with his reputation as editor of *Inside Science Fiction*, voted the world's best sf fanzine of 1956, and an intimate of everyone who really mattered on the American science-fiction scene.

When the world didn't actually come to an end, Ron was too embarrassed and too broke to return to New York. Instead, he multiplied his credentials into the deputy editorship of *Squire*, a down-market

Playboy rip-off then just starting up under the editorship of a neurasthenic Canadian named Jack de Lissa.

Squire operated out of a tumbledown backstreet building not too far from my old workplace at Central Station. It was there that I approached Ron for advice after my first few weeks of freedom. How should I launch my career as a full-time professional writer?

Squinting across a desk so piled with paper that he was almost invisible, Ron startled me by saying, 'If you're not doing anything, we could use some help here.'

About then, Jack walked through the office carrying a large Nikon camera, heading for the makeshift photo studio at the rear of the building. A pretty girl in a very short robe followed him.

'Come on through,' he said to Ron. 'I need someone to work the lights.' He glanced at me with a smirk. 'Bring your friend.'

I didn't need any more encouragement. Over the next year, I held lights for photo sessions – well, someone has to do it – wrote ill-informed articles about orgies and harems, composed letters to the editor – those we received were either obscene or illiterate – and penned the text that accompanied the nude layouts.

This last was a useful introduction to the real

business of writing for a living. Jack rejected my first effort. 'Who gives a fuck that her name's Sheila Smith and she's an unemployed typist?'

'But . . . that's what she is.'

'So what? Make something up. She won't care. Bright writing, John. That's what we need.'

I returned with a fanciful bio of one Sensualda la Farge, of Martinique descent, who collected Siamese fighting fish and enjoyed playing Chopin in the nude.

'That's the stuff,' Jack said. 'You might have a future in this business, once you grow out of this science fiction crap.'

If science-fiction fandom was my high school, Ron Smith and *Squire* were my university. Not long after I started working with him, Ron explained that he and Cindy had an 'open marriage'. He was free to indulge in unlimited extra-marital affairs – as was she, he pointed out magnanimously, in whatever spare time she could find between looking after their son, doing the housework and earning a living making and selling silver jewellery in Sydney's street-markets.

Ron, a mere five feet tall, only needed a bowler hat to become the image of Toulouse-Lautrec. Despite this, or perhaps because of it, and notwithstanding the fact that, as he confessed at every opportunity, his dick was in proportion to the rest of his build, he was a persistent, energetic, successful seducer – living proof of the truism that, if you ask every woman you meet to have sex with you, you'll get your face slapped a lot, but you will also get a lot of sex.

Under the guise of trawling for models to pose for *Squire* centrefolds, he engineered a series of piquant and often bizarre situations in which I, as his faithful confederate, participated enthusiastically. My virginity was given up in a blizzard of flesh.

Of all these events, the strangest was what I'll always remember as the Blue Movie Meeting.

'There's going to be a meeting,' Ron told me one morning. He grinned with a shark-like display of his slightly buck teeth. 'About making a porno movie. I got us invited, pal.'

'Someone's always talking about making blue movies,' I said dismissively.

'Yeah, but this is for real, buddy.' He named a prominent journalist. 'And he's got Shad Chase on board!'

With the Australian film revival yet to come, Shad's was as big a name as the local industry could boast. His experimental shorts appeared periodically at film society screenings, and he was known to be working on a feature of impeccable impenetrability. Obviously any meeting with his support wasn't to be missed.

Ron and I dutifully turned up at an address in the fashionable Edwardian suburb of Paddington the following Saturday morning. A dozen people lounged around in the long downstairs room, squatting against the wall or slumped on paisley bean-bags. An unacknowledged gentility kept us from the low double bed standing in Saturday sun at the other end of the room, alcoved in a white-curtained bay window, like an altar.

Our host moved easily around the room in a madras caftan and sandals, filling tumblers from a flagon of inky claret. He was about thirty; good-looking, slight and balding a bit. Sun from the curtained window fuzzed his outline.

'Natalie's made some chilli. It'll be done in a sec. Glad you could come.'

I looked sideways at Ron. He sat hunched, arms locked around his knees. He was watching Shad. Tall and skinny with an air of vagueness about him, he had arrived with two men and a girl – members of his co-operative. The girl and Shad sat together. He squatted easily on his haunches with his back against the wall, glancing around every few seconds with a calm I learned to recognize as a grass high but which at the time looked like Olympian ease. She sat on the seagrass matting, her legs stretched out in front of her. I recognized her from Shad's movies. Her print dress was thigh-length and, when she bent her knees, I found myself staring at pastry-white flesh above green stockings. Ron lifted his glass and drank half the wine in a gulp.

'Chilli. Bowls, everyone.'

Natalie, the journalist's mistress, circulated with a large earthenware bowl and a ladle. She too was a Shad Chase star. I remembered her fleeing in slow motion down deserted city streets, pursued by nameless terrors, and wearing nothing but a wet sheet.

'She's as bad a cook as she is an actress,' I muttered to Ron, mouth full of munchy red beans.

Ron nodded, but he was still looking at Shad's girl. Her dress hitched even higher as she made a platform for her food. Shad refused the chilli, but exchanged a sleepy smile and a few words with Natalie as she stooped before him, holding a bowl out like an offering.

'When you've eaten,' said the journalist, 'we'll get down to business.'

It still took half an hour. By then, smoke hazed the air and the booze had been flowing. After a brief lecture on the perils of censorship, the journalist wound up.

'Making a really good erotic film would be a perfect way to concretize our position. A piece of what Marcuse would call "cultural terrorism". Now, I've already discussed the project informally with some of you. Shad has prepared an outline script. I'd like him to read it for us. As a basis for discussion.'

Shad fished in the back pocket of his cords and stood up with a tattered sheet of paper.

'Yeah. Well.' He looked around the room. 'This is just an outline, OK?'

'I think we all appreciate that.' The journalist was sounding a tad impatient.

'Yeah. OK. It begins on a beach.' Shad looked down at the paper, but didn't read from it. 'There's a whole lotta people there. Not surfers. I mean, couples. Naked. Girls. In the sun. Then, suddenly, out of the trees, all these people arrive.'

He looked around for encouragement.

'They're wearing costumes. Suits of armour. Crinolines. But incomplete, y'know? I mean, the girls just have skirts on, and the men don't wear pants. Maybe there's a goat too, and a donkey. Anyway, they all run into the surf and start to play around and frig one another, and like that.'

The room was silent. Smoke curled like incense from a cigarette forgotten in the tin lid used as an ashtray.

'Now, down the beach comes this guy. Big Prick.' Gratified by the laugh, Shad waited for it to die. 'He stands there, and all the women on the beach look at him. He gets down and he fucks one of the women. The others watch. Then the other people come up out of the surf and he fucks them too. Everyone fucks.'

He stared at the page, then turned it over, as if looking for something he'd left out. Then he sat down.

Around the room, people clapped. Not warmly, but not without enthusiasm either. Shad's two colleagues led the applause. The girl, I noticed, didn't move. She had the distant look of the girls Ron and I helped photograph for *Squire*.

'Any comments?' The journalist fooled with his pen. The top sheet of paper on his clipboard was blank. Natalie sat beside him, legs crossed, examining her nails, no expression on her high-cheekboned Slavic face.

Then a voice chirped out, 'I wondered if Shad had any particular location in mind.'

'Uh, there's lots of beaches,' he said. 'Down south.'

'Have to be pretty private.'

'No problems, mate.'

'Shad,' the journalist said. 'One thing. Costumes.'

'You can rent them.'

'Well, I know. But won't that cost a lot?'

Natalie looked up from her nails. 'I can handle the costumes,' she said.

The journalist drew a circle on the paper and began filling it in. He didn't look at her. 'That's fine. That was my only doubt.'

'It isn't mine.'

Ron's voice beside me made me start. Suddenly, everyone in the room was looking at us.

'Like, where the hell do we get all those people from?'

Shad pointedly glanced around the room. Someone giggled.

'Oh, sure.' Ron's voice went shrill, as it did when he was annoyed. 'All of us just get up there on some beach and fuck our brains out. Right?'

Shad looked away, not embarrassed but dismissive. 'If this is supposed to be a protest against censorship,' Ron went on, 'does it matter what sort of porno movie it is? Why not just two people? You don't need donkeys and armour and all that crap.'

I recognized my cue.

'Surely,' I said, 'the real question is, who of us here is prepared to strip off and fuck on camera?'

Shad stood up abruptly, skinned off his roll-neck sweater, dragged down his cords and underwear in one expert thrust of hooked thumbs, kicked off his sandals and stood stringily naked.

From the corner of my eye, I saw Natalie begin to do the same. Before her heavy breasts were free of her sweater, Shad gathered her in the crook of his right arm and hustled her to the bed. Shad's girl was barely a metre behind them, hauling her dress over her head. And Ron bolted like a runner from the blocks, starting after her pale back.

A double bed will hold a surprisingly large number of people. By the time I'd risen to my feet and walked down the room, six naked bodies competed for space on the mattress. Shad and Natalie rocked in oiled silence, faces buried in each other's neck, a demonstration of coitus as classic as the drawing in any manual. Ron knelt naked by the girl's shoulder, kissing her ear. One of her long legs dangled off the edge of the bed. The other rested on the shoulder of Shad's cameraman and business partner. Two more men, having carefully adjusted the venetian blinds, were climbing out of their trousers. More were drifting away. In the centre of the bed, the journalist reclined with a taut look about the eyes. He was only an inch from his mistress's shoulder but they were separated by a world. His pale, hairless body was faintly flushed across the chest. His penis rested limp across his testicles. He seemed to be listening to some faraway music.

Of course, no film was ever made. In a land where it was always afternoon, to talk about something offered more amusement than actually to do it. And if, in the process, you could get high or drunk or laid, that was enough. Perhaps, one day, Australians would make films, censorship would be abolished, marijuana legalized and aboriginal land rights restored, along with all the other items on the liberal wish list. At that moment, I decided I didn't want to wait that long.

Postscript to Part One

IN 1969, IN WHAT SEEMED AN INEVITABLE MOVE, I
left Australia for Europe. In those days of
stratospheric air fares, methods of getting to Europe
were limited, and often adventurous. My friend John
Brosnan travelled in a London double-decker bus
which trundled as far as Greece before breaking
down. A few others took a freighter to Yokohama,
transferred to the Trans-Siberian Railway and made
the interminable trip across the Soviet Union,
culminating in a bus ride across the ice to Finland and
then a train to London.

Most of us, however, scraped together the few
hundred dollars for a berth on one of the liners plying
between Australia and Britain, a thirty-day trip that
inched around the world, each degree of longitude
snipping an hour off the day, so that we descended
inexorably into night, only re-emerging into daylight
as the Isle of Wight hove into view. Our boat was the

old SS *America*, now refurbished and renamed the *Patris* by a Greek company that subdivided the once-spacious cabins, the better to squeeze in more passengers. Clive James came across on such a boat, and has movingly described in his book, *Unreliable Memoirs*, the experience of sharing a cabin with six rugby league players and the crankshaft. If one of them wanted to get up, all the others had to go back to bed.

The trip was nobody's idea of fun. Periodically the engines stopped, leaving us motionless on an oily sea, overtaken by lazily paddling sea turtles with gulls perched on their shells while distant clanking sounds suggested fundamental repairs taking place below.

Enough of the old infrastructure of the *America* remained to hint at the great days of the luxury cruise. Bouillon was served on deck every morning at eleven, but from a samovar-like heater dented and scratched over decades, and with porcelain cups replaced by paper ones. The attractive little cinema showed only two films, which, recycled interminably, had become a storm of scratches. The library contained some turn-of-the-century tomes on colonial administration and hundreds of battered mysteries that could have come from the Junee Railway Institute.

The *Patris*'s itinerary – Fiji, Acapulco, the Panama

Canal, Miami, Southampton – belonged to the Thirties too, though the entirely Sixties passengers would have been happier in Bali or Penang, getting drunk and laid. One night, I overheard a young man enquiring conversationally of the girl in the deckchair next to him, 'If I came and rooted you one night, and you couldn't see who it was, would you know it was me?' After a thoughtful pause, she said, 'Dunno. Try it and see.' Most spent the stop-overs in bars, seeing who could down the most of the local brew. In Miami, when a drunken group stormed what looked like the last bus back to the ship, the driver simply accelerated away in panic.

During the thirty-day passage, I struck up a friendship with a lugubrious Italian with the finely drawn profile of a Lorenzaccio, who spent the mornings practising Chopin on the piano in the forward lounge. Over paper cups of bouillon, he confessed he'd emigrated four times, but always returned to Florence, as he was doing now. His wife and children remained in Australia, however, and even he recognized he'd be back eventually. But I felt no such thing. In leaving Australia, I wasn't leaving where I belonged so much as going towards it.

My library remained with my long-suffering parents. When they came to move house, a friend offered to help. Tottering back and forth with countless cartons, he paused, breathing heavily, to ask what they contained.

'Books,' my father said.

After another twenty loads, with still no end in sight, the friend overcame the Australian taboo against inquisitiveness. 'Do a bit of reading, do you, Jack?' he asked.

In Europe, I felt immediately at home. The films, magazines, newspapers and books we saw in Australia anything from a month to a year late were here available so fresh that nobody had yet decided what to think about them. I'd finally got to where the action was. In Paris, the city still bore the marks of the events of 1968; patches of cobbles torn up, graffiti scrawled across walls – events that, in Australia, would have been the subject of debate for a decade, but here were already being effaced by a culture voraciously eager to move on. It was the same in cinema. Back in Sydney, we'd still been discussing the hand-held camera and improvised dialogue of the *nouvelle vague*, but I saw no signs of either in the latest François Truffaut, *L'Enfant sauvage*, set in nineteenth-century rural France, or Resnais's *Je t'aime, je t'aime*, a science-fiction movie. For the French, the New Wave was old news.

My last job in Australia had been a contract to write publicity material for the Australian Commonwealth

Film Unit, now Film Australia. Taking advantage of its impressive headed notepaper, I'd written to all the major European film festivals, advising them that Mr John Baxter would be travelling in Europe on a fact-finding tour, and would like to attend. Most wrote back with generous invitations to be their guest.

And so it was that in the summer of 1970, my girlfriend and I packed a tent into the back of a battered Volkswagen and bumbled across Europe, sprucing ourselves up before arriving at the Festival Director's office in Berlin or Venice to learn which four-star hotel we'd been booked into. And this is how I came to be sitting on the Lido di Venezia, chatting to John Coleman, film critic of *The New Statesman*, in the gardens of the Hotel Quattro Fontane. From where we sat we could hear the distant flump of Adriatic waves. Down the road was the Hotel des Bains, used by Luchino Visconti as a location for *Death in Venice*. Visconti was in Venice to premiere the film but was staying at the Gritti Palace, on the landward side. John Ford was at the Excelsior, not a hundred metres away, having reached the Lido via the same *vaporetto* as us. Sitting in the velvet Venetian night, listening to talk of legends from the lips of people who, a few weeks ago, had been near-legends themselves to me, was dizzying. Caught in some neural loop, the title of a film by the Finnish director Jörn Donner ran through my mind. *Adventure Starts Here Adventure Starts Here Adventure Starts Here . . .*

PART TWO

CHAPTER EIGHT

The Old Country

'England, Home and Beauty.'

Captain Cuttle on his values in Dombey and Son *by Charles Dickens*

A FEW SATURDAY MORNINGS AFTER WE HAD MET FOR the first time, Martin Stone and I found each other again in Swiss Cottage market. We were to do this often over the next twenty years, bumping into one another in odd corners of the world, like paper boats, borne along on a river of books, that briefly share the same eddy.

I offered him a coffee and, leaving the long-suffering Ruth to mind the stand, he led me across Finchley Road to a café where the pink Formica tables were scratched white and the grey coffee arrived in Pyrex glass cups and saucers.

'Found any more Greenes?' he asked.

'I found some,' I said. 'I didn't buy them.'

He nodded in understanding. The prices asked by West End booksellers for even relatively recent Greenes were sobering. In selling me *Our Man in Havana* and *Two African Journals* for a fiver each, Martin had done me a big favour. You wouldn't find either in a regular shop for less than £20.

'Henry Pordes has a beautiful *Stamboul Train*, in the wrapper,' I said. Pordes, situated in Charing Cross Road, London's traditional 'book street', had a stock the eccentricity of which was only rivalled by its inflated prices.

'They bought it from me,' Martin said. 'Found it in a car boot in Stepney. It's not as good as it looks. Somebody left a newspaper clipping inside.'

Newsprint is so acidic that, over time, it stains bookpaper anything from a light beige to mahogany brown. In the worst cases, the brittle page crumbles as if crisped in a fire.

'But a beautiful wrapper,' I said.

'Yeah. Nice wrapper.'

'What were you doing in Stepney?'

Martin blew on his coffee. The silence lengthened.

I changed the subject. 'Found anything good lately yourself?'

'I bought an Arthur Machen collection. And a nice limited edition of Lautréamont, in vellum, signed by the translator . . .' He reeled off more names – titles I half knew, in editions limited to ten signed copies . . .

original gravures laid in ... bound in calf ... bound in morocco ... bound, for all I knew, in the underwear of Mata Hari. His goblin face, normally a deadpan mask pierced by a pair of watchful eyes, lit up as he described a particularly obscure edition of Thomas Browne's *Urn Burial*. Running books was more than a matter of buying to resell. This was passion.

'Well,' I said, as I paid for the coffee – a small price for the lesson – 'if you ever come across any more Greenes, let me know.'

He looked at me speculatively. 'Ever go to Camden Passage on Thursdays?'

I knew Camden Passage, a paved alley lined with antique shops, just off the Angel in Islington, north London, and the site of an antique street market on Saturdays. I didn't remember it having any bookshops.

'What happens there?'

'Thursday mornings, there's a book market.'

'What time?'

Martin shrugged. It was a silly question. Runners recognized only one time. 'Early.'

The sun was just coming up the following Thursday when I arrived at Camden Passage. Stripped of the Saturday crowds, the narrow lanes reverted to the time of Jack the Ripper. Shopfronts, their windows webbed with security grilles, crowded in on the wet flagstones. The shops themselves were choked with mahogany furniture, murky portraits and over-decorated silver. Whoever called Victorian society 'claustrophilic' could find living illustration here.

At the far end, sheltered by an overhang, half a dozen trestle tables bowed under thousands of books. A few men hung about, some with fags in the corners of their mouths, others with hands cupped around steaming polystyrene cups.

Over the area hung that unmistakable and electric atmosphere, inseparable from all shared and illicit male pleasures, of complicity. It flows between gamblers in a betting shop, homosexuals loitering in a public lavatory, punters cruising the street whores from Sydney to Amsterdam. I felt the instant excitement that hasn't diminished over many decades and countless markets.

Martin himself, by far the scruffiest of the group, with the rattiest fag and the steamiest coffee, was so authentically a part of this environment that one half suspected him of being Alec Guinness, made up and costumed for one of his greatest performances. Obviously unsurprised to see me there, he said without preamble, 'Got something you might like.'

He led me away from his table to where a lanky man in a black beret and a brown duffel coat sat on a folding steel chair, reading.

'Got that Greene?' asked Martin.

The man marked his place and put down the book. Next to his coffee cup was a small pile of thin new books, all the same. Neither the title of the book, *Lud Heat*, nor the writer's name, Iain Sinclair, meant anything to me.

He reached under the table and resurfaced with a book the size of a paperback, in a tattered brown wrapper. I recognized Herbert Read's novel *The Green Child*, reprinted in 1970 by Chatto & Windus, with an introduction by Greene. It was part of a series called 'The Landmark Library', an uninspired attempt to produce hardcovers at paperback prices. I'd seen a few copies, and, while I didn't actually own this title, it wasn't particularly rare.

Martin took it and, nicotine stained fingers trembling – not, as I now knew, with excitement so much as last night's hangover and the morning's recuperative toot of cocaine – opened it.

Spidering across the khaki flyleaf were a few wavering words in minute handwriting, with the even more tentative signature of Greene himself.

'How much?' I was already reaching for my wallet.

I drove home to Highgate in a daze, the Greene on the seat beside me. Still to come was the ritual of 'shelving' – placing the book with the now-lengthening line of Greene titles, in chronological order, with a lightly pencilled note on the flyleaf giving the price paid and the date purchased. Then came the detective work of deciphering the dedicatee's name: was it 'John' or 'Joe'? A friend of Greene's, or some stranger who cornered him at a publisher's party? And with each step grew the comforting sense of ... well, belonging. But belonging to what?

The universe of most dealers and runners, no matter in what city they live, shares something of the vision of New York drawn by Saul Steinberg in his famous 'View of the World from Ninth Avenue', which was first published on the cover of *The New Yorker* on 19 March 1976. A few blocks of Manhattan, his home turf, loom large in the foreground, rich in detail, but after that the world Dopplers away across a hinterland featureless except for a few high-rises, randomly distributed, that stand in for Chicago and Los Angeles. Beyond them stretches an indeterminate Pacific, with an undifferentiated Asia on the far side.

The places where he buys and sells circumscribe the bookman's world as surely as the hunting ground and the watering hole define that of the wild animal. A Parisian *bouquiniste* may haunt suburban *ventes aux enchères* to stock his little stall by the bank of the Seine, but never visit the Hôtel Drouot, the city's biggest auction house, nor the *brocantes* held every weekend throughout Paris. A Manhattan runner will work the street markets and charity shops of Greenwich Village but venture no further uptown than 14th Street, let alone into Brooklyn or Queens.

Accuse them of laziness or a lack of enterprise and you'd get a barrage of protest. One book worth $100 unearthed after a week of searching, they'd insist, is worth less to them than a hundred $1 books bought in a single afternoon. What if there *were* good books to find in Brooklyn or Neuilly or Newport Pagnell? Would there be enough profit to cover the train fare? How would they haul them back? Also, where would they store them? Their wives were already giving them hell . . .

Weekend car-boot sales were springing up all over London, mainly in car parks, and there were still plenty of suburban bookshops, but most runners couldn't be bothered to check them out. It was easier to trawl the reliable sources. Nor was there any incentive to leave London in search of new customers, since the dealers and collectors who were their main clients would find their way to Camden Passage, as I had done.

If a runner extended his 'turf' at all, it was only to take advantage of markets and charity shops near his home. Iain Sinclair and the Dalston dealer Brian Troath both routinely checked the Saturday-morning market known as 'the Waste', on Kingsland Road, and sometimes found good books among the dodgy video cassettes and leather jackets 'wot fell off the back of a lorry, guv'nor'.

Another group cruised the dustbins and skips of Soho, a patch so lucrative that runners operated an *ad hoc* roster like the one imposed by beggars on Hungerford Bridge, which led from Embankment station to the Royal Festival Hall. Actors crossed frequently, and were always good for a pound or two if the beggar recognized them and said, 'Good luck tonight, Sir George.' Time on that patch was rationed to an hour.

Soho's most prized skips were those behind Wardour Street, where film companies tossed out old movie stills, scripts, posters, publicity items, and sometimes original sketches for ad layouts, or off-cuts from the films themselves. The ad items found their way almost instantly to two shops on the fringe of Soho, Fred Zentner's Cinema Bookshop and Danny Posner's Vintage Magazine Shop, from where they speedily entered the international market.

Martin Stone, Iain Sinclair, Driff Field and a few other more ambitious dealers ranged across Britain and even, occasionally, the Continent in their search for books. Top American dealers like Peter Howard of Serendipity Books in San Francisco even flew Martin to the US, provided him with a car and driver, and sent him out scouting for rarities. For almost every London runner of the Seventies, however, the world was encompassed by the weekly book market at Camden Passage, the big general second-hand and junk market of Brick Lane (actually Cheshire Street, near Liverpool Street railway station, in east London), and the Saturday morning book market on Farringdon Road, near Fleet Street. Books bought at Brick Lane or Farringdon Road at the weekend were sold on Thursday at Camden Passage – and, as Arthur Seaton said in Alan Sillitoe's *Saturday Night and Sunday Morning*, 'the rest was propaganda'.

Once visited, the London street markets were never forgotten. The smell, the look, the atmosphere, left as indelible a mark as the dust that tattooed itself into the pads of one's fingers from hours of handling old paper, ancient leather and wood.

Around 4 a.m., anonymous and battered Ford Transit vans started to nose into Cheshire Street. Their arrival electrified the runners bent over tables or crouched by the blankets where some amateur had spread his stock. Before each van stopped moving, a helper crouched in the back pushed open the doors. Beams from twenty torches probed the interior as dealers jostled for a look at furniture, silver and glass gleaned from a week of house clearances and country auctions.

This wasn't *Antiques Roadshow*. There was no time

to turn the piece over and look at the marks. Decisions were instant and instinctive. 'That chair on the left,' somebody yelled, waving a handful of fivers. Another scrambled inside, flinging himself across a Sheraton-style settee and defying anyone to dislodge him. It was here that the legend of the 'divvy' flourished; individuals so attuned to the subtleties of patina and craftsmanship that one glance was enough to identify a masterpiece or dismiss a fake. The skill, which can appear quite magical when demonstrated by a master, was nicely depicted in one of the BBC's *Lovejoy* episodes. Confronted on live TV by half a dozen pieces on a small table and asked to spot the £1,000 item, Lovejoy, after glancing over the objects, all modestly valuable, dramatically whips off the cloth to identify the true treasure as the table itself.

Books didn't interest divvies unless they were seventeenth-century or earlier. At Brick Lane they sold last, if at all, and a few runners and collectors, working from opposite ends of the market, scooped up what there was.

Farringdon Road, however, was only for books. It was run by George Jefferies, who inherited the pitch from his father. Under an obscure law, the right to sell on the busy Farringdon Road could only pass from father to son, and as each family relinquished its pitch, the council gained slightly more control, until only Jefferies remained. When George died, his son decided to go into the used-camera business, leaving the council free to redevelop and modernize everything. (Ironically, he decided he didn't like the camera business, and is back selling books.)

Aware of Jefferies' methods, dealers arrived at Farringdon Road early each Saturday, and hovered round the old flat-bed drays on which he arranged his stock, covered with tarpaulins. Promptly at nine, he appeared with the first of a number of enormous canvas sacks all filled with books, which he upended on the footpath. Dealers descended on them like crows on a carcass, grabbing armfuls of books going for 5p each. Finds were ferried across the footpath and piled against the low brick wall. These heaps were sacred; to interfere with them meant at least an argument, at worst a punch-up. Everyone had seen blood spilled.

When all the bags had been emptied, Jefferies whisked the tarpaulin off the first of his drays, exposing his slightly better books, which went at £1 each. He enjoyed toying with his clients, particularly those who had offended him. He'd wait until his adversary was occupied with one cart, then dart to the other end and pull off the tarpaulin, giving his competitors first chance.

Some of Jefferies' stock came from West End dealers like Maggs, Quaritch and Sotherans, who found it convenient, when they bought a big private library, to skim the best titles and discount the rest to George. He also haunted 'the rooms', as dealers called the auction sales. After delving briefly into each of a dozen tea chests, he'd estimate their resale value and bid accordingly. Dealers who hoped nobody had noticed the £200 Evelyn Waugh first edition at the bottom of Box 5 found themselves outbid by Jefferies, who offered a thousand pounds for all twelve boxes, knowing he'd profit by selling everything at a quid a pop. Resignedly, they'd go along to Farringdon Road the next week and wait until the end of the morning, when George 'auctioned' the week's better items – a process that consisted of holding up a book, shouting 'What's it worth? A fiver?' and pitching it over the heads of the crowd to whoever yelled loudest.

Booksellers outside central London relied for stock on a weekly magazine called *The Bookdealer*. For decades, the mouthpiece of British bookselling had been *The Clique*, which, as the name implies, was a specialist publication for professionals with large city shops. In the Fifties, Fudge & Co. introduced *The Bookdealer*, aimed at the small operator who worked from home and couldn't afford advertising or postage. As reading matter, *The Bookdealer* didn't even rival *Bradshaw's Railway Guide*. Printed on thin but unyielding paper, like the debased currency of some Communist satellite, it contained double columns, set in minuscule type, listing the books for which subscribers had been asked by clients, or which they needed for stock.

Other dealers perused the lists and, if they could fill the want, completed a slip (supplied in quantity with each subscription), adding address and price, and mailed it to the magazine's office. There, someone – I visualized a Bob Cratchit-like clerk, in green eyeshade and celluloid sleeve protectors – bundled it with other responses and mailed them to the advertisers, who could contact the seller direct if they wanted to buy the book. This Dickensian method combined maximum effort with minimum results, but it had the merit of being cheap, and what most small dealers had in greatest quantity was time. As a result, *The Bookdealer* flourished, driving *The Clique* out of business.

A few big shops, like Waterstone's, filled pages with their wants, but the typical advertiser was a lady in a country village who operated as 'Bide a Wee Books' or 'Elderberry Cottage Antiques' and wanted nice clean books about rose growing or astrology – but at 'Realistic prices, please!' Some preferred to pay in postage stamps, since it saved the few pence of a postal order or cheque.

Queries like 'Waiting for Good-oh. Becket?', 'Poetry of Arthur Rambo' and 'Richard Hillary, *The Last Enema*' betrayed the frightening ignorance of the average *Bookdealer* subscriber. Peake was routinely misspelled 'Peek', Nabokov as 'Nabokoff' or 'Nabucov', Genet as 'Jenny'. Plainly, some hadn't read any fiction since *Fanny by Gaslight*. Others were, by contrast, almost too clever. Every issue featured a few appeals for priceless rarities like firsts of *A Clockwork Orange*, *Lord of the Flies* and *The Catcher in the Rye* – always, of course, 'dust-wrapped copy only'.

Professional runners loathed *The Bookdealer*. News that some 'armchair dealer' had scored a coup by these methods could drive them to fury. When Don Bell, through good luck and persistence, argued his way into the notoriously restricted back room of a Paris bookseller and emerged with a first edition of *Dracula* which he then sold to John Wronowski at Lame Duck Books in Boston for thousands of dollars' profit, Martin complained bitterly. It was not so much that Don found it on his 'patch', but at the sheer fluke that had won him entry to a dealer who had resisted all Martin's cajoling. I could see his point. Pure chance offended someone who made his living from exercising a painfully acquired skill.

But then using that skill at someone else's expense was all the more pleasurable. In *The Ninth Gate*, Polanski's film of *The Dumas Club*, Dean Corso demonstrates one such dirty trick, known as 'nailing a library'. Negotiating with the in-laws of a collector now paralysed by a stroke, Corso buys a rare *Don*

Quixote for cash at a fraction of its worth, then, as he leaves, gives an inflated estimate for the remaining books, killing any chance of profit for his competitors.

Most dealers are more generous, but it's only human to take pleasure in outdoing a colleague. As La Rochefoucauld put it, '*Dans l'adversité de nos meilleurs amis, nous trouvons toujours quelque chose qui ne nous déplaît pas*' – 'In the adversity of our best friends, we always find something that does not displease us' – usually paraphrased as 'It is not enough to succeed; your best friend must fail'. I never saw Martin happier than the afternoon when, on a tip from Phil Wood at the San Francisco Book Company in Paris, we visited the home in suburban Paris of Yiddish poet and left-wing activist Dora Teitelboim, who'd died a few months before.

'There's nothing there,' Phil told us. 'We got the lot. But you're welcome to try.'

The decaying 1920s villa looked like it would fall down if someone removed its picturesque web of rat-infested ivy. A man and his nephew, distant relatives of Teitelboim from Israel, were gutting it in preparation for a major overhaul. They agreed that Phil and his helpers had probably taken anything of interest, but invited us to rummage in the ruined living room where books and magazines were heaped on a makeshift table improvised from a door.

I picked up a slim volume from the top of the heap and saw, with a pleasurable shock, that it was inscribed to Teitelboim by legendary editor and publisher Nancy Cunard. There was more of the same further down in the heap, and, as we discovered over a convivial vodka and fearsomely black coffee in the ruined kitchen with the new owner (an ex-general in the Israeli army, as it turned out), in a basement filled with dusty filing cabinets where Phil's guys never looked. These proved to be full of her personal copies of obscure books published in Argentina with contributions from the likes of Jorge Luis Borges. It was wonderful to find the books. It was even better to find them when somebody else had not.

It seems natural now that I should have graduated from collecting books to dealing in them. It was Martin, of course, who initiated me into the craft.

'Danny Posner knows where there are some Greenes,' he murmured to me one afternoon after I'd known him for a few months.

'Where?'

'Um. Well. There's a problem. He wants fifty for the address.'

'Fifty pounds? Is it worth it?'

'He says it is. He says there are other things too. A lot of books.'

Unspoken was the implication that, because of Martin's chronic penury, I would have to front the money for any purchase, splitting the profits with him afterwards.

'Sure,' I said. 'Call him up.'

Every dealer longs for the Big Buy. Bookshops that advertise – as almost all of them do – 'libraries bought' are not so much expressing a willingness as a hope. They dream of rooms, houses, warehouses of books; hecatombs of print; enough books to drown in. In *Cadillac Jack*, the main character is tempted by an invitation to buy the contents of the Smithsonian. While this is a slight exaggeration, there are plenty of bookdealers who would make an offer on the Library of Congress.

Which is why Martin and I found ourselves one night not long after standing on a windy street corner off the Archway Road with £50 in used notes.

Danny Posner had launched his Vintage Magazine Shop a few years before in tiny premises just off Cambridge Circus, a rat's nest of old magazines and newspapers, arranged in dusty piles, and festooned with showbiz paraphernalia. Life-sized 'standees' of Sean Connery as James Bond and cut-outs of Sid James and Barbara Windsor from the *Carry On* films jostled with promo items for defunct rock groups.

How did Danny know that Connery, an ex-swimwear model and milkman, would transcend his beginnings to become the idol of millions? Probably the same way he knew to feature prominently in his cluttered window, six years before *Alien*, a poster for the 1973 Emerson, Lake and Palmer album *Brain Salad Surgery* designed by obscure Swiss designer H. R. Giger. Danny later confirmed his business acumen. Moving to more spacious premises in Brewer Street, Soho, he tripled his prices, and, shifting his main stock into a warehouse, launched a profitable business renting to movies and TV. In 1970, however, he was just another small-timer looking for a profit.

'This had better be good,' Martin said when he showed up. I gave him the cash.

'It is,' he said, counting the money. 'I only wanted the magazines. But these people have got lots of books. In wrappers.'

He strolled back to the tube station with our – my – fifty, and we looked at the address.

'The bastard!' I said. The house was in Highgate – not fifty metres from where we stood.

The following night, we made an appointment to see the books.

One in a row of three-storey detached homes built in the Twenties, the house and garden had the shabby look of a place run to seed, belying the red MGB sports car parked in front. The car's owner opened the door, a young man of the type known as 'Hooray Henry', in yuppie uniform of pressed jeans, flannel shirt, Hush Puppies, no socks, and – my God! – a cravat.

'You're the book chaps, yah?'

'Yah,' I said. 'I mean, yeah.'

'Come in, come in. Haven't much time. Lots to do.'

He led us into the front room, lined floor to ceiling with big books in uniform leather bindings. Sorting papers was a girl dressed in the female equivalent of his outfit; same jeans, same shoes, same no socks.

'These are the book chaps, sweet,' he said.

She spared us an uninterested glance and went back to the papers.

'The house belonged to my fiancée's father,' he said. 'I'm helping her with the sale. Now these,' he went on, waving around the walls, 'are *not* for sale. A valuer from Sotheby's will be here tomorrow. That understood?'

Martin nodded enthusiastically, groping at the same time for his tobacco pouch and the makings. I looked around the books with my best poker face. Even I knew that bound volumes of the *Proceedings of the British Dental Association* were worth about as much as telephone directories. Both he and the Sotheby's man were in for a *mauvais quart d'heure*.

'The rest are upstairs.' He led us up the staircase. At the top was a large room lined with empty shelves, in the middle of which was a neat parallelepiped, two metres by one by one, of the books that had been on them. 'You can have any of these. See if there's anything you want. I'll be downstairs.'

As his steps receded, Martin, nodding with pursed lips, as if listening to an unheard voice, picked up one of the books. It was a first edition of P. G. Wodehouse's *The Heart of a Goof* in its original gaudy dust wrapper with its golf motif. I'd seen one less good in a catalogue at a hundred pounds.

There were more underneath, all in their wrappers. Eric Ambler novels, Sapper, Taffrail, John Buchan – and Graham Greene; my heart jumped as I spotted the near-diaphanous wartime cover of *A Gun for Sale* and the plain cream one of his first novel, *The Man Within*.

'Boots rebinds,' Martin said, peeling off the Wodehouse wrapper to reveal the plain cloth cover. 'Boots rebound everything, but they kept the dust wrappers. At the end of the year, they put them back on and sold the books at a shilling each.' He turned the spine to me, showing the 'one shilling' label.

'What are they worth?'

'The books? Ten quid each, maybe. The wrappers . . .' He shrugged. 'Hundreds.'

'Each?'

'Well, the Wodehouses anyway. And the Greenes. The Buchans . . .'

We tried to calculate a total, but hadn't got far when the young man bounded up the stairs again.

'Well, what do you think? Anything here you can use?'

'Oh dear, oh dear . . .' Martin muttered. In moments of stress, he betrayed his middle-class origins by descending into a variation on the maiden-aunt's fluster that sat oddly with his boho look. He didn't quite wring his hands, though he came close. 'I suppose . . . two hundred quid for the lot?'

Said with more confidence, the sum might have seemed almost insulting, but Martin's nervousness, not to mention his wardrobe, suggested that £200 was all he had in the world.

'And you'll take them away – tonight?'

'Car's outside,' I said, not revealing it was a Fiat with the cubic capacity of a shoebox. I took out my chequebook. 'Who do I make it out to?'

We spent an hour ferrying the books to the car, convinced that at any minute he'd realize the treasure he was giving up. Each trip just made the experience more intense. If there is anything more pleasurable than not giving a sucker an even break, I don't know what it is.

It never occurred to me that Martin might think the same way, even though people warned me getting money out of him was a major headache. Week by week, 'our' books melted into the stock that crammed his Cannon Street Road home. Deals were either in progress or about to be closed, or had been closed but the cheque hadn't cleared, or, if it had cleared, the funds were momentarily tied up on some other buy.

In the end, I just helped myself to the Graham Greenes, though only after a contorted argument in which I recognized the twitching paranoia of cocaine.

'They're worth a couple of bills,' Martin grumbled as I stowed the books in my bag.

'But I put up the money to buy them!'

'You'll get your money.'

'When?'

'It's there, it's there . . .' With a mangled cigarette, he waved towards the future prosperity which, for all runners, recedes more speedily the closer they approach it.

'Well, let me know when it arrives. We can tote things up then.'

I didn't see him for a few weeks. When I did, he was his usual amiable self. But no money was forthcoming, and the books we'd bought were never mentioned again.

CHAPTER NINE

A Regional Collection

BERNARD: Americans are a very modern people, of course. They are a very open people too. They wear their hearts on their sleeves. They don't stand on ceremony. They take people as they are. They make no distinctions about a man's background, his parentage, his education. They say what they mean and there is a vivid muscularity about the way they say it. They admire everything about them without reserve or pretence of scholarship. They are always the first to put their hands in their pockets. They press you to visit them in their own home the moment they meet you, and are irrepressibly goodhumoured, ambitious, and brimming with self-confidence in any company. Apart from that, I've got nothing against them.

Tom Stoppard, New-Found-Land, *1976*

ONCE YOU SET OUT TO COLLECT AN AUTHOR, YOU can't do it by halves. You may tell yourself you'll confine yourself to the early novels of Joseph Conrad or the poetry of Kingsley Amis, but a pristine *Almayer's Folly* from Conrad's later years or Amis's first novel, *Lucky Jim*, will tempt you, and after that you're lost.

To avoid this, you can collect books around a theme or literary movement, and even pick and choose within it. 'American expatriate writers in Paris', for instance, offers almost unlimited variations. Refine it, if you like, to 'American female expatriate . . .' or 'African-American expatriate . . .' Why not, for that matter, 'gay and lesbian expatriate . . .' or 'post-World War II expatriate female African-American . . .'?

If you draw your limits carefully enough, you need never beggar yourself for a first edition of Hemingway's *In Our Time* or Gertrude Stein's *The Making of Americans*. Instead, you can spend your money on Chester Himes's *Pinktoes* ('African-American expatriate . . .'), which, though, like *Lolita*, it was published by the Olympia Press, costs a hundredth of the price, or the Calder & Boyars edition of *Girl on a Motorcycle* by Pieyre de Mandiargues, translated by Alexander Trocchi ('Scottish beat-generation post-World War II expatriate . . .').

Better still is a collection based on your home town, or, if you're fortunate enough to have them, literary relatives or friends. If you're lucky, this means access to first printings and limited editions, all lengthily inscribed, as well as to proof copies, letters, even manuscripts, all of them for free. And generally the author is not only flattered to be asked, but glad to find a sympathetic listener who, unlike his own wife and children, accepts that, when he's staring out of the window and smoking, he's really working.

I'd started a few of these mini-collections already. One was devoted to Derek Jarman, the designer and film-maker whom I first met when I was writing my book about Ken Russell, *An Appalling Talent*, in the early Seventies.

The first movie I saw on British soil was Ken Russell's *Women in Love*, and it was pure luck that, not long after, I found myself writing the biography of its director, with his enthusiastic co-operation. A London film buff had invited me to a screening of a Thirties film called *Under the Red Robe*, about Cardinal Richelieu. In the discussion that followed, I vigorously defended the latest re-telling of this story, by Ken Russell in his film *The Devils*. The only person to agree with me was a soft-spoken American named Gene Phillips. We arranged to have lunch the next day, and, much to my astonishment, he turned out to be a Jesuit priest – and, moreover, Ken Russell's spiritual advisor. With his recommendation, gaining an entrée to Ken's home and inner circle was no problem at all.

Derek Jarman had designed the incongruous white-tiled sets for *The Devils*, and when I began the interviews with Ken for my book he and Derek were working on a production of Peter Maxwell Davies's opera *Taverner* for Covent Garden. Derek created some startling designs; chimpanzees in bishops' mitres, characters who appeared female from one side, male from the other. Ken proposed to lower all doors into the House to a metre. Patrons would enter on hands and knees, to confront the carcasses of freshly slaughtered animals hanging on the walls, and monks and nuns fornicating in the aisles.

I was never optimistic about the willingness of Covent Garden to accept this plan, and when Ken and Derek returned from the make-or-break meeting it was clear they'd been turned down. Derek had prepared an exquisite notebook containing his original costume designs, heightened with red and gold gouache. He also had a folder of rough sketches, and a copy of Maxwell Davies's libretto. As they came into Ken's front room, he started to drop them into the wastepaper basket.

Feeling like Hurd Hatfield in *The Left-Handed Gun* snatching souvenirs of Paul Newman's gun-fights, I said, 'You're not throwing those away?'

He looked at them in surprise. A painter can think as little of a superseded sketch as I do of a discarded manuscript page.

'They aren't going to do the opera. Not with us anyway.'

'Let me buy them from you.'

He held them out to me. 'Have them, John. They're no use to me.'

They became the nucleus of a collection that finally comprised some of his sketches for the sets of *The Devils*, the manuscripts of all the screenplays he co-wrote with Russell, first editions of the books he produced until his early death from Aids – and even one from after. *Reliquary* was assembled by hand at Prospect Cottage, Dungeness, Derek's windswept seaside home almost in the shadow of the nuclear power station. There are 200 numbered copies, of which mine is No. 148. It's an oblong box, 18 cm by 12 cm by 4 cm, shrink-wrapped, containing, apparently, photographs, reproductions of paintings, a scrap of a Sandy Powell robe Derek wore, and a stone charm from the pebbled beach. I say 'apparently' because my copy is still in the original shrink wrap. It's worth more that way, of course – but keeping it intact also, in my mind, preserves something of the charming man whose life and death inspired it.

Among a dozen such mini-collections, my favourite was compiled in the mid-Seventies when I was visiting professor at Hollins College, near Roanoke, Virginia.

I'd been to the United States many times, but it never occurred to me to live there until I looked up from a pile of documents in the British Film Institute

Library one day in 1974 to see a man of about my age leading a crocodile of dazzling young women on a tour of the information department.

In what seemed only a few months, he was back again, with a different but no-less-attractive group. He was, the staff told me, a professor of film and theatre named Atkins from an American college for women who brought students on cultural trips to London.

On his next trip, Tom Atkins left a note for me at the BFI. He was interested in Ken Russell, and wondered if I could arrange a meeting. Ken agreed, and I became friendly with Tom and his wife Mary-Ellen, also a professor at the same school, Hollins College. When we had lunch together on his next trip and he explained that, having decided to take a semester off to write a book, he needed someone to do his job, it wasn't until dessert that I realized he was asking me.

Visiting professor! Heady stuff for someone who left school at fifteen. But when I arrived in Roanoke, in the winter of 1974, my first thought was that I'd made a big mistake. The nineteenth-century colonnaded buildings and two-storey student houses scattered across the wooded slopes reinforced the impression that nothing of significance had happened here since the Civil War – or, as I quickly learned to call it, the War Between the States – and that the only book on the curriculum was probably *Gone With the Wind*, for a TV remake of which Hollins could have doubled as a set. Faculty and students alike had deserted the snow-covered campus for the Christmas break. From the window of Tom's – now my – office, the buildings appeared linked by narrow paths in the foot-deep snow. I went outside and put my palm on the wet grass. It was warm. The 'paths' marked a network of steam pipes that kept the empty buildings from freezing.

Virginia was rich in literature. Little, however, came from Hollins. Though it was shortly to have its intellectual stature lifted with a Pulitzer Prize, until 1974 its sole gift to the written word was Elizabeth Meriwether Gilmer, who in 1896, as 'Dorothy Dix', became the world's first newspaper agony aunt.

This fact took a little finding, since Hollins didn't trumpet it. And who can blame them when Dix offered opinions such as this one: 'So many people think divorce a panacea for every ill, who find out, when they try it, the remedy is worse than the disease'? At a college where every student seemed to have at least two sets of parents, it was an uncomfortable adage. One girl already referred to her fiancé as the man who would be 'my first husband'.

The only local writer of any reputation was Nelson Bond, a hack for pulp magazines like *Air Aces*, *Thrilling Wonder Stories* and *Spicy Detective* in the

Thirties and Forties who retired there to become a local pundit, book collector and occasional dealer. He maintained an informal support group of fans and drinking buddies, called – false modesty was not a fault of Nelson's – the Nelson Bond Society.

But Bond too was out of town, so I borrowed Tom Atkins's spare car, an old cream Ford Fairlane that cried out for a whip aerial, soft dice dangling from the rear view mirror and flames painted down each side, and began exploring on my own, starting with downtown.

Everyone warned me against this. Roanoke's middle class had retreated to a ring of well-tended suburbs. Any surviving cinemas, drugstores, second-hand shops, supermarkets and liquor stores mainly served a large African-American community that had migrated here to work for the railroads, only to be left high and dry by their retreat. Welfare kept the town alive, supporting a black population frustrated enough to give Roanoke the nation's eleventh-highest per-capita murder rate.

Black faces watched – suspiciously, it seemed – as I parked and walked a couple of blocks on the wide footpaths with their cracked, tilted cement paving slabs. Desolate even at midday on a Saturday, the town provided no evidence to contradict its best-known, indeed *only* celebrity quote. Comedian Eddie Cantor, passing through in the Forties, rolled his trademark pop eyes and muttered, 'It looks like a graveyard at midnight.'

The junk shop I'd spotted on my first pass was also run by a black man. He sat at the back, presiding over an empire of cracked plates, dented pots, chipped enamel mugs, stopped watches, sun-blasted advertising displays, and – most interesting for me – a few shelves of books.

Regarding him narrowly, I made for these. But the shelves contained what you'll find on almost every bookshelf in every shop in the south of the United States: paperbacks from the Fifties and Sixties, and book-club editions of best-sellers from twenty years ago. Even if you had wanted the Dell edition of Steinbeck's *Cannery Row* or the Book of the Month Club *Man in the Grey Flannel Suit*, you would not have bought these copies. Pages spilled out of the so-called 'perfect-bound' paperbacks, while the cheap book club paper was flaking away relentlessly to dust.

I eyed the proprietor covertly. What if I left without buying anything? Would he pursue me down the cluttered aisle, waving the rusted – and almost certainly fake – cavalry sword hanging above his head? I grabbed the one item worth having, a movie tie-in edition of Mae West's *Diamond Lil*, based on her baldly-titled Broadway play *Sex*. Its endpapers were covered with library stamps and the dust wrapper was glued to the cover, but Mae's gaudy portrait was not without charm. I walked the bare board floor to the desk.

'Uh, how much is . . .'

That was all I got out, since the rat-trap mouth expanded in a blinding grin.

'Waaalll, hell – you *can* talk!' he gabbled in a falsetto drawl. 'I saw this guy comin' in, guy I don't know, never *seed* him before. I wonder, "Who's this guy?" But you don't say nothing, you just go over there and start looking at them old books. So I wait, and I watch, and I think, "Well, he *got* to say somethin' *some* time." But no, you just go through them books, looking at them useless ol' books like they was interestin' or somethin', and here I am just waitin' . . .'

There was a lot more of this: Tennessee Williams in blackface, crossed with Eddie Murphy doing Truman Capote, every second syllable accentuated with camp scepticism or pushed into the stratosphere – 'But *nooooooo*' – in theatrical surprise. Half an hour later, when I escaped, *Diamond Lil* in hand and 25c poorer, I hadn't got in more than a dozen words.

'Oh, ol' gay Lee,' said Jim Ayers, one of the other theatre professors, when I described the incident later. 'He's one of the town characters.'

Why should homosexuality be nominated as Lee's main identifying characteristic? Was it so rare, to be gay in the south? Was Lee in fact the 'town gay', like the 'token black' of the TV series, maintained like a mascot to prove Roanoke's liberalism? Truman Capote and Tennessee Williams made no secret of their sexuality, but both of them lived in New York. Maybe, here in the quieter corners of the South, it really still was 'the love that dare not speak its name'.

I soon learned otherwise. I'd bought a large print of a picture by Jamie Wyeth called *Draft Age* to decorate my bare office. It showed a boy in dark glasses and jeans leaning against a street light. I pinned it to my wall and got to work, hardly noticing that the faculty was drifting back after the vacation – not, at least, until one of them, a bachelor from the English department, put his head round the door.

'Hello. Just thought I'd look in and welcome you.' He asked me to his home for tea and, as he left, looked admiringly at *Draft Age*. '*Love* your picture.'

The following morning, another male colleague called. Then the professor of dance and movement, who wore leather trousers. If there was ever anything he could do, he said, patting my knee, I only had to ask. Before long, I decided to take down *Draft Age*, and oddly enough the visits tailed off.

A month combing thrift shops, book exchanges and second-hand stores for fifty miles around turned up almost no books worth having. The failure mirrored my growing disappointment with Hollins. After writing all day with only a frozen stretch of Tinker Creek and some lacklustre willows to contemplate, I'd return to my apartment and nod off watching the 5 p.m. re-run of *Streets of San Francisco*, *Mod Squad* or *Ironside*. Waking just in time for the closing credits, I'd cook something in the enormous kitchen, experimenting with the exotic ingredients available from the local twenty-four-hour supermarket, watch a commercials-riddled movie on TV, read, go to bed.

But things began to look up when spring brought the return of that local institution, the swap-meet. In the North and around larger towns, garage sales are the norm, with people spreading their junk on the lawn and sidewalk. The South, more reticent, prefers the semi-public swap-meet, which usually takes place in a car park or, in the case of Hollins, a drive-in cinema.

Few places more precisely embody desolation than a drive-in by daylight. The undulating asphalt spiked with speaker posts reveals itself nakedly as made for machines, not people. A Petri dish probably looks the same to a bacterium – vast, empty, but with an insistent sense of being watched.

On this chilly Saturday morning, a few dozen sellers had parked on the sunny side of the drive-in, a tide of cardboard boxes lapping at the tailboards of their station wagons and the dented bumpers with their peeling stickers: HONK IF YOU LOVE JESUS, PASS WITH CARE: DRIVER CHEWS TOBACCO, IF TAXES DON'T GET YOU,

RADAR WILL and the ubiquitous VIRGINIA IS FOR LOVERS.

Swap-meets demonstrate America's almost heartbreaking optimism. Box after box is exposed to public view in the touching belief that someone will fall on these corroded wrenches, cracked cups, jam jars of rusted screws, yellowing newspapers and empty shotgun shells with coos of delight.

Books don't figure much at swap-meets, less out of an aversion to literature than because of weight, and their susceptibility to damp. This morning, five cartons turned up nothing more interesting than a paperback of the mildly salacious crime story *A Hard Man is Good to Find*, which appeared to have spent part of its life stuffed in someone's hip pocket. Most of the others were swollen with moisture, their pages glued into inseparable slabs.

The sixth box looked no more promising until a slightly outsize item caught my eye. I teased it out. The cover had no illustration, just some text in minute type on a paper so soft and grey as to be barely decipherable. But I did puzzle out 'Gertrude Stein' and above it, so faint as to be almost unreadable, the title: *transition*.

My chilled and grimy fingers could barely catch the edges of the cheap rough-cut paper. The title page had hardly been sullied since it rolled off the press in Paris half a century ago.

3. *transition*   June 1927

Gertrude Stein, Georges Ribbemont-Dessaignes,
Elin Pelin, Alexander Blok, Morley Callaghan,
Kay Boyle, Georg Trakl, James Joyce, Margery Latimer,
Philippe Soupault, Man Ray, Hart Crane,
Pavel Tchelitcheff, Georg Doro, Allen Tate,
Velko Petrovitch, Laura Riding, Robert Sage,
Rhys Davies, Eugene Jolas, Gustav Davidson,
André Masson, Bryher, Michail Zostchenko,
Kurt Schwitters, John Mitchell, Berenice Abbott
Principal Agency: SHAKESPEARE and CO.
12, rue de l'Odeon, Paris, VIème
Price: 10 francs
50 cents.

It was issue No. 3 of the legendary literary magazine distributed by Sylvia Beach at Shakespeare and Company in Paris: the magazine that first published Ernest Hemingway's short stories, James Joyce's experiments, the early poems of William Carlos Williams, that introduced Kurt Schwitters, Yves Tanguy and the Surrealists to America. How did such an item end up here, in a Virginia swap-meet? *Anything can be anywhere . . .*

The owner sat on the tailboard of her old Ford Estate, feet dangling in ancient stained trainers. I grabbed two more paperbacks at random, sandwiched the *transition* between them, and held them out to her.

She parked her cigarette in one corner of her mouth and, squinting against the smoke, shuffled the books. I looked for the first time at what I'd chosen. One was a devotional book by the sanctimonious Norman Vincent Peale. The other was *A Hard Man is Good to Find*. Well, maybe she'd think I just had catholic taste.

'Ten cents for those,' she said, setting the paperbacks down beside her. She leafed through *transition*. Her calloused fingers found the title page. Surely even *she* would know these names. 'Allen Tate,' she said. 'Came here once. To the library.'

'Is that right?'

For the first time she caught my accent. 'You English?'

'Yes. From London. I'm teaching at Hollins.'

'Niece of mine went there.'

'Uh-huh.'

She nodded, looked back down at the magazine, and noticed the price.

'Fifty cents. Lot of money back then.'

'I suppose so.'

'*Lot* o' money.' She closed it decisively. 'Say a quarter for the three?'

I handed over a 25c coin before she could change her mind.

Driving back to the college, I glanced occasionally at the treasure, lying on the passenger seat in splendid isolation. The morning sun made the dull cover gleam. Maybe I'd give Hollins another chance.

In the end, Hollins itself provided a solution to my collecting dilemma. Though none was famous, Hollins did have its share of writers. Why not collect their works? Start, in fact, a regional collection?

I began with the poet William Jay Smith, emeritus professor of English, who was taking one of his frequent sabbaticals. This was fortunate for me, since I'd inherited his campus apartment. Bill Smith enjoyed an almost iconic standing at Hollins. The English department continued to list him on staff even though he was kept away most of the year at foreign literary conferences, visiting professorships and even a spell as Poetry Consultant at the Library of Congress in Washington – the US equivalent of the Poet Laureate.

His first visit, the February after I arrived, threw the faculty for a loop. A reading was hurriedly arranged in the college's most prestigious location, the Green Drawing Room. 'We're having a few people over afterwards,' John Moore, the department's Joyce scholar, murmured in my ear, before rising to introduce Smith with respectful references to the Library of Congress, his translations of Hungarian poetry, and various new books – the latest of which, *Venice in the Fog*, was, he mentioned pointedly, on sale at the college bookshop. I knew: I'd already bought a copy.

Smith himself, tall, distinguished, prosperously bulky in his tailored three-piece suit, didn't hide his dislike of the room. It sat directly under a large dormitory, the plumbing of which ran along the ceiling over his head, periodically gurgling and clanging. 'The *worst* place to read poetry . . .' he said with a sigh, before cursorily thanking Moore for his introduction – mistaking him for Lex Allen, the department's modernist.

Smith shrugged the gaffe away. *It's been a long time, and one meets so many people . . .* Lots of them rated a mention in the next hour: Jim Dickey; Larry Durrell; Robert Graves; Dick Wilbur. Introductions were peppered with drop-dead asides – 'my French wife . . . working with Illic in Budapest . . . our Paris apartment', culminating in the *coup de grâce* – a reading of the entire text of *Venice in the Fog*.

Cats go masked: white-veiled, bulging flower shops float
    off, barges bearing the remnants
Of bridal festivities . . . I touch their perfume as they
    move away; and from here in the room gaze down
On the bridge below and the shops beside it held in
    marbled water, veins of mist cutting
Through it while my pen on the page cuts through
    veined layers of consciousness . . .

In the front row, the English department, uniformly drab in worn corduroy and shiny tweeds, like a flock of sodden birds on a telephone wire waiting for the storm to pass, hung its collective head. What had *they* done? Articles for the scholarly press. A few pages of that habitually uncompleted novel. And not one veined layer of consciousness between the lot of them.

All the more puzzling then that at the get-together afterwards, of the sort scorned by Reynolds Price in his *New York Times* obituary of James Dickey as a 'punch-and-cookies English department reception' (though in this case substitute weak tea and brownies), Smith should have taken me aside and asked to meet privately the following day.

I found him in an office hastily requisitioned from the most junior member of the English department. He was on the phone.

'What *is* the honorarium, Jean?' he was asking. His expression as he nodded me to a chair suggested what he thought of her reply.

'Well, one is *so* busy at the moment . . .' A pause. 'Oh, you think you might be able to improve on it? Well, in that case . . . Yes, let's talk again . . . I *can* call collect, can I? They *are* looking after your expenses on this thing, I hope? I don't want *you* to be out of pocket . . .'

What did he want with me, this international literary hired gun? Maybe he needed someone to wash his car.

'John, why I wanted to talk to you . . .' He sighed. 'I have a son . . .'

For the next hour, Bill Smith exposed his life in the sort of confessional detail that so alarmed Bernard, the British civil servant in Stoppard's *New-Found-Land*.

His first marriage had ended in divorce. As part of the settlement, his wife retained his treasured poetry collection – a loss he regretted more than the divorce. (As a collector, I could sympathize.) He was happy in his second marriage, to a younger and more resourceful French woman, but now his children had returned to haunt him. One son had recently overdosed on amphetamines in Austria and thrown himself into a river. He was due at Hollins in a few weeks to recuperate. He liked movies. Could he audit my classes?

'Well, naturally.'

Smith beamed in relief. 'John, how can I thank you?'

As much to fend off the unexpected warmth of his smile, I held up the copy of *Venice in the Fog*. 'You could inscribe this.'

Which he did, very warmly. My regional collection was launched.

Bill Smith might have the kudos, but the man who really ran the English department was Richard Dillard. Lanky, donnish, permanently amused, Richard behaved like a jester left to manage the court while the king and queen were out of town; his crooked grin and boyishly raised eyebrows scrawled 'misrule' across every expression. Born in Roanoke of an old southern family, he was both a charismatic teacher and, though middle-aged and balding, a campus heart-throb. Students literally *loved* Richard, and he reciprocated, to the extent of marrying two of the most talented.

His one novel, *The Book of Changes*, and three books of poetry displayed an eccentric sense of humour and an enthusiasm for antique pop culture, ranging from Sherlock Holmes to vintage horror films. *The Night I Stopped Dreaming About Barbara Steele* took its name from the British actress who cowered through numerous Italian vampire pics, and Fellini's *8½*.*

The dust wrapper for *The Book of Changes* was

* 'I *read* that book,' Steele said to me years later at a Hollywood party, pouting. 'It hardly said *anything* about me.' At the same party, actor Paul Sand gushed, 'I was in Rome in '75 and my friend told me you lived in the next apartment building. We got out the binoculars and there you were, on the roof, wrapped up in something large and brown.' Steele raised an eyebrow and, with impeccable timing, purred, 'A man, I hope, darling.'

designed by Edward Gorey, not yet famous for his work on the Broadway *Dracula* and PBS's series *Mystery*. Ignorance of Gorey's work did nothing to elevate me in Richard's eyes. Nor did my book collecting, an explanation of which earned a sceptical look, particularly when I remarked that, every time one opened a first edition, its value dropped $5. The copy of *The Book of Changes* he gave me was inscribed, 'An autographed copy you needn't be afraid to read! But read at your own risk . . .' Another one for the collection, along with copies of the books of verse.

Ranging the demarcation zone between the faculty and the student body was Meta Anne Doak, known to everyone as Annie, a former student of Richard's who had become his wife. With her straggling blonde hair and permanent uniform of jeans, baggy T-shirt and trainers, she could have passed for the instructor in basket weaving. Nobody took her seriously – a grave mistake, as it turned out. After an attack of pneumonia in 1971, she'd decided to 'experience life more fully'. About the time I arrived at Hollins, she was confiding to her journal, 'It is still the first week of January, and I've got great plans. I've been thinking about seeing. There are lots of things to see, unwrapped gifts and free surprises. The world is fairly studded and strewn with pennies cast broadside from a generous hand. But – and this is the point – who gets excited by a mere penny?'

She started camping out on nearby Tinker Mountain and by Tinker Creek, watching raccoons come down to wash, following muskrats on their hunts, making detailed notes on both the large and the small – ants' nests, the egg cases of preying mantises, but also the nocturnal forest ('A blind man's idea of hugeness is a tree').

Picking the brains of the faculty about botany, entomology, theology and classical mythology, she would not, being Annie, have been too precise about why she wanted this information. When her book *Pilgrim at Tinker Creek* became a best-seller in March 1974, making Annie Dillard a household name and winning her the Pulitzer Prize for Non-fiction, certain professors, stabbing their fingers at some botanical or hydrological datum, muttered bitterly, '*I* gave her that.'

The Dillard marriage didn't survive her success. Within a few months, Annie was living on an island on Puget Sound, as far as one could get from Virginia without leaving the country. My souvenir of her, and another item for my regional collection, was a paperback edition of *Pilgrim* inscribed with typical reticence: 'For John Baxter, cheers . . .'

Years before, Richard had cajoled the English department into adding a movie course to the curriculum, arguing that it would help students to understand different modes of story-telling. Called 'Film as Narrative Art', it was really an excuse to show his favourite horror films, and the work of Fellini and Ingmar Bergman. Enrolment was invariably huge.

In the first class, Richard always expounded his Chicken Theory of Cinema. This was based on a report he had read of a group of Peace Corps volunteers trying to teach tribal Africans about mosquito eradication. They used a documentary film to explain what should be done, but found it difficult to stage a discussion afterwards, since none of the Africans remembered any part of the film.

'Do you remember *anything*?' they asked.

Finally a woman cautiously raised her hand. 'There was a chicken,' she said.

General agreement greeted this. They ran the film again – and, indeed, a chicken pecked in the background while, closer to camera, a scientist discoursed on the perils of stagnant water.

As Richard explained it to his students, every film had a chicken, if you looked hard enough. Sometimes it was 'Subtle Chicken', like the game of Chicken in *Rebel Without a Cause*. Newcomers wandering into a screening of Ingmar Bergman's dour movie *Shame* without knowing the Dillard theory were startled when the class exploded with applause as Liv Ullmann and Max von Sydow, about to leave their home, paused to ask one another: 'Should we take the chickens with us?'

Richard was a shrewd enough teacher to know that searching for chickens would keep his students' minds on the movies. Once they had the habit, he could get down to serious teaching – until the final examination, when he occasionally set Roman Polanski's *Cul-de-Sac* as an essay topic. (It takes place almost entirely on a chicken farm.)

Richard's film class had no more faithful followers than Hollins's handful of male graduate students, pursuing a one-year postgraduate Master of Fine Arts degree. There was a Foreign Legion air about this group, which included the scion of a distinguished Virginia literary family who was working doggedly through a first novel that would have had to bear comparison with the work of his famous uncles and cousins and an ex-Vietnam Cobra pilot and son of an air force general who slept with a .45 under his pillow and had set up his bedroom so that the first thing he saw on waking was a poster-sized photograph of a gunship control panel. Ostensibly they were drawn by the Creative Writing Course, though, for most, the very remoteness of Hollins was the main attraction – that, and the presence of six hundred bored and attractive young women, almost all with their own bedrooms.

The liveliest of this group was Jon Stephen Fink.

With his goofily sharkish grin and an LA accent that could cut sheet steel, Jon Stephen managed to double as campus clown and resident intellect; sometimes both at the same time. A graduate of CalArts, the Los Angeles university funded by Walt Disney, he'd reacted to its relentless triviality by becoming a poet. His Poundian verse, dense with Old Testament imagery and a plangent Gnosticism, clashed with his glee in elaborate practical jokes, always at the expense of the English department, with which he was permanently at war.

Periodically, its staff published *The Hollins Critic*, an austere leaflet celebrating some literary figure. With the help of fellow grad student Garrett Epps, Jon Stephen wrote and printed a fake edition devoted to Holly Martins, pulp-writer stooge of racketeer Harry Lime in Graham Greene's *The Third Man*. The parody was impeccable, down to references to Martins' *The Oklahoma Kid*, *Death at Double X Ranch* and *The Lone Rider of Santa Fe*, and their themes of 'lost innocence, conflict with the self, the closing of the range, the dangers of smoking loco weed'. The cover sketch by the *Critic*'s regular artist Lewis Thompson even showed Joseph Cotton as Holly in Carol Reed's movie.

Maybe half a dozen people on campus got the joke, and I was the only one who seemed to find it funny. The English department regarded it as an insult. Of course, I was delighted to add a copy to my regional collection.

That summer, Hollins held its Literary Festival. The star guest was Richard Adams, author of the best-seller *Watership Down*, detailing life in the English countryside as seen by a community of rabbits.

Jon Stephen should have sensed that his plan for a special welcome for Adams flirted with disaster, but his success with the *Critic* tempted him to overplay his hand. He hired two costumes, and managed to cajole a girlfriend, Ellen Harwich, into wearing the other. Since they couldn't drive in the costumes, Richard Dillard agreed to take them to the airport when he met Adams.

And so it was that, when Adams walked into the one-room arrivals hall, he saw two giant rabbits sitting on a bench, one clutching a handbag filled with carrots, the other reading *Playboy*.

Adams acted as if they weren't there.

'I wonder if that has anything to do with you,' Richard said tentatively.

'No, they're publicizing something,' Adams said. 'I've seen them in other towns. Is the car through here?' He led the way outdoors.

Unable to think of an alternative, Richard followed, and drove his guest to the college. The plan had been for Jon Stephen and Ellen to return with him. Now they were stranded at the airport, dressed only in rabbit suits, with no money.

Having managed to get back to Hollins in a taxi, whose driver took pity on them, Jon Stephen and Ellen haunted Adams, sitting prominently in the audience at his readings and lurking in his wake. In every case, Adams ignored them. He'd had his fill of questions like 'Why rabbits?' and simply acted as if everyone took his furry heroes as seriously as he did. Only when they arrived pushing the dessert trolley at that evening's faculty dinner in Roanoke's only 'French' restaurant ('Our Specialty. Roast Prime Rib with *Au Jus*') did he sullenly acknowledge their existence.

It was a victory of sorts, but a hollow one. His taste for practical jokes dulled, Jon Stephen turned to the less treacherous world of the written word. Though he went on to publish such novels as *Further Adventures*, *If He Lived* and *Woke Up Laughing*, his first book – undeclared wars are always the hardest to end – wasn't a novel or even a book of poetry but a spoof work of film theory called *Cluck! The True Story of Chickens in the Cinema*. And of course a signed copy of that went into my regional collection as well.

I came to Hollins for a semester and stayed for eighteen months. Instead of the novel he meant to

189

write, Tom Atkins and I collaborated on a piece of scientific speculation, *The Fire Came By*, which became a best-seller. I made a few enemies there, mainly among the faculty, and a lot of friends, almost entirely among the students, one of whom, Joyce Agee, I married and took back to London with me – not quite 'collecting Hollins' like Robert Bloch's 'collecting Poe', but near enough.

Two decades later, with my third wife, Marie-Dominique, whom I'd also met at Hollins, I moved into the very building in Paris where Sylvia Beach lived when she ran Shakespeare and Company, and from where *transition* was distributed. Might that discovery in a Roanoke flea market have played some part in jolting me onto the path to Rue de l'Odéon? For someone to whom books mean so much, it's hard, in retrospect, to believe that such things happen by chance.

CHAPTER TEN

With the Rich and Mighty . . .

'I have an unsigned first edition. They're the
rare ones, aren't they?'

Lewis (Peter Sellers) to Probert (Richard Attenborough) in
Only Two Can Play*, the film adaptation of Kingsley Amis's* That
Uncertain Feeling *(1962). Script by Amis and Bryan Forbes. (The line
doesn't appear in the book.)*

THE BEST FISHING, AS EVERY ANGLER KNOWS, IS FOUND
where other fishermen are not. It's the same with books.
You *can* build a collection by competing at public sales,
reading catalogues or lining up at signing sessions. But
for real quality you need an edge, and none beats being
part of some public enterprise where writers congregate.

For me, the road to rarities was BBC Radio. In the
Seventies and Eighties, my work as critic, commen-
tator and writer/presenter of radio documentaries
yielded numerous gems.

191

Does asking for an autograph degrade you in the eyes of an interview subject? Some journalists think so. They prefer to be considered as colleagues of the interviewee, not fans. Being Australian, and thus, as far as the British were concerned, occupying the lowest spot in the pecking order, I would never be considered an equal by anybody. If anything, an Aussie brashness was expected. So when the opportunity arose, I pursued my collecting shamelessly.

Not that I was alone in this. Many journalists and critics automatically push their copy of your book across the table after an interview for signing, sometimes on the pretext that their son or nephew is a fan. (To see a radio person lost for words, ask them, 'Oh, what's his name?') Presenters in the United States, of course, never bother. The stock phrase, 'I haven't had a chance to finish your book,' means they haven't read it or, probably, even seen a copy. Possibly they may not know how to read. But Roy Plomley, creator and long-time presenter of the BBC's *Desert Island Discs*, owned hundreds of books inscribed by his guests, from Nobel Prize-winning physicists to boxers and celebrity cooks. Others still living have even larger collections. Sheridan Morley, seldom off air or out of the papers over the last thirty years, must have thousands of signed books.

A missed opportunity for obtaining a signed copy can be traumatic. BBC producer David Perry once accompanied critic Christopher Ricks to Paris to interview Samuel Beckett, who, as usual, refused to be recorded, but did agree to chat. They met in the coffee shop of an unprepossessing modern hotel on the Boulevard St Jacques near Beckett's apartment, and, after an hour, Perry began to regret that he hadn't brought at least one copy of *Waiting for Godot*, since Beckett had proved more than amiable. As he was lamenting this, Ricks reached under the table and produced not one book but an attaché case bulging with first editions. 'And Beckett signed all of them!' says Perry, still, after all these years, chagrined at the memory.

Such lack of foresight puts people like David squarely on one side of that divide between those for whom collecting is a natural extension of what they read and those for whom interest in the book ends when they close it. When Anthony Burgess, responding to David's query about where he could be contacted, wrote his name and address and a signature on the flyleaf of *1985*, the novel they had just been discussing, it never occurred to David that Burgess was not only being co-operative but signing the book. Not long ago, when I asked after it, he admitted that the last time he had seen that copy it was propping up his son's mini snooker table. Now it seems to be lost for ever. 'I don't think signed books are my forte,' he confessed morosely.

David was one of the producers of Radio 4's arts programme *Kaleidoscope*, in those days broadcast live at 10.30 p.m. on weekday nights. I did my first BBC review almost as soon as I arrived in England in 1970 and, except for 1975 and 1976, spent in the United States, have never been off the air for very long since. Between 1971 and 1975, the 'Beeb' occupied a large segment of both my working and social life. Many of my friendships and not a few affairs germinated in the hothouse atmosphere of Broadcasting House, a few of them 'bolting' into unexpectedly luxuriant forms, though the ferment brought its share of tragedy too.

Jacky Gillott, one of the *Kaleidoscope* presenters who'd become a friend, inscribed my copy of her novel *The Head Case*, then drove down to her home in Cornwall and committed suicide. Around the same time, Jan Dawson, editor of the British Film Institute's *Monthly Film Bulletin*, for which I also wrote, killed herself as well. Neither had seemed particularly distressed at our last meetings. If suicide was indeed a cry for help, why had I not heard it? Gerald Priestland, the BBC's Religious Affairs correspondent at the time, and a victim of clinical depression himself, attributed the reticence, tranquillity, even apparent happiness of people like

Jacky to their sense of predestined and inevitable death. 'Others may think you are fortunate,' he wrote, 'but *you* know it is all an empty fraud, and that one day the hollow balloon will burst, you will be found out and your crime exposed. What crime? You don't know; you only know you are guilty; and you can hear them coming down the corridor to get you. The penalty, of course, is Death and you might as well be your own executioner.'

I'd always found it easy to talk to people like Jacky and Jan, and they, apparently, to me, so my failure to have foreseen disaster, whatever Gerald said about its inevitability, depressed me acutely. Nick Carraway, the priggish narrator of *The Great Gatsby*, prides himself on a character so unjudgemental that it had 'opened up many curious natures to me and also made me the victim of not a few veteran bores. The abnormal mind is quick to detect and attach itself to this quality when it appears in a normal person, and so it came about that in college I was unjustly accused of being a politician, because I was privy to the secret griefs of wild, unknown men.'

The passage struck a dispiritingly familiar chord. On the infrequent occasions I went anywhere in fancy dress, I wore a clerical collar and a black suit. Inevitably, within ten minutes, I would be sitting in the corner as someone poured out the story of their life. It should have been obvious that I was destined to write biography, but I was still loyal to speculative fiction and movies.

From the start, radio felt like my natural home. I had the knack of affecting enthusiasm on cue, useful if you were to sit down late in the evening to discuss some film or book, and indispensable if you'd just raced up Regent Street from a Soho preview theatre, scribbling your notes under streetlights. On one occasion, a critic, sprinting out of the Royal Court bound for the studio, saw a chauffeured Rolls-Royce idling on the other side of the road. *At last*, he thought, *a little appreciation*.

Bending to the window, he said to the driver, '*Kaleidoscope*?'

The driver sniffed. 'Kenneth Tynan, sir.'

Kaleidoscope fielded a notable team of presenters, though the 'voice' of the programme was Paul Vaughan's. Relaxed to the point of languor, Paul always gave the impression he would rather be playing Mozart on his clarinet than dealing with the artistic trivia that passed across the desk. An intelligent man, he'd been invited to join one of the high-IQ group socials but turned them down – '*Silly* people.' I suspect he thought the same of us. During one break, I noticed he'd doodled some anagrams of the programme's title on his notepad. They included 'Look, I'd escape' and 'Cloaked, I pose'.

Paul was at the microphone the night I dried up in the middle of a review, able only to croak 'I'm sorry . . . I'm sorry.' In his memoirs, he suggests I was drunk. Unfortunately, much less glamorously, I'd succumbed to a new cold medication. Getting a drink in Broadcasting House was, in fact, all but impossible before a broadcast, a tradition reinforced by anecdotes of presenters sliding glassy-eyed under the table after lubricated lunches. The ban survived until an aged Dame Sybil Thorndike and her equally venerable husband Sir Lewis Casson agreed to be interviewed in the Sixties. A few minutes before air time, Sir Lewis asked for a drop of something to steady his nerves. Told that alcohol was barred from the premises, he got up and headed for the door, in search of the nearest pub. A panic call to Security brought a guard with a flask of medicinal brandy from the first-aid cabinet.

Following this near-débâcle, it was decided that drinks should be provided for guests – but, except in emergencies, only *after* the broadcast. The drinks trolley was actually locked, and only the producer had a key. As a result, writers and artists who would normally have made off into the night after their *Kaleidoscope* appearance sat about in the control room over a gin and tonic or two, and discoursed. I routinely picked up the newest book by that night's guest and got him or her to sign it. My collection swelled with personally – and often amusingly – inscribed first editions by Tom Stoppard, John Braine, J. G. Ballard, William Empson, Clancy Sigal, Anthony Burgess, Norman Mailer, Thom Gunn, James Baldwin, Roald Dahl, Lynne Reid Banks, John Updike and, most notable in terms of both quantity and quality, Kingsley Amis.

Amis, of course, appreciated the post-broadcast drink more than anyone, particularly after the trolley was augmented with his favourite single malt. The fact that we knew some of the same people in the science-fiction community, particularly Harry Harrison and Brian Aldiss, made me confident enough, after he'd signed *The Alteration*, to ask if we could meet again, and if I could bring my other first editions for him to sign.

He agreed, though the plan came badly unstuck. There were two pubs called the Flask in north London, one in Highgate, the other in Hampstead. After sitting for an hour in the near-empty Highgate one, I realized my error. There was nothing for it but to send a grovelling letter of apology, asking if he could *possibly* make another date.

('With the rich and mighty,' they say, 'always a little patience,' to which I'd add, 'and a great deal of abasement.' If it embarrasses you to fawn, you should be collecting bottle tops or beer labels.)

Fortunately Kingsley forgave me. A lifetime of

drinking had made him sympathetic to lapses of memory and concentration. Privately, no doubt, he categorized me as one of the 'shags' and 'shits' who troubled his life.

Since my first abortive attempt at a meeting with Amis, the licensee of the Flask in Hampstead had died. Amis disliked the 'gentrification' embarked on by the new owner, and now hung out in the nondescript Coach and Horses on Heath Street, where, shuffling in twenty minutes late, he found me the following Monday evening sitting over a half of lager and wondering if this time *he* had got the place wrong.

It was hard to reconcile this figure with the man I remembered. At fifty-seven, he appeared twenty years older. (In a letter to Philip Larkin later that year, he confessed the almost total loss of his once prodigious sex drive.) Stooped, almost shambling, he was myopic without his glasses, which he put on in the doorway before peering around uncertainly. Obviously, he was a regular. It wasn't only the suited business types who smiled and said hello but the men in grimy work jackets.

Subsiding into the other side of the booth, he looked with distaste at my lager.

'What will you have?' I asked.

'Oh, a pint of mixed dry and sweet cider.'

This was the tipple of perhaps the most famous

literary drinker of his generation? Certainly the one who had written most about the joys of alcohol. I ordered it, and watched him swallow half.

By way of explanation for his fragile condition, he said, 'I had a session at the Garrick last night. I got one of those letters, you know: "Dear Kingsley, You may recall certain boozy nights after the war . . ." He was the cook at a club I used to belong to. I bought him a few drinks from time to time. So we had dinner. But after dinner, out came those dreadful dog-eared manuscripts. "A few pieces I've done. Appreciate the benefit of your advice on these . . ." What can you do? I don't mind giving someone a few beers and slinging him a copy of one of my works, but that's *awful*.'

The cider was gone. I said, 'Another of those?'

He looked at the empty glass as if he was wondering how it had got there.

'Good Lord, no. A double Teacher's, with just a drop of water.' The cider evidently acted as a cushion against the assault to come.

When I returned with our drinks, he was digging into the bag of books I'd brought. The quantity obviously surprised and flattered him. Also the fact that all retained their dust wrappers, preserved under plastic covers.

On top was *Take a Girl Like You* in the standard Gollancz lemon-curd cover. Amis's name appeared at top and bottom in red, with the title in between. Otherwise, the wrapper was blank. The front inner flap bore no blurb summarizing the plot, and there was no author's bio on the rear flap – which is also true of *The Anti-Death League*. In 1960, at the height of Amis's first success, Gollancz didn't feel the need to say anything more.

'Do you know where this title comes from?' he asked, opening the book and poising his pen.

'No.'

He started to write 'All the best to John Baxter, Kingsley Amis', then continued down the page:

> Take a girl like you down to New Orleans
> Dress you in a dress of red.
> Buy you a house on the back of town, baby.
> Buy you a folding bed – yeah,
> Buy you a folding bed.
>
> Josh White

I took the book reverently and put it on the bench beside me.

Once in a hundred signings, an author writes something on the flyleaf other than 'Best wishes'. A few months before I'd done a piece about book signings for a series of talks called, austerely, *Words*, which were meant to plug the gaps in concert broadcasts on Radio 3. I'd urged writers to let their imagination go when inscribing books. They should say whatever came into their minds, even if it meant continuing over onto the front endpaper; details of arguments with editors, dissatisfaction with the text, errors of typesetting, explanations of how that title, character or venue was chosen. 'Regards' or even the somewhat embarrassing 'Love' (favoured by writers as diverse as James Baldwin and Roald Dahl) weren't enough. I concluded: 'We take your love for granted, as you do ours. Give us *words* instead.'

Anyone would have thought Amis had heard the piece. The inscriptions flowed. 'My not very good second book' on *I Like It Here*; a notation on the *Collected Poems* that the editor has got two in the wrong order; 'I like this one best' on *The Anti-Death League*. I hardly dared speak for fear that the river would dry up, but as long as the double scotches kept coming, so did the dedications.

Some books still had on the flyleaves the price I'd paid for them.

'Bloody hell,' Amis said, seeing I'd laid out £60 for *My Enemy's Enemy*, his rare collection of short stories.

We got talking about prices as he kept signing. Some writers resent the fact that a book that once retailed for ten pounds now changes hands for a hundred. A few won't sign unless they think you bought the book at the list price. Getting books signed can uncover unsuspected prejudices. Brian Aldiss wouldn't sign proof or review copies, on the grounds that we got them for free, with no profit to him. I startled him by explaining that a dealer would sell a proof or a copy with a review slip for more than a simple first edition.

Richard Hooker, author of *M.A.S.H.*, the basis of the phenomenally successful film and TV series, was so furious at having sold the film rights for only a few hundred dollars that he never again signed a copy of the book. One can understand his resentment.

When I asked Bob Bloch to inscribe my first edition of *Psycho*, he sighed. In 1959, his US publisher Simon & Schuster sold the paperback rights for $3,000, of which it kept half. Then the film rights went for a trivial sum to an anonymous company which, they discovered too late, belonged to Alfred Hitchcock.

Simon & Schuster received the paperback money in April of 1959 but didn't pay it to Bloch until his next royalty statement, in January 1960. This had a direct effect on his family at the time, as he reveals in a letter to his friend, the editor Vernon Shea.

My trip to Milwaukee with Sally Ann disclosed that the simple orthoplasty commanded a high fee: the deal would run to about $550 for an operation performed under local anaesthetic and involving less than 2 days in hospital – as opposed to about $225 for a complete hysterectomy, for example. Balked at this at the moment, the more so when we learned that the venture would involve at least three trips down there and run over into Sally's school term. So maybe next year . . .

Bloch eventually profited handsomely from new editions of *Psycho* following the movie's success, but the fact that a publisher's accounting methods could impinge on the health of his family never ceased to rankle. 'The old complaint of the negro: "First to be fired, last to be hired", can often be paraphrased to fit the situation of the lesser writer,' he told Shea. As for the fact that a signed copy of the Simon & Schuster first edition of *Psycho* now commands $4,500, this might have tested even his famous sense of humour.

Amis had no such problem; he just found it interesting, and a little flattering, that people cared enough about his books to pay that kind of money. It also tickled some commercial instinct, since he invited me to his home a few weeks later to 'look at a few books' that he 'might want to sell'.

That day, his old friend and collaborator Robert Conquest opened the door. Kingsley, he explained, was still in bed, crashed out after the launching of a new wine at the Portuguese embassy the previous night. After half an hour, he appeared, looking pale and unwell, but rejecting my suggestion that we call it off – probably because he was seldom in any better shape anyway.

Any hopes of the first edition of *Lucky Jim* in a dust wrapper were dashed when I saw his meagre shelves. He did, however, have the American first of his book of science-fiction essays, *New Maps of Hell*, which appeared a year before the Gollancz printing. Also some copies of *The Darkwater Hall Mystery*, a pastiche of Sherlock Holmes written for *Playboy*, but shortened by them. The tiny Tragara Press in Edinburgh had done a handsome limited edition of the full text. Kingsley had three of the 165 copies produced, and I said I would like two of them – one for myself, and one for my friend, the dealer and collector George Locke, to whom Holmes was dearer than life itself.

How much? Amis and Conquest exchanged a baffled look; neither had the slightest idea. Finally Kingsley said, 'Fifteen quid for *New Maps*? And a tenner each for the others?' I had the cash out before he could change his mind. Today, a copy of *The Darkwater Hall Mystery* sells for £120 – if you can find one. My copy, inscribed by Amis, is worth half as much again.

Once the ice was broken, both men entered into the game, fuelled by more single malt. Amis and Conquest had the customary writer's blind spot about their own first editions. Even Graham Greene, who treasured the books of Ezra Pound and Evelyn Waugh, hardly kept any copies of his own novels, and the few he did have were in a ruinous state.

Most writers, however, are interested to hear what their books fetch from collectors, since it tells them something about their popularity. Amis was no exception. For the same reason, he studied his royalty statements – not the sums involved, but the number of copies sold. '*Lucky Jim* is always at the top,' he told me, somewhat morosely, 'then the newest book.' It bore out the common assessment, he thought, that his whole career had been a slow, albeit profitable, slide downhill.

'What else of mine have you found lately?' he asked.

I mentioned a couple of his letters I'd bought from autograph dealers.

This was closer to home. Both men pricked up their ears.

'*Interesting* letters?' Amis asked.

'Not really. To a PEN editor, giving her rights to reprint a story. That sort of thing.'

'You could *make* them interesting, I suppose,' said Conquest.

'Put in a PS, you mean?' Kingsley mused. ' "By all means reprint the story. PS. By the way, how about a fuck?" '

We all laughed, but Amis would not have been the first writer to collude with a dealer to 'doctor' an item and make it more saleable. When the market is suddenly swamped with books inscribed to a variety of literary stars, one is entitled to be suspicious – as I am of two copies of Michael Moorcock's novel *Mother London* currently on offer in a London catalogue, though I don't doubt that, in this case, the inscriptions are a Moorcock joke. Maybe he does know V. S. Naipaul, to whom one copy is inscribed, but even though Moorcock lives in Texas, has either man ever set foot in Clarksdale, Mississippi, where he is supposed to have signed it? I'm even more doubtful about the second. Had I been the rigorous and severe George Steiner, I don't think I could have parted with a book inscribed, '*Auf Wiedersehen*, sweetheart. Yours forever, "Frosty", Cambridge.'

'Real' fake inscriptions are seldom funny. They betray themselves by being too obviously what the buyer would like to see. Nineteenth-century French collectors bought dozens of letters purporting to be from Julius Caesar, Alexander the Great and Christ. They were so full of lofty sentiments that nobody wondered why all these men wrote in impeccable French.

The conversation wandered off into the afternoon. Amis had just been to Scotland on a tour of distilleries, and had happy memories not only of the booze (and in particular the private stock of one manager: 'a very . . . interesting whisky. I could become *fascinated* with that whisky'), but of Scotland itself. His hosts insisted he visit Glencoe. The ancient battleground moved and chilled him, he said – the gathering mist, the rain, the sense of doom. Conquest, who had written the definitive history of the Stalinist terror, and had visited more than his share of mass graves, looked down into his glass.

One rationale of book collecting is that it brings you close to the writers you admire. Mostly this is a fantasy, but Amis was one case in my collecting career where it came true. However briefly, and with whatever alcoholic encouragement, I had been admitted to a place most people never penetrate.

Or had I?

As I was leaving, Kingsley, passing the shelves, pulled something else from a heap of papers. 'Here, you might as well have this.'

It was a Jonathan Cape book proof, recognizable by the generic snot-green paper wraps with the company's emblem of an urn filled with fruit and the initials 'JC'. The title and author's name are printed plainly at the top and 'Uncorrected Proof' at the bottom.

This one said '*You Only Live Twice*' and '*Ian Fleming*'.

'I used it when I was writing *The James Bond Dossier*,' Amis said.

The first page of text and the blank facing it were covered with notes in his rounded hand. Others were scattered through the text.

Proof copies of any of the Bond novels sell, when they sell at all, for anything from £700 to £2,500. And with Amis's notations . . . ? I had to be holding at least £3,000 in somewhat uncertain hands.

'But . . . how much?'

'Oh, take the bloody thing.'

Did I just *want* to feel that he sensed the proof's worth; that, in giving it to me, he was offering a lesson in relative values? If a book was worth more as a collectable than for its content, what did that say about him as a writer? Perhaps I should have responded nobly by replacing Fleming's exercise in sex and snobbism back where Amis had tossed it years before . . .

Ah, well, at least I didn't sell it. If he wanted to make a point about the values by which writers ruled their lives, I could do no less for collectors. Along with all the books he signed for me, I have the Fleming proof still.

Had I still harboured ambitions to write science fiction for a living, England would have fanned my ambition to white heat. Not for the first time in my writing career, however, I found myself losing interest in something just as I gained access to its inner circle. Fortunately, the London science-fiction community had no shortage of burned-out cases and perennially promising talents, and since I was as keen a collector of science-fiction first editions as ever, the writers and fans accepted me amiably enough, though my tendency, noted by Kingsley Amis, to linger all night over a half of lager meant I was always looked on a little askance.

This cut both ways, since science-fiction and fantasy writers don't make the best company. Those who aren't scholarly and dull are usually in some way psychologically maimed. 'All the great fantasies, I suppose, have been written by emotionally crippled men,' wrote Damon Knight, the doyen of science-fiction critics. '[Robert E.] Howard [author of the stories about Conan the Cimmerian] was a recluse and a man so morbidly attached to his mother that when she died he committed suicide. [H. P.] Lovecraft had enough phobias and eccentricities for nine: [A. B.] Merritt was chinless, bald and shaped like a shmoo.* The trouble with

* Who today remembers the shmoo, one of the better inventions of Al Capp for his comic strip *Li'l Abner*? Wide-eyed, pear-shaped and mute, the little shmoos yearned to be eaten. They were so anxious to please that their flesh assumed the flavour of whatever the eater desired.

Conan is that the human race never has produced and never could produce such a man, and sane writers know it; therefore the sick writers have a monopoly of him.'

None of the writers I met qualified for the description 'sick', but, for many, a career on the margins of literature had taken its toll. In his long career, Harry Harrison, for instance, had dabbled in just about every form of fiction from comic-book dialogue balloons to a 'Saint' novel ghosted for Leslie Charteris. The result was evident in his books. His novel *The Stainless Steel Rat* and its sequels squirmed with his cynicism, as did his *Deathworld* trilogy. 'Slippery' Jim diGriz of *The Stainless Steel Rat* is a cosmic con man whose larcenous skills are co-opted to help govern the galaxy, while, in the *Deathworld* books, colonists land on a planet where every plant and animal is bent on their destruction. Only in the third book do they discover that both flora and fauna can sense the emotions of the invaders; registering Man's innate hostility, they return it with interest. The message of both series is clear: everyone in authority is a crook, and everything is out to get you.

Compact, irascible, a growling terrier with a bristling moustache and beard, Harry always reminded me of a tiny dog defending his kennel against wolves. True to this image, the Harrison family dog was a diminutive Jack Russell terrier to which he gave the name Otar, after a giant Norse warrior from one of his stories. Harry had lived in half a dozen countries, from Denmark to Mexico, fetching up in the late Seventies on a mountaintop in County Wicklow called Kestrel Ridge. From this eyrie, he sent out messages urging everyone to accept the exemption from income tax offered to all professional writers and artists who agreed to settle in Eire and make it once again the 'nest of singing birds' it had been at the time of Joyce and Synge.

A few dozen writers, including Frederick Forsyth, Susan Howatch, Lonnie Coleman and myself, would make the move, as would Kyril Bonfiglioli. 'Bon' was a corpulent bon viveur whose roomy hollow legs operated in inverse proportion to the amount of single malt poured into them. He met Harry via Bruce Montgomery, who wrote Firbankian crime stories about a detective named Gervase Fen under the name 'Edmund Crispin'. *The Moving Toyshop*, *Love Lies Bleeding*, *Frequent Hearses* and *The Case of the Gilded Fly* are all now much collected. He also edited a series of discriminating *Best SF* science-fiction anthologies for Faber & Faber – like most science-fiction anthologies not collected at all – and earned a living composing film music, mainly for the *Carry On* comedies.

Both old Balliol men, Bon and Montgomery

regarded themselves, like André Breton, pope of the Surrealists, as too serious to be amateurs but too lazy to be professionals. Bon, in particular, worked only when time and money were in too short supply for him to continue pursuing a good time. Starting as an art dealer, he drifted into editing Ted Carnell's old magazine *Science Fantasy* when, like *New Worlds*, it was bought by Roberts & Vinter in 1964. The new owners, hoping to retain the old audience while at the same time attracting paperback buyers, put both magazines into card covers and handed editorial control to Bonfiglioli and Mike Moorcock, neither of whom any rational management would have placed in charge of an office raffle.

Such are the ironies of literature, however, that Moorcock proved an editor of brilliance. From a disordered crash pad near the Portobello Road, he almost single-handedly remade British visionary fiction, injecting Carnell's timid futurism with the virus of the counter-culture. William Burroughs shared space in the new magazine with Tom Disch, and J. G. Ballard with Mervyn Peake, while Brian Aldiss, an H. G. Wellsian visionary reborn as a modern Peter the Hermit on speed, preached the crusade of a millennial Europe in audacious novels like *An Age* and *Barefoot in the Head*.

Bon, on the other hand, edited *Science Fantasy* with the abstracted air of someone who would much rather be doing something else, as indeed he often was. Clinging to Balliol like a truffle to a tree root, he occupied a twenty-seven-room mansion in north Oxford, once the seat of a bishop, while an antique Rolls-Royce sagged elegantly at the kerb. *Science Fantasy* did launch writers such as M. John Harrison and Chris Priest, and gave house room to the Calvinist imaginings of Keith Roberts, who also drew most of his covers, but the majority of Bon's discoveries soon wandered away to find their level in rock, advertising, movies or crime.

When Bon arbitrarily renamed the magazine *Impulse*, everyone could read the writing on the wall. Fortuitously, he spotted an unrecorded Tintoretto in a country house sale, bought it for £40, sold it for £40,000, and took the profits to Jersey. This left *Impulse* in the uncertain hands of Keith Roberts, from where it passed to J. G. Ballard. Jim lasted six days, after which Harry Harrison played caretaker until *Impulse* merged with *New Worlds*, a marriage of convenience that became a suicide pact.

Meanwhile, Bonfiglioli, unmoved and at ease amid the Channel Islands' millionaires, reinvented himself as an author, turning out camp comic crime novels. P. G. Wodehouse collided with Ian Fleming and Dornford Yates in his stories featuring Charlie Mortdecai, dodgy London gallery owner, con man and sometime secret agent. 'This is not an autobiographical novel,' he said of the first book, *Don't Point That Thing At Me* (1972). 'It is about some other portly, dissolute, immoral and middle-aged art dealer.' *Something Nasty in the Woodshed* (1976) and *After You With the Pistol* (1979) followed. So did a picaresque historical tale, supposedly based on an ancestor, called *All the Tea in China*. But none of the profits from the Tintoretto or the novels stuck to his fingers. He fetched up on Kestrel Ridge in 1979, bringing only a well-cultivated thirst and the clothes in which he – barely – stood up. The Harrisons sheltered him for a few months. Not in the house, however, but in a caravan that Harry, as if to underline the finite nature of his hospitality, kept parked just short of the sheer drop to the Meeting of the Waters below.

Bon finally found an attractive cottage close to the border with Ulster, the peppercorn rent for which should have roused his suspicions. Walking into the local pub that evening, he was taken aback to hear conversation fall away to silence. Fronting up to the bar, he ordered 'a pint and a Paddy' – Irish whiskey with a beer chaser. The barman ignored him. So did everyone else. After a few dry and awkward minutes, Bon fled.

A few enquiries the next morning elicited the explanation that should have been obvious. The previous tenant of his cottage had been a flagrant

British Army plant. They had tagged the new occupant as another of the same.

The thought of spending the rest of his time in Ireland drinking alone was too much for Bon. The next night, he returned to the pub and, in the same silence, located without too much trouble the local 'hard man', a flint-eyed fanatic who managed things for the IRA.

'You think I'm a Brit spy,' he said shortly. 'I'm not, and I can prove it.'

The man eyed him cautiously.

'Think about it, man,' Bon went on. 'What age would you take me for? Well, I'll tell you. I'm fifty-six. Now, if I was in the British Army, what rank would I have achieved by this time? I'd be a major, wouldn't I? Even a colonel. Do you really think they'd put a major or a colonel in a miserable posting like this?'

The IRA man took another pull on his pint. Then, looking at the barman, he said, 'Give my friend here a drink.' The rest of Bon's time in Ireland was a blur. He never published another book in his lifetime, though he was working, desultorily, on a thriller, *The Great Mortdecai Moustache Mystery* (since completed by Geoff Brown), when he died, a well-worn sixty-two, in 1985.

In retrospect, my time in London came to an end on an evening in 1979. Trailing Harry Harrison from country to country had been his long-suffering wife Joan. To celebrate their quarter-century of marriage, Harry decided to throw a huge party. Since only a few people had succumbed to the lure of a non-tax Ireland, it took place in London, just around the corner from Sloane Square in the Irish Club.

The party, like the live-tax-free-in-Ireland plan, proved generous in impulse but flawed in execution. The club welcomed Harry's demand for a totally open bar; booze, they assured him, would be unlimited. Though they promised to have a go, they were less confident about his request for a buffet of Indian and Chinese food, neither being popular in the spud-and-stout culture of Ireland.*

The Harrison party began at 6 p.m., and most people came direct from their offices. Ordering a drink, they gulped half of it before discovering that, taking Harry at his word, the barmen were serving brimming tumblers of booze with only a trace of soda or tonic. After turning to the buffet and finding it inedible, they took another drink. And another. Within an hour, every guest was paralytic. Mark Barty-King, urbane director of Granada Publishing, whom I had never known to raise his voice, was in a

* When I lived in Dublin, food inspectors closed down the local Chinese takeaway after finding half a butchered Alsatian in the kitchen. It re-opened soon after, the owners having argued they would never waste perfectly good dog on the Irish, but reserved it for the family.

near-screaming row with Kingsley Amis's then-wife, Elizabeth Jane Howard. Amis himself, drunk and sprawled in an armchair, stared in bemusement at film historian John Brosnan, who, no less pie-eyed, was berating him for failing to agree to be interviewed for his new book.

When John, as was his custom, quietly passed out a short time later, my wife and I carried him home and put him to bed on the couch. Watching him dead to the world, oblivious of the hangover to come, I almost envied him. London was no town for someone who only drank lager, and not much of that. To borrow a metaphor from my book hunting, it was an eddy, not a stream; no matter how far or fast you travelled, it would always be in a circle. I recognized the familiar itch to be somewhere else, with new people, new ideas . . . new books.

CHAPTER ELEVEN

The End of the Affair

There was always a moment during the writing – usually
about midway through the script – when one despaired and
said, 'For God's sake, let's chuck this up!'

Graham Greene on writing screenplays

BETWEEN 1976 AND 1980, JOYCE AND I LIVED IN
London almost full time, with a brief tax exile in
Dublin, and some excursions to the United States and
Australia. We bought an apartment in Highgate, on
the high ground above north London, which I started
filling with books – many by Graham Greene.

R. A. Wobbe published *Graham Greene: A
Bibliography and Guide to Research* in 1979 and I spent
hours browsing the close-set pages. Obscure editions
swam through my dreams like women.

I stalked Greene through London. When I read

that the Samaritans was to hold a fund-raising auction, for which many authors, including Greene, had contributed signed books, I rang immediately.

'Hello. I want some details—'

I didn't get any further. '*Hello!*' said a soft male voice, plangent with understanding. 'How are you this evening?'

'Uh, fine, thanks. I just want to know about this auction—'

'Could I have your name, please?'

I gave it. 'But all I really want—'

'Now, John, what would you like to talk about?'

'Well, Graham Greene.'

This threw him momentarily. 'Graham Greene, the *writer*?'

'Yes, I read in the *Evening Standard*—'

'I don't think I've ever read any of his books,' he said, recovering quickly. 'Which is your favourite?'

'Look, you don't understand. I'm not calling for help. I want some information—'

'Of course you don't need help, John. Now calm down.'

'I *am* calm.'

'No need to get angry.'

'*I'm not angry . . .*'

The Samaritan system worked. If I'd been thinking about suicide, I'd have dropped the idea by then.*

Being known as a 'player' earned me access to the stream of gossip that bubbles below the world of books like a subterranean river. Leads came from unlikely places. With his wife Candy, Al Reuter, whose jagged axe-murderer smile and hulking build belied his kindly nature, dealt in Royal Family memorabilia from a rat-hole of a shop off the Finchley Road.

''Ere,' he said. 'Saw some Greenes las' week. Din' want 'em meself, but she's probably still got 'em.'

His tip led me to the daughter of film producer John Stafford, who was interested in selling some of the books Greene had signed for her father. Stafford, whom Greene once called ruefully 'too nice a man to be in the film business', produced movies of his *Loser Takes All*, *Across the Bridge* and *The Stranger's Hand*, all of them traduced by bizarre executive decisions, often involving the choice of a director or star from Italy, where Stafford usually went to scrape up a foreign partner. *Loser Takes All*, inspired by Greene's brush with movie mogul Alexander Korda, described

---

* And yes, I did get the book – one of the three hundred numbered and signed copies of *How Father Quixote Became a Monsignor*, part of what Greene at the time called 'a novel that will never be completed', though he did publish *Monsignor Quixote* in 1982, to considerable success.

how a young accountant, quixotically rewarded by his millionaire boss with a honeymoon in Monaco, gambles both his future and his wife, and nearly loses both. The role of the colourless bean-counter cried for somebody archetypally English, like Alec Guinness, so, naturally, Stafford cast Italian matinée idol Rossano Brazzi.

A few days later, I spent the morning in Stafford's old home in a seedily genteel corner of west London. His middle-aged daughter, limp and colourless as a house-dress washed to exhaustion, had hung on to first editions of *The Quiet American*, *The End of the Affair*, *A Visit to Morin* and a rare proof copy of *A Burnt-Out Case*, all inscribed to Stafford or his wife Dorothy. I emerged a few hours later with all of them, and wove my way to the tube station, rubber-kneed from having shared most of a bottle of neat gin, drunk at room temperature from one of those little tumblers painted with brightly coloured flowers in which processed cheese used to be sold. Greene would have approved.

Gossip also led me to bookseller Robert Chris and his disordered den in Cecil Court, the bookshop-lined passage that cuts through London's theatreland. Resembling nothing so much as a bullfrog, Chris had occupied the shop for forty years, and knew Greene from the old days. Greene, according to the scuttlebutt, dropped in on Chris when he was in

London, and probably used him, in a somewhat cleaned-up version, as the model for the KGB-contact bookseller in *The Human Factor*. I spent some unpleasant hours browsing his battered stock, thick with dust, all the time both hoping for and dreading the moment when light from the door would be blocked by the stooped figure of Greene, but, except for Chris's ogre of a wife, almost nobody else came near the place.

Chris was happy to reminisce about Greene. They'd met in the Thirties, when the Greene brothers would spend Saturdays browsing for Victorian detective stories. They remained friends while Graham wrote his first novels and became film critic for the magazine *Night and Day*, which aimed to bring the sophistication of *The New Yorker* to London. In 1937, Greene notoriously reviewed John Ford's *Wee Willie Winkie*, making disparaging remarks about Shirley Temple, then just nine years old. Neither Greene nor *Night and Day* anticipated that Twentieth Century Fox might sue for libel on Temple's behalf. They bankrupted the magazine and inflicted £1,500 damages on Greene. According to Chris, Greene came by his shop that day in a panic, announcing that he was leaving for Mexico, perhaps never to return. Chris urged him to stay in London, and even lent him some money (if true, a notable first for a bookseller), but Greene went anyway, returning the next year to write his novel *The Power and the Glory*, and *The Lawless Roads*, his account of the persecution of Mexican Catholics by the left-wing anti-clerical government.

It was Chris who directed me to Maggs on Berkeley Square, one of the temples of the rare book trade. Normally I shunned West End shops like Heywood Hill, Sotheran's, Bertram Rota and Maggs, Suppliers of Books to the Gentry and the Royal Family. Even if they had the kind of books I wanted, I almost certainly couldn't afford their prices.

But Bob Chris held them all in contempt. 'They think they know it all,' he said, 'but nobody knows *everything*.'

It was a crucial insight. Many treasures aren't found in skips and thrift shops but on the shelves of specialists. Someone who knows the exact value of Dickens's *Bleak House* as originally published in monthly parts will probably underprice a first edition of Dashiell Hammett's *The Glass Key*. In a piece for *The New Yorker*, Calvin Trilling described how a runner had found in Larry McMurtry's Booked Up an edition of Louis Hémon's *Marie Chapdelaine*, one of the cornerstones of Québecois literature, which McMurtry had priced at a fraction of its value.

Maggs only had one Greene of interest – a first

edition of *The Lawless Roads*, without a dust wrapper, at £150.

'It's inscribed,' the assistant pointed out.

There was the spidery dedication. 'For Gervase Matthew . . .'

Gervase Matthew? The Jesuit priest to whom Greene dedicated *The Power and the Glory*? The name meant a lot to me, but obviously not to Maggs. The special relevance of the signature, missed by their cataloguer, doubled its value.

Over the next few years, Greene visited Bob Chris a few times, though never while I was in the shop. I left books with him to have signed, which Greene did, though always to Chris himself, inscribing them 'from his ancient old friend'. With the brass face of the true dealer, Chris sold my own books back to me at about two-thirds what they'd fetch on the open market. And I was happy to pay.

Among these books was an uncorrected proof copy of *A Burnt-Out Case*. It led me into that jungle of variants that can be a trap for many collectors.

The incomplete is always alluring. When I was a kid going to movies at the Coogee Boomerang, the magic began even before the film itself when a rippling oblong of light appeared at the far end of the cinema. It was some years before I realized that this was just the first few feet of the film which the projectionist, either out of inattention, laziness, or professional embarrassment at the scratched and riddled print, elected to project onto the curtain. Sometimes he didn't 'pull the tabs' – the proper technical term – until halfway through the credits.

As art historians X-ray pictures to see *pentimenti*, film historians dig through out-takes to create 'directors' cuts', and literary critics study manuscripts, so bibliophiles collect proofs. The proof is the first impression of the text taken after the typesetter has turned the manuscript into type. It's the larval state of a book and, like most larvae, isn't much to look at. Traditionally, half a dozen proofs were done on cheap paper, in long sheets called galleys. The printer and, if he was lucky, the writer then checked the text, correcting errors with marginal code marks. An obliging publisher might allow the writer to make a few additions, while living in fear of striking another Marcel Proust or James Joyce. Both regarded galleys as just a cleaner version of their manuscript. They not only rewrote the text but added new material in the margins, and spilling onto other pages. You could almost sympathize with the printer, who had to start all over again each time.

Pity too the French country printers to whom Sylvia Beach sent the text of James Joyce's *Ulysses*. She thought their typesetters wouldn't be as scandalized by the language as their English-speaking colleagues had been. They weren't. But they also couldn't read much English, and, even when they did understand it, couldn't read Joyce's writing. It took eight impressions before Joyce, Beach and their friends dug out the crabgrass of typos.

Most writers couldn't be bothered reading proofs, which is why so many first editions are identifiable by their printing errors. Only by checking whether your copy of the Scribner's edition of *The Great Gatsby* has 'chatter' in line 16 of page 60, 'northern' in line 22 of page 119, 'sick and tired' misprinted as 'sick in tired' on lines 9 and 10 of page 205 and 'Union Street station' in lines 7 and 8 of page 211 can you differentiate the first from later printings. On true first editions of *Doctor Jekyll and Mister Hyde*, the printing date on the front wrap, 1886, is changed in ink by hand to '1887', which was the true year of publication. On second impressions, they printed the date correctly – so copies that give the correct year of publication are the 'wrong' ones.

When everyone was done tinkering, the printer pulled more galleys, but this time chopped the long sheets into normal pages and bound them in cheap paper covers. In the great days, a proof like this was regarded as the first edition *of* the first edition – the next best thing to the manuscript. Distribution of these 'bound galleys', sometimes called 'uncorrected proofs' to cover any errors the printer didn't spot, tended to be limited and restricted. The cover designer got one, the publicist, and maybe a few influential critics or editors – even the author, provided the office boy didn't sell them all out the back door.

Variants could still creep in, even after the corrected text had been sent to the printer. Jonathan Cape printed a few copies of John Fowles's novel *The Collector* in black cloth, but switched to brown for the main printing, making the test copies twenty times more valuable. Dust wrappers varied as well. George Orwell's *Nineteen Eighty-four* appears in both a pink and a green dust wrapper, but nobody knows which came first. Kingsley Amis rewrote the 'blurb' copy for his novel *Girl, 20* before publication, but copies with the first version occasionally turn up. When Michael Haggiag of Aurum Press published *The Tree*, a collection of Frank Horvath photographs with text by John Fowles, the cover copy misspelled Fowles's novel *The Magus* as *The Magnus*. Haggiag conscientiously reprinted the cover, but an American dealer bought the discarded jackets, which Fowles collectors now pursue.

Certain proofs assumed mythical status. Mostly, they were for novels that succeeded beyond all expectation. How many proofs were struck for Sylvia Plath's novel *The Bell Jar*, published pseudonymously as by 'Victoria Lucas', or for Anthony Burgess's *A Clockwork Orange*? A dozen? Twenty? And how many were tossed in the bin by uninterested reviewers? What about that thriller an editor of Jonathan Cape published as a favour to his old pal, a London foreign correspondent? If there were any proofs of Ian Fleming's *Casino Royale*, I don't know anybody who has ever seen one. Should one turn up, the value would be astronomical – considering that a copy of the book itself in its dust wrapper would set you back £25,000 in today's market.

The rarest proofs belong to books that never got published, or were much changed between proofing and publishing. In the middle of my most passionate period of collecting Greene, I was jolted when, around 1977, George Locke, who dealt in science fiction from a basement in Sackville Street, flashed a proof bound in plain brown paper and said, 'This might interest you.' It was the proof of Greene's first successful novel, *Stamboul Train*. And the first version – *this* version – had been withdrawn by the publishers when J. B. Priestley decided the popular novelist in it parodied him, and threatened to sue. It was pulped, and Greene rewrote the text.

George didn't realize this proof was any more valuable than any Greene proof of that period, and I was not about to tell him. Though maybe he suspected something, since he refused to sell it to me, on the pretext of creating a 'retirement fund' of books for his wife Rita that were more readily converted into cash than the penny dreadfuls and first editions of *The Worm Ouroboros* and *Varney the Vampire* that were his stock in trade. Six months later, having just received a big advance for a new book, I arrived in his shop with a wad of tenners fresh from the bank and, explaining that I wanted to 'buy myself a present', started to lay them down on the counter one by one. I got to £110 before George groaned, 'All right, all right, it's yours.'

American publishers cottoned on to the trade in proofs and began to make 'limited editions' and 'collectors' editions'. Proofs, reborn as ARCs – Advanced Reading Copies – flooded the market. Some companies distribute more ARCs than the first printing of the actual book, and ARCs of popular writers like Ed McBain or James Lee Burke are a drug on the market, effectively worth nothing. On the other hand, when Gollancz produced two limited-edition proofs for J. G. Ballard's *Empire of the Sun*, the first a facsimile of the manuscript with Ballard's corrections, the second with those corrections set in type, both became highly collectable.

Proof hysteria survives in a few corners of the

market, notably eBay, where the following listing appeared in December 2001:

The Women of Provincetown, 1951–1922 by CHERYL BLACK /Publisher: University of Alabama Press/ Pub. Date: April 2001/(UNCORRECTED/ADVANCE/ PROOF) 1ST EDITION UNREAD NEW CONDITION SEALED IN PLASTIC. Every year, just before Christmas I go through my collection and come up with some GEMS! These rare collectable proof editions make great stocking stuffers! It is rare enough to find an uncorrected proof let alone one that is from an extremely small publishing company so it is an extremely rare copy! If YOU can find another proof copy let ME know where! For those of you who don't already know, the rarest form of a published collectable is an uncorrected, unedited, advance proof. These hard to find collectable proofs are only sent to editors or reviewers. These books are sent to editors, the language is cleaned up, the stories are toned down or eliminated entirely – many of them are written in (not this one) by editors (there are many editors – not one) and then many of the copies are destroyed. Finally let me stress that because so very few proof copies are made the price on a rare proof (marked and stamped as such with pre-publishing data etc.) can only go through the roof. (A Harry Potter proof copy recently sold on eBay for over $1000 – the first edition of the same book is still available in bookstores for around $12.) I wish

I had a scanner so you could see the beautiful cover artwork and condition of this proof edition! Bid now!! Before it's too late!! I only have one copy. When it's gone it's gone!!\

Full marks for saleswomanship but none for scholarship. A proof of that vintage and of so obscure a book is worth almost nothing.

By the early Eighties, my Greenes had spread along the wall of our living room and into the bedroom, and acquired a taxonomy and biology of their own. At night, one could almost imagine the books rustling and rubbing against one another like a colony of insects. At its silent behest, I reorganized the collection constantly, 'mating' titles in new configurations; alphabetical order, then chronological. Titles like *Journey Without Maps* or *Brighton Rock* with all their foreign editions; then the inscribed books together; then all those from the same publisher. Collectors of almost anything periodically go through the same process. The hero of Nick Hornby's *High Fidelity* does it with his records.

Around this time, it dropped into my mind that, further to unify the collection, I should have a bookplate – the label you stick in the front of a book to show it belongs to you.

Bookplates have a mixed reputation. Collectors

always own a few from the libraries of other people. We steam them out, then usually discard the book, wondering why anyone would put a plate into a Book Club edition of *More Raunchy Rugby Songs*.

Bookplates were just beginning to revive as an aid for lazy but successful writers who didn't care to sit around in bookshops waiting for punters. Instead, they signed plates, which sellers pasted in. Many collectors spurned these, the existence of which spawned the neologism 'flat signed'. A signature 'flat signed' on the page is regarded as more authentic, and thus more valuable, than one on a plate.

(My objection to pre-signed plates was less to the authenticity of the signature than to that of a plate which says 'Ex Libris' and is signed by the author. Is the book supposed to be from his library? If so, what does he want with a signed copy of his own book? More mysteries for the bibliophiles of the future to unravel.)

Some famous artists had designed bookplates. Aubrey Beardsley, for instance. Norman Lindsay made it enough of a specialty to have a book devoted to his designs. I owned an enigmatic one done by Max Ernst for the film historian Georges Sadoul, a fellow-traveller of the Surrealists. The most delicate I ever found was by glassmaker René Lalique. Printed on translucent paper in pale brown ink, it was barely readable – not terribly efficient as a means of identifying a book.

But was it ever meant to be? Originally, a plate discouraged people from swiping your books. Seeing that stern 'Ex Libris' – 'from the library of . . .' – was supposed to ensure that borrowers returned your property, like those mantras children put in school textbooks – 'If by chance this book should roam / Box its ears and send it home.'

But if a plate is meant as protection, why make it decorative? It would be enough to put, 'This book belongs to X. Please return promptly.' Or just that blunt warning one sometimes finds scrawled across a pastedown, 'Stolen from X.' People who go to the trouble of having a bookplate designed and gumming it into every book don't, as far as I can see, much mind if the book does end up on someone else's shelves. Bookplates advertise that the owner is important enough to rate a library. Like putting the family crest on the silver, it does less to protect the silver than show that you have enough for it to be worth protecting.

In practice, a bookplate is as sure a sign of new money as the library itself. Scott Fitzgerald was right when he had Nick Carraway and Jordan Baker, exploring Gatsby's house during one of his vast parties, find a drunk admiring their host's well-filled bookshelves.

'What do you think?' he demanded impetuously.

'About what?'

He waved his hands towards the book-shelves.

'About that. As a matter of fact you needn't bother to ascertain. I ascertained. They're real.'

'The books?'

He nodded.

'Absolutely real – have pages and everything. I thought they'd be a nice durable cardboard. Matter of fact, they're absolutely real. Pages and— Here! Lemme show you.'

Taking our scepticism for granted, he rushed to the bookcases and returned with Volume One of the *Stoddard Lectures*.

'See!' he cried triumphantly. 'It's a bona-fide piece of printed matter. It fooled me. The fella's a regular Belasco. It's a triumph. What thoroughness! What realism! Knew when to stop, too – didn't cut the pages. But what do you want? What do you expect?'

Jay Gatsby would have had a bookplate, for sure. Probably, like most of the plates affected by self-made men of that time, it showed a sunset over a tranquil country landscape, seen through a mullioned window, with a briar pipe smoking on the sill, and a pen lying across a half-finished letter.

Or maybe it was one of those 'Much have I travelled in the realms of gold' jobs, with knights skewering dragons, centaurs cavorting, seas foaming, and maids languishing under sad cypresses. Artists sold a lot of these to movie stars of the Twenties and Thirties; Rudolph Valentino had a particularly pompous example which, while it would have suited a copy of *King Solomon's Mines*, looks odd in some of the books you find it in. I happen to have it in his lavish gilt and red-morocco-bound copy of *Exhibition of Female Flagellants in the Modest and Incontinent World*.*

This is not to say that all movie people are without taste. The director George Cukor, who had a large library – though mainly of books given to him or related to his movies – commissioned an austere plate from Paul Landacre. It showed simply the front of his Hollywood home, and was elegant enough to provide the cover for the catalogue of his collection issued by George Houle when he sold it in 1986.

But the design of most bookplates is pitiful. Why would anyone choose to have such a thing in their books? Probably the answer lies in the fact that, unless you want one 'off the peg' – like the generic items that used to be given away by book clubs, or

---

* When I showed this to erotica expert Michael Neal, he plunged his nose into the open book and sniffed like someone savouring a large burgundy. 'Ah, yes. Published in Paris,' he said. 'There was a later American printing. This is authentic.' What did he smell? I didn't like to ask.

which you can still buy, in lots of fifty, pre-gummed – plates have to be commissioned. And, having commissioned a design, you're committed to using it, for fear of offending the artist – almost always a friend. There isn't even the option that comes with portraits, of hanging it in the dark corner of the guest bedroom. However horrible, the bookplate has to appear on every book you own.

Finding some of these bookplates can be like discovering a squashed frog in a book (and don't think *they* don't turn up. And much worse.) Fear of such a conclusion frustrated my first attempt at commissioning a bookplate. London bookseller David Bunnett was friendly with Francis Bacon. He often told stories of hanging around Soho's Colony Room with Bacon and such grotesques as Nina Hamnett and 'Iron Foot Jack'.

Would Bacon, I asked him, design me a bookplate? David promised to ask, and, after much prodding, said that Bacon had agreed, for a fee of £1,000. But I wouldn't own the artwork afterwards; that would still belong to Bacon.

I thought about it. The cost wasn't the problem, so much as concern that I wouldn't like the result. Would one care for a screaming pope on every book? I was heavily into collecting science fiction and books about the cinema, and while Bacon's existential anguish might square with the first edition of Brian

Aldiss's *Greybeard*, on the pastedown of Robert Heinlein's *Have Spacesuit, Will Travel*, or *Call Me Lucky*, the memoirs of Bing Crosby, it could clash. And, having spent that kind of sum, one could hardly not use it. Finally, I took the coward's way out, pleading poverty.

It was a good lesson that a bookplate should be emblematic; consonant with the books in which it appears. I began to think about art from people a little closer to my literary interests. Ron Graham, the Australian collector and, briefly, publisher of science fiction, commissioned a plate from his favourite fantasy illustrator, Virgil Finlay, who, happily, was still alive, and sufficiently productive to design him one – though using an illustration from his golden period in the Thirties, rather more attractive than his later, less precise efforts.

Not long afterwards, at the World Science Convention in Brighton, I saw some beautiful work by a Californian sculptor who specialized in creating tiny skeletons of imaginary animals. If ever a man had his future in the film business, it was he, and no doubt he ended up there, since he never responded to my suggestion that a two-dimensional version of one of his elegant skulls, with its intricate geometry of multiple horns, jaws and elongated eye sockets, would look good on my books.

Well, it was starting to come into focus. Probably

good rather than great art. And probably having something to do with the books in which it would be used.

The British 'pop' artist Allen Jones was my next candidate. I'd always liked his arrogantly sexist work with its slick airbrush surfaces and candy colours, his strutting women with their jutting breasts and rocket thighs. And I had an introduction to him, since, through one of those series of coincidences that characterize the book business, I had acquired not one but two copies of one of his early lithographs, the interestingly named *Left-Hand Woman*.*

Cruising the Saturday morning flea market in The Waste, off the Balls Pond Road, my friend Brian Troath had found a signed limited edition of a book about sculptress Elizabeth Frink.

'Are you interested in pictures at all?' the seller enquired as he wrapped the book in an old page from the *Sun* and shoved it into a plastic bag. Slowing down his blink rate to the reptilian, Brian said he'd been known to buy the occasional daub. The Frink book, explained the man, came from the warehouse of a bankrupt printer. As well as the books, he'd bought a roll of pictures. He offered to bring them

* There was no masturbatory connotation, as in 'left-handed reading'. He had done a *Right-Hand Woman* too. The titles just referred to which side of the picture the lady in the black neoprene jumpsuit was crouching.

round. A few days later, Brian called me with that forced calm one learns to associate with someone who can barely suppress the impulse to jump up and down making high-pitched squeals.

I went round to his home. A fat roll of paper lay on his kitchen table. Carefully, he unrolled it, sheet by sheet. First, an instantly recognizable David Hockney; an old man with a long nose, sitting in profile in an upright chair. Then a lithograph of two hands. Signed 'The hands of God. Henry Moore.'

A Barbara Hepworth, two Graham Sutherlands, two copies of Allen Jones's *Left-Hand Woman*, a Ceri Richards inspired by Dylan Thomas's 'The Force That Through the Green Fuse Drives the Flower', an Edward Bawden of Smithfield meat market . . . and so on. Twenty lithographs in all, almost all signed, and in some cases inscribed to the distinguished but now defunct Curwen Press. Various Curwen clients had supplied them for a book about the press, *Artists at Curwen*. After that, they'd gathered dust while the company died around them, and finally been sold as waste paper.

I put up the money to buy them, and kept the Hockney and the Allen Joneses as my share. Jones hadn't signed either, which is how I came to be climbing the stairs to his Charterhouse Square studio.

Artists' homes often look like they've been ransacked by the Armageddon chapter of Hell's Angels. But Jones lived in pristine minimalist splendour, his apartment dominated by one of his controversial statues of a woman in stilettos, stockings and garter belt – not the one on all fours, supporting a coffee table, but the one standing upright. The figures looked life-sized in pictures, but were actually about ten per cent larger than life, and thus a little daunting. Maybe the feminists had it wrong: Jones wasn't objectifying women – not entirely, anyway. He was saying something about their power too.

Jones was interested enough in where I'd got the lithographs not to mind signing them for me. It helped that I arrived with my collection of other books about, or illustrated by him; evidence that I was an enthusiast, and not just looking to make a couple of items more saleable.

After that, he showed me some more of his work, including trays of lithographs, almost clinically filed, annotated, recorded. Some were tiny – the size of a bookplate . . .

I almost opened my mouth to suggest it. But this clearly wasn't the moment. I'd established myself in Jones's eyes as a mid- to lower-level fan, someone sufficiently house-trained to be accommodated. To become a client would demand an entirely new relationship – more intimate in some ways, less in others. The artist asking his model out for dinner must face the same dilemma. It would be simpler, I decided, to terminate this contact, and re-establish another to discuss a bookplate. But I never did.

In part, it was the question of content. Did I want a left-hand woman, or any of her sisters, on all my books? Also, I associated Jones's work with colour, and simply couldn't imagine a colour bookplate. They exist, but they're rare.

And, by then, I'd seen enough bookplates to know how little I knew about what they should look like. I don't know yet. Probably the best answer is a completely blank one. It would show people you owned a good library, but deny them the material to categorize you. But here's the problem – who would I get to design it?

The whole question became academic in the summer of 1981. I had just delivered the manuscript of a new novel to my English and American publishers. Both had responded with a long list of suggested changes, and, since none of the changes appeared on both lists, I faced a summer effectively rewriting the book twice – and this before the days of computers, when such jobs can be achieved almost at a key stroke. Sitting in the front room of our Highgate apartment, I began to sense the presence of my books at my back as a sort of burden.

Debra Peattie rang. A student at Hollins during my tenure, she was now a biochemist, and had been on attachment to the Imperial Cancer Research Fund. She was returning to America and had a generous house-moving allowance. Was there anything I wanted shipped to the east coast?

An hour later, Denise Bethel rang from New York. Another Hollins graduate, in her case in art history, she'd passed – hurriedly – through a phase as curator of the Edgar Allan Poe Museum in Richmond to become, she now announced, head of the Rare Book Department at the New York auction house Swann Galleries. Did I have anything I'd like to sell?

I turned and looked at the Greenes. The fledgling that had once been a pleasure to nurture had grown into a giant cuckoo absorbing my energy and funds. What could I reasonably expect to add to the collection? Better copies of the novels perhaps, with newer dust wrappers. Some letters; manuscripts even – but these were rapidly being priced out of my range.

And if I ever met Greene . . . ? The encounter with Allen Jones had clarified the nature of the collector's relationship with the object of his interest. As Kingsley Amis had shown me, I could be a fan or a friend, but not both. I decided that, if I ever did meet

Greene, I'd rather not do so with one of his first editions in my hand.

The decision took place automatically, as it usually does in these cases. 'How would you like to sell my Greene collection?' I asked.

CHAPTER 12

Bookshop Dreams

After love, book collecting is the most exhilarating sport of all.

Bibliophile and dealer A. S. W. Rosenbach

SELLING MY GREENE BOOKS – WHICH SWANN
Galleries did, on 24 June 1982 – didn't diminish my
enthusiasm for collecting. If anything, those empty
shelves were a silent invitation. And I had, after all,
realized an average 200 per cent profit – if you didn't
count the hundreds of hours spent tracking down the
books.

Though I didn't attend the sale, for fear that last-
minute regrets might have driven me to fling myself
across my books, sobbing, 'Don't take my babies
away!', in the early Eighties I was spending more and
more time in America, and thus in American
bookshops. Taking Josef von Sternberg's advice, and

building on what I'd learned at Hollins, I began to collect American authors and illustrators less easily exhausted than Greene. Edward Gorey, for instance, still hadn't been widely discovered. Frances Steloff's Gotham Book Mart in New York, which published his little books and acted as a point of contact for the few collectors, always had a pile of limited editions by the cash register, often signed by him. I bought most of them, at prices which, today, appear ludicrously low.

One occasionally glimpsed Gorey drifting around Manhattan *en route* to the ballet, his only recreation: he attended the New York City Ballet six nights a week, almost always sitting in the same seat. A gangling figure in ankle-length raccoon coat and sneakers, he could have stepped out of one of his creations – *The Fatal Lozenge*, perhaps, or *The Gashlycrumb Tinies*, an alphabet featuring twenty-six sinister children. 'N is for Neville,' he captioned the image of a pale child, just a tiny head with hollow eyes, staring through the window of a vast moated grange, 'who died of ennui.' But I only began to collect him after seeing him interviewed, reluctantly, by Dick Cavett, a night-club comedian who remade himself as the thinking man's Johnny Carson. Cavett – or at least his researchers – latched on to the fact that Gorey drew the covers for Doubleday's paperback reissues of Henry James.

'What do you think of James today?' Cavett asked.

An expressionless Gorey replied, 'I loathe every word he wrote.'

Cavett nodded sagely. 'Yes, I share your ambivalence,' he said.

Gorey soon became one of the most sought-after designers of the Eighties, but the second of my new enthusiasms, Lafcadio Hearn, remained relentlessly obscure. An American born on the Greek island of Lefkas (hence the name), he became the first Western author to settle in and write about Japan, a country he chose because his appearance – he was very short, and one eye bulged like that of a horse – excited no comment from the Japanese, to whom even the handsomest Westerner was as grotesque as a Martian.

Other writers of similar obscurity attracted my attention, and began to fill the shelves: Horace McCoy, author of realist and crime novels like *They Shoot Horses, Don't They?* And the American humorist of the Twenties, Don Marquis, who wrote comic verses in the persona of Archy, an *avant garde* poet reincarnated as a cockroach, and featuring Archy's friend Mehitabel the cat, who may or may not in a previous life have been Cleopatra. In a parody of e.e. cummings, Archy wrote entirely in lower case, since he had to dive head-first onto the typewriter keys for each letter, and never found a way to make capitals.

In the long term, however, the most fun came from collecting the publications of the Olympia Press, the English-language publishing house directed in Paris in the Fifties and Sixties by the spectacularly shifty Maurice Girodias.

'Published in Paris' was a cliché of porn, but for Olympia and its companion series Ophir, Othello and Ophelia, it happened to be true. Girodias more than any other modern publisher earned Paris its reputation as the world capital of one-handed reading. Yet he also had literary pretensions, and his attempts to finance literature by publishing pornography (and, occasionally, financing pornography by publishing literature) must be unique. No publisher ever struck more concisely the balance between heightened consciousness and lowered trousers. For every *Lolita*, *Ginger Man*, *Naked Lunch*, *Ticket That Exploded*, *Watt*, *Molloy* or *Thief's Journal*, there was *The Loins of Amon*, *Until She Screams*, *The Debauched Hospodar*, *How to Do It*, *Sex for Breakfast*, *Bottoms Up* and *Lust*.

Girodias's father, Jack Kahane, had launched the Obelisk Press before World War II and published a number of mildly naughty novels, including Henry Miller's *Tropic of Cancer*, for which young Maurice designed a lurid cover, with a giant crab carrying a nude woman. Obelisk also published Miller's sequels *Tropic of Capricorn* and *Black Spring*, James Hanley's *Boy*, Frank Harris's *My Life and Loves*, and Cyril Connolly's *The Rock Pool*. In his introduction to Patrick Kearney's bibliography of the Olympia Press, Girodias calls himself frankly 'a second-generation Anglo-French pornographer'. His publishing decisions, he claims, were in the best Obelisk tradition: 'The connecting link is clear enough: anything that shocks because it comes before its time; anything that is liable to be banned by the censors because they cannot accept its honesty.'

Eroticism is deeply embedded in publishing, book selling and, above all, in book collecting. Many bibliophiles dream about acquiring books before they start to collect. In one of my earliest dreams, which recurred until my late teens, I discovered a tea chest brimming with American colour comics, the antithesis of the consumptive editions produced for the Australian market. I was in good company, as it turned out, since, in 1973, Graham Greene wrote, 'I don't know how Freud would have interpreted it, but for more than thirty years my happiest dreams have been of secondhand bookshops.' I could have helped him with a Freudian explanation, since I once asked a psychiatrist friend what he made of this fantasy. 'Oh, a common dream of puberty. It's all sexual.' I didn't doubt him. To have found the comic books, only to lose them on waking, dramatized the same sense of inadequacy as did those fantasies Freud called 'student dreams' which arrive later in adolescence: the exam where you can't answer even one question; the train that carries you past your destination; the realization that you are in the middle of the main street but your trousers aren't. For an adolescent to visualize a tea chest of comic books and wake to find them on his shelf was as good as being guaranteed an unfailing morning erection – a powerful incentive to collect.

And perhaps also to buy. Because the buying and selling of antiques is innately erotic, a fact on which BBC TV's *Antiques Roadshow* and its international versions trade flagrantly.

Antiques Roadshow exaggerates, even parodies, those stages that the act of selling shares with the act of seduction: mystery, collusion, anticipation, revelation. Its experts, riding into town like the gunmen of *The Magnificent Seven*, bring with them a sense of arcane knowledge. To share it, punters stand in line for hours, sometimes in the cold and rain; and, even when they get inside, checkers reject all but the choicest items. Finally, only when one of these catches the eye of an expert are they invited to a consultation on camera.

These encounters are distinguished by a quasi-erotic call and response that the more telegenic regulars have honed to a fine edge.

'Now what have we here?' they demand, jovially. 'Have you had it long? Is it a family piece?'

The owner stammers out the little information she possesses, which the expert normally brushes aside.

'No, it isn't Chinese. It's Japanese . . .' With much flourishing of the loupe, and pointing to illegible signatures, minuscule silver marks and tiny painted letters on the underside of pots, the intimacies of the owner's family piece are thoroughly exposed. 'So,' says the expert coquettishly, 'we come to value. What did you say your mother paid for it?'

She names a very small sum.

'What if I told you it was worth . . . five hundred pounds?'

No! Five hundred? She sucks in her breath. In control now, the expert presses ahead. 'Then what if I told you it was worth a thousand pounds?'

By now, her surrender is total. He can do with her as he pleases.

'But what you really must do . . .' The pause is agonizing. '. . . is insure the item . . .' Yes? Yes? 'for . . . five thousand pounds!'

The TV audience shares the prolonged throb of orgasm.

There follow a few seconds of post-erotic languor, the expert smirking, the punter trying to steady her trembling knees, the viewers murmuring,

'Did you hear that? Five thousand quid. For that pot? We should really check the attic . . .'

It remains only to bring the encounter gracefully to a close. Some experts do this better than others, with a consoling pat on the arm, or an even more affectionate final caress of the object itself. Others can't resist extorting a final self-congratulatory spasm. 'You didn't expect that, did you?' they murmur. ('Was it good for you?')

Unfortunately, buying and selling first editions doesn't induce the same ecstasy as dealing in impressionist oils or Georgian silver. Sex is conspicuously lacking from bookshop novels; George Orwell's *Keep the Aspidistra Flying*, for instance, and Brian Aldiss's *The Brightfount Diaries*. Even 'bibliomysteries' such as the Bernie Rhodenbarr stories of Lawrence Block or John Dunning's highly touted series that began with *Booked to Die*, generally confine themselves to nastier passions.

I did, it's true, in the late Seventies, spend a disturbing half-hour in the vast basement of a movie memorabilia store under Greenwich Village, a head-scrapingly low space awash with movie stills and posters that slipped under my feet as I shifted my weight – the Junee garage multiplied by a hundred – while the pale young man who slept in a grubby nest of blankets and pillows at the back described with anatomical precision where and how and how often he had 'done it' in this cellar with young heroin addicts: whether male or female didn't seem to be an issue, given the carnal voraciousness of his reminiscences. Back at the shop itself, it took me a few visits to realize that the furtive men who arrived from time to time carrying TVs or cameras weren't leaving them for safekeeping: the owner was also a fence. Hubert Selby Jr and John Rechy didn't need to invent much for novels like *City of Night* and *Last Exit to Brooklyn*. As it says on Christopher Wren's tomb in St Paul's, 'If you seek his memorial, look around you.'

One of the few good bookshop sex scenes appears in Howard Hawks's 1946 film of *The Big Sleep*. Unable to bluff his way into Arthur Gwynn Geiger's porn library, Humphrey Bogart crosses the street to a bookshop managed by the young Dorothy Malone. When he asks her about variant printings of *Ben-Hur*, she knows enough to check a bibliography and establish that no such editions exist. One thing leads to another and, with nobody likely to come into the shop during an afternoon downpour, she hangs out the CLOSED sign, and she and Bogart repair to the back room with a bottle of rye.

The scene doesn't appear in the novel. There, the shop assistant, a middle-aged woman with 'the fine-drawn face of an intelligent Jewess', gives Marlowe a frosty reception, and though she consults the bibliography for him, sends him out into the rain. Frankly, this is more like reality. During languid afternoons in bookshops, the presence of someone attractive at the desk or browsing the shelves can ignite fantasies, but it would need to be a very dull shop indeed before a real collector would stop thinking about books and begin to contemplate sex.

Sadly, books in themselves lack sex appeal. Even collectors of erotica primarily acquire the books not to read but as objects, and, on this level, *120 Days of Sodom* is no more tantalizing than the *A-Z Guide to London*. And, while the marks of silversmith Paul Revere or the crossed swords of Meissen china exercise an hypnotic fascination for silver and porcelain collectors, the letter 'A' under the colophon or the bracketed (1) on the last text page by which Scribner's and Appletons respectively indicate a first edition induces no such thrill.

The more flamboyant a book's subject, in fact, the more its publishers pursue drabness. James Joyce dictated a blue cover with white lettering for the Shakespeare and Company *Ulysses* to suggest the ocean and rocks of Greece, but the discretion of his design meant that far fewer copies were confiscated by customs or postal inspectors. Likewise, the sage-green paper covers of Olympia's 1955 two-volume first edition of *Lolita* appeared so ordinary that an inattentive American customs officer stamped the first copies 'Passed for Circulation in the USA', and unleashed a publishing phenomenon.

The phrase 'mailed in plain wrapper' soothes the ears of the nervous collector more than Mozart. Visitors to Paris in the Thirties snatched up the complimentary paper covers supplied by bookshops like Gibert; covered with anodyne ads for school supplies, they would mislead any censor. Richer collectors had the books rebound, so that *Tropic of Cancer* could arrive in America or Australia bound as *Structural Engineering* or *Wisdom of the Philosophers*. And the number of times tourists returned from Mexico with packets of miniature pornographic comics disguised as a pocket testament earned the booklets the nickname 'Tijuana Bibles'.

Once a collector got his treasure safely home, he sometimes indulged himself by making the book even more erotic – with a sexy bookplate, or, occasionally, a provocative binding. After author Paul Bourget used Laure Hayman as the basis for the character Gladys Harvey in his novel *Cosmopolis*, she gave a copy to her friend Marcel Proust bound in the flowered silk from one of her petticoats.* In a British exhibition of the Eighties, a London binder exhibited

---

* S. J. Perelman parodied this in *The Pants Recaptured*, where the contemporary male subject of such a novel has a copy bound in a pair of his underpants.

a volume bound in black vinyl, with a life-sized breast moulded on the front cover, and a three-dimensional white hand (detachable) cupped over it. Others have gone further still. In 1886, *The Book Fancier* noted, 'A Russian poet is said lately to have offered to the lady of his affections a collection of his sonnets bound in leather – human leather – which the poet himself furnished! On falling from his horse one day, he broke his thigh, and being obliged to undergo amputation, he had the skin carefully tanned and reserved for some purpose of the kind.'

What the trade calls delicately 'anthropodermic bindings' are rare but not unknown, though, for obvious reasons, nobody is in a hurry to admit they own them. The Library of Congress owns a *Scrutinium Scriptuarum* of Paulus de Sancta Maria, believed to have been printed at Strasbourg by Johann Mentelin before 1470. The previous owner, a Dr Vollbehr, who presented it to the Library, noted on a card: 'The old wooden boards were covered with human skin in the 19th century.' Harvard Law Library acquired a copy of the second volume of Juan Gutierrez's *Practicarum Quaestionum Circa Leges Regias Hispaniae* (Juan de la Cuesta, Madrid, 1605–6), inscribed, 'The bynding of this booke is all that remains of my deare frend Jonas Wright, who was flayed alive by the Wavuma,' but nobody has been able to identify John Wright or prove that the vellum-like binding is of human origin.*

Better authenticated is a book in the collection of the Boston Athenaeum. *The Highwayman* was written in prison by James Allen, alias George Walton, alias Jonas Pierce, alias James York, alias Burley Grove, a burglar, bank-robber, horse-thief and highwayman who, in 1833, shot John Fenno Jr on the Salem Turnpike during a botched robbery. A buckle on Fenno's suspenders deflected the bullet, and Allen was arrested and jailed. Fenno's bravery so impressed Allen that he asked for him to be presented with a copy of *The Highwayman* bound in his own skin. When Allen died in July 1837 and his body was given to Massachusetts General Hospital 'for anatomical and pathological studies', enough epidermis was removed for the purpose. Local binder Peter Low tanned it to look like grey deerskin, and created a classic gold-tooled binding with the inscription '*Hic Liber Waltonis Cute Compactus Est*' ('This book by Walton bound in his own skin'). Fenno accepted the gift, which a descendant presented to the Athenaeum. And as recently as 2002, a Paris book fair exhibited the tanned chest skin of a

---

* The Wavuma at least exist, an east African people who, though warlike – Henry Stanley shot three of them with an elephant rifle when they attacked him during his search for Livingstone – aren't known for flaying captives.

man executed for murder in 1904, who'd asked for it to be preserved for its tattoos.

Clients for bindings in human skin may not be battering down the door, but erotica in general has always sold vigorously, and attracted celebrity clients. John Barrymore and Rudolph Valentino both owned a number of rare and sumptuously bound erotic books. The French actor Michel Simon had one of the world's biggest collections. So, traditionally, did King Farouk of Egypt, though when his palace was invaded after his overthrow the looters dismissed his famed library as consisting 'mostly of cheap paperbacks' – unaware that almost all erotica, including the rarest, aims for cheapness and drabness.

There is no aspect of human sexuality which does not have its collectors. Offering a book about hanging, the guillotine, flaying or mummification on the Internet is like dropping a piece of rotten meat into a tidal pool. Within minutes, the pale crabs creep out to nibble. Scores of dealers serve the erotica market, some specializing in flagellation, homosexual or 'Uranian' literature, others in even more singular tastes. Dealers in erotica come in all shapes and sizes. Plump, balding and genial, Michael Neal, bibliographer and connoisseur of what he amiably calls 'filth', would look at home in the blue-and-white-striped apron of a London butcher. Patrick Kearney, bibliographer of the Olympia Press and author of *A History of Erotic Literature*, a north-country Englishman transplanted to California, still looks and sounds like someone who takes his holidays at Frinton-on-Sea – unlike Michael Goss of London's Delectus Books, who's sharp enough to double Johnny Depp in *The Ninth Gate*.

Starving American and British expatriates, male and female, were the backbone of the Girodias operation. They wrote the novels or 'translated' the classics, often embellishing them shamelessly with new erotic material. John Coleman had already confessed to me at Venice years before that he'd been on the team. So was the poet Christopher Logue, who, as 'Count Palmiro Vicarion', assembled volumes of bawdy ballads and dirty limericks. Gregory Corso contributed *American Express*. As 'Frances Lengel', another beat-generation poet, the Scot Alexander Trocchi, wrote *White Thighs*, and, since the imagination of noted sexual motor-mouth Frank Harris ran out after only four volumes of *My Life and Loves*, Trocchi composed a fifth in a pastiche of Harris's rambling style.

Iris Owens ('Harriett Daimler') and Austryn Wainhouse ('Pieralessandro Casavini') both had later careers under their own names, as did Terry Southern, co-author of *Candy*, and Chester Himes, the African–American writer of *Pinktoes*. Canadian poet John Glassco already had a minor reputation when he agreed to complete Aubrey Beardsley's *Under the Hill* for Olympia. Having a legitimate author on the payroll went to Girodias's head. *Under the Hill* appeared in a limited edition of 3,000 copies on watermarked paper, bound in green moire silk, which must have puzzled American tourists nervously asking *bouquinistes*, '*Quoi de neuf chez Olympia Press?*'

Although Girodias generally avoided any French literature not long out of copyright, he did publish the first English-language editions of Raymond Queneau's *Zazie dans le métro* and Pauline Réage's *Histoire d'O*. Like most Girodias decisions, the one to publish the sadomasochistic *Histoire d'O* was audaciously conceived and ham-fistedly executed. Needing a translation in a hurry, he commissioned newcomer Baird Bryant, later 'Willie Baron' of *Play This Love With Me*, and his wife Donny, neither of whom knew enough French for the job. The result, riddled with howlers, mangled Réage's coolly reticent text. Instead of having one of his regulars like Austryn Wainhouse redo it, Girodias rushed the book into print, and, when the purple-covered first edition sold out, produced a cheaper one in Olympia's standard green covers. By then, American and British customs had got wind of the title, so Girodias, who'd reprinted *Candy* under the title *Lollipop* to mislead the censors, decided to do the same for *The Story of O*.

His new title? *The Wisdom of the Lash*.

Naturally it was banned everywhere, and remains one of the most elusive Olympia titles. By then, however, Graham Greene, J. G. Ballard and Susan Sontag had praised the book, leading to the appearance of austerely dignified editions from prestigious publishers such as Grove Press. Not for the last time, Girodias had snatched defeat from the jaws of victory.

Who was 'Pauline Réage'? Only a few people knew, one of them being Jean Paulhan, editor of France's most eminent literary monthly, *Nouvelle Revue Française*. It was an open secret that the book had been written for Paulhan. He even contributed a prefatory essay, 'The Happiness of Slavery', in which he called the book 'the wildest love letter any man ever received'.

Paulhan died in 1968. In traditional French fashion, his family and friends followed the coffin on foot to the grave. Leading the cortège were Jacqueline, his daughter-in-law, and Dominique Aury, Paulhan's long-time mistress and for years his deputy at *Nouvelle Revue Française*.

Seeing a huge wreath of flowers on top of the coffin, with no card attached, Jacqueline Paulhan drew an obvious inference. 'You know,' she said, leaning towards Aury, 'those flowers have to be from Pauline Réage.'

Aury, then sixty, soft-spoken and discreet, best known for her translations of English novels like Evelyn Waugh's *The Loved One*, and for editing a major anthology of religious verse, looked oddly at the other woman. 'But, Jacqueline,' she said, '*I'm* Pauline Réage.'

By the time Aury died in 1998, her book had sold millions in numerous languages, been the subject of some mediocre but commercially successful movies, and scores of imitations.

It also inspired a world-wide middle-class enthusiasm for masochism. Merchants of 'marital aids' watched in astonishment as whips and manacles outsold vibrators and edible undies. Stars like Madonna played with the wardrobe of bondage, and conferred on it a showbiz gloss,* as did the discovery of a pair of handcuffs in Kylie Minogue's luggage at Heathrow airport (whether or not they were, as she claimed, just the 'fun' handles of a handbag), and the

---

*An interesting collection might be made of literature associated with bondage and self-strangulation, starting with William Burroughs and the erotica written, as 'Anne Rampling' and 'A. R. Roquelaure', by Anne Rice, author of *Interview with the Vampire*, and proceeding, by way of Michael Crichton's *Rising Sun* and Peter Barnes's *The Ruling Class*, both of which include the death of a 'gasper', to the work of two notable victims, actor Albert Dekker, star of fantasy films like *Dr Cyclops*, and cartoonist Vaughn Bode, whose work inspired Ralph Bakshi's animated version of *Lord of the Rings*.

death in 1997 of her one-time lover Michael Hutchence, apparently from sexual self-strangulation.

Throughout the Sixties, Aury sat demurely at dinner parties and listened to other writers hint broadly that they were actually Réage. The beautiful and promiscuous painter Leonore Fini was confidently named as the 'real' O because one of her bird masks inspired an episode in the final chapters. Never one to shrink from publicity, Fini had herself photographed in the mask, and produced a series of erotic lithographs for a special edition of the book.

Another candidate, novelist Alain Robbe-Grillet, even faked a Réage introduction to *L'Image*, a sadomasochistic novel by his fiancée Catherine, written as 'Jean de Berg'. After all, he reasoned, was Réage going to come forward to accuse him of forgery? When *L'Image* came out, 'de Berg' agreed to be interviewed on TV, but only if she could hide her face in a half-veil. Her appearance incognito bolstered the general belief that 'de Berg' was also Réage.

Aury urged Paulhan to scotch these rumours without giving her identity away. He and Jerome Lindon, the boss of Editions de Minuit, which published *L'Image*, were old friends, and played *boules* every Sunday. Over their next game, Paulhan said he doubted the authenticity of the Réage introduction. A German expert in the new-fangled science of computers claimed he could identify literary fakes. Why didn't they let him settle the argument?

Lindon agreed, and, a few weeks later, asked Paulhan for the result.

'Well, I'm puzzled,' Paulhan said. 'He tested the introduction and the text of both *L'Image* and *Histoire d'O*.'

'And?'

'He says the same person wrote all three.'

Even when literary historian John de St Jorre publicized Réage's identity in 1994, her motives in writing *Histoire d'O* remained obscure. By then, I'd started to collect editions of the book, and was keeping an eye on its growing fandom. Roissy, the village where she placed the cult's secluded château, has become a place of pilgrimage, though most of her locations have long since disappeared under France's largest air terminal. There are Roissy societies across the United States. 'Our events are structured as a social event,' says one website, 'with the highlight being a dungeon party on Saturday night. In the past we have had pajama parties, a *Story of O* theme party, and educational demonstrations of technique and style.' You can even take a Roissy cruise; three days in the Caribbean, including a party in a private villa on Paradise Island ('limited equipment will be available'). British associations like Sisters of O try to go beyond holiday high-jinks. 'We are female slaves owned in totality by The Cloister,' proclaim its anonymous creators. 'We are slaves in all aspects of our lives; its property to do with as it will, our lives lived out in the shadow of its control, under the watchful eyes of our sisters.' Its website offers a list of British S&M service providers which ranges from An Old English 9 ('Scene and dungeon furniture') and Aristocuffs ('A one-stop perv shop specializing in BDSM, leather, fetishwear, toys etc') to Zipper ('Gay sex shop with leather, rubber, books, bondage gear').

The more fixated fans of *Histoire d'O* often baffle those artists and readers who simply enjoy its elegance of style or find inspiration in fetishist imagery. British painter Stefan Prince devoted some years to a series of large canvases inspired by the book, and started his own website (StoryofO.co.uk) – which, not surprisingly, attracts its share of cranks. 'I just received a book called *Carnal Knowledge* as a gift from two obviously "new age" fetish/occultists in Texas,' he told me once. 'They claim *Story of O* is based on truth and that Roissy refers to the Orders of the Rose-Croix, the Rosicrucians.'

Girodias's crooked methods ensured that his writers regarded him with, at best, amused tolerance, at worst, downright hatred. Samuel Beckett in his quiet way despised him. J. P. Donleavy was so furious at his claiming all rights to *The Ginger Man* that he bought up the bankrupt Olympia to reclaim his copyright. After relocating in New York, Girodias relaunched it using American writers, some of whom, like poet Diane de Prima and science-fiction author Barry Malzberg, had excellent literary credentials. In Paris, Girodias had published no gay books at all except Cocteau's anonymous *The White Book*, but in New York they became the backbone of the line. Otherwise, his publishing decisions remained gloriously ill-advised. He published *Inside Scientology*, an exposé that attracted the wrath of the increasingly powerful followers of L. Ron Hubbard, and the manifesto of SCUM, the Society for Cutting Up Men, invented by the crazed Valerie Solanas, who shot Andy Warhol, and planned to do the same to Girodias.

Most disastrous of all, however, was *President Kissinger*, a book idea cooked up by Girodias in 1974 after the American Olympia Press had gone terminally bankrupt. The work of a number of hands, including Girodias's, it purported to be the biography of Henry Kissinger, written after his election as President – actually impossible: you have to be born in the United States. The middle section rounded up his known life, but Girodias recruited five other writers, including one of his regulars, Marco Vassi (*Contours of Darkness*, *The Gentle Degenerates*), to fill in the gaps. According to an unpublished auto-biographical sketch excerpted in Patrick Kearney's *A Bibliography of the Publications of the New York Olympia Press*, Girodias asked Vassi to invent Kissinger's sex life. His adolescence posed no problems but in Kissinger's young adulthood, Vassi admitted he got carried away with his own inventiveness.

> I described him having an affair with a German girl in whose closet he discovers an S.S. uniform. She confesses to him that her brother has been in the Gestapo, and their subsequent sex scene has her wearing the uniform and Henry a frilly French maid's outfit, with him walking around on his hands and knees while she straddles his back and whacks him with a riding crop. Maurice wanted to cut this scene but I grew indignant and challenged him to live up to his reputation as a fearless eroticist.

The book was printed with Vassi's scenes, and all copies shipped to a warehouse. Two days later, according to Vassi, Girodias and his wife were stopped on their way to dinner with friends by men claiming to be state and federal police. They 'found' a quantity of cocaine in the car, but told Girodias he wouldn't be charged if he left the country immediately. The American government has a different story; according to the Immigration Service, an interview with Girodias turned up the fact that his visitor's visa had expired, and he was told to leave the country. Either way, by the time *President Kissinger* hit the shelves, Girodias had fled back to France.

Shortly after this, Girodias sold his two-volume autobiography, *The Frog Prince*. After that, nothing until his death in 1990 – or so I thought, until Rick Gekoski sold me the manuscript of Girodias's last work, *Atlantis*; of all things, an unpublished science-fiction novel. It was accompanied by a portfolio of correspondence, mostly letters written by Girodias to Nick Austin, editor of Grafton Books, badgering him to publish it. Nobody did. Good old Maurice, wrong to the last.

CHAPTER THIRTEEN

Without Whom . . .

Australia is Switzerland, but it would like to be Texas.

Film director Dusan Makavajev, in conversation

BOOKS ARE FOR EVER, BUT BOOK PEOPLE CHANGE, and none more so than the London runners and dealers who had become my friends.

Iain Sinclair was already writing his first novel, *White Chappell, Scarlet Tracings*. When it was published in 1987, the dedication would read, in part, 'to Martin Stone, always ahead'. (This puzzled Martin, who wrote below it in my copy 'though of what he has no idea'.)

Much of the book would detail book-buying forays across the British Isles as chauffeur to Martin and Driff Field, and it opens with a comprehensive description of pausing by the roadside for 'Nicholas

Lane', alias Martin, to vomit the previous night's meal.

Regurgitation featured in most encounters with Martin, who remained unregenerately self-destructive. A neglected ulcer was steadily devouring the walls of his stomach. Most of his teeth had fallen out, as had much of his hair. The residue lurked under an increasingly tattered black beret, a sordid accessory which, Ruth confided, remained clamped in place until only a few seconds before they went to bed for the first time.

An increasing proportion of his income went on cocaine. It was nothing to drive around London while he chopped coke on the little mirror carried for the purpose. He continued to do with relentless absorption even when a traffic jam stuck us in front of Holloway Road police station.

Martin and Ruth had a house in Cannon Street Road, in the most dilapidated corner of east London, with a second building out back that had once been a balloon factory. It so bulged with books that he might have been there still had the whole floor of the balloon factory not collapsed at the height of a rave, dumping guests into the space below. This coincided roughly with the collapse of the marriage. Ruth took their daughter, and proceeded resourcefully to make a life of her own. Martin announced he was giving up book dealing and returning to music, a decision solemnized on film, when director Chris Petit included Martin, Driff Field, Iain and a number of other denizens of the London book and crime worlds in his film *The Cardinal and the Corpse*.

Joyce and I attended the inaugural gig of Martin's relaunched career at Dingwalls, a club in an ancient brick warehouse next to Camden Market. Before a standing-room-only audience, and barely visible through a fug of sweat and grass fumes, Martin stepped forward, struck a chord, and all the lights blew. While technicians fiddled, a young American picker roused the crowd to frenzy with an extended and pyrotechnical blues. Martin wasn't heard from that night, or for many nights after.

In 1983, Joyce and I went to Australia for what was intended to be a year. Around the same time, and more hurriedly, Martin also left London for Paris, one step ahead of a scandal in which cocaine played a large part. It would be a decade before we met again.

Superficially, returning to Australia seemed a good idea. An old friend, Brian Hannant, had just co-written the Australian cinema's biggest hit to that time, *Mad Max II*, aka *The Road Warrior*. Producers were queueing up to finance his first film as a director. Did I have any ideas for science-fiction movies? And, if I did, would I collaborate with him on writing one?

Having left just before a programme of tax

incentives engendered *Picnic at Hanging Rock*, *My Brilliant Career* and other superior films, I arrived back in time to see the whole scheme sinking into a morass of recrimination, bad debts and graft. Desperate to assert some kind – *any* kind – of national identity, rival federal and state film commissions invested fortunes in almost any project, no matter how feebly thought out.

Too few people of talent were chasing too much money, and audiences, insofar as there had ever been any for Australian movies, were melting away. At the première of a working-class teen rock musical, significantly held in Parramatta – jockstrap on the belt of the industrial suburbs that flanked Sydney to the west – and in the presence of Prime Minister Bob Hawke, Phillip Adams, media pundit and sometime film producer, suggested that film-makers should no longer aim for 'bums on seats' but 'minds in gear' – a frank confession of failure.

Government funding of literature had met with more success. Since only an idiot would imagine writing could make you rich, most applicants were sincere and talented. Frank Moorhouse, once a contributor to the lowly *Squire* magazine, had emerged as a major voice, as had Peter Carey, David Malouf, Thea Astley, Elizabeth Jolley and Les Murray, while Patrick White continued to mutter dourly from his secluded home overlooking that gem of

Victorian colonialist garden design, Centennial Park.

Even science fiction had won a toe-hold on respectability, and old friends like Lee Harding were now full-time professionals. Crime writing too was well established with the work of Peter Corris, with whom I became friendly and whose work I started to collect. I also accumulated a collection of Peter Carey's works. Early books like *The Fat Man in History* and *Bliss* could still be picked up for a few dollars, and, since Peter and I ran into each other often – Sydney was, in literary terms, a small town – one never lacked opportunities to have him sign them.

'What should I put?' he asked.

'Just say, "Without whom . . .",' I joked – but he took me at my word, and that's how all his early books are inscribed.

I should have taken my own advice and systematically amassed a regional collection. A shelf of signed David Maloufs, David Irelands, Elizabeth Jolleys and, of course, Patrick Whites, would by now have zoomed in value by a factor of ten. But I simply didn't like their work enough. While most people read the moderns, I rediscovered Henry Lawson and Xavier Herbert. If I read new writers, it was people like Gerald Murnane, whose *Tamarisk Row* and particularly *The Plains* recalled that tradition – but who, significantly, never took off as a collectable author.

While I was away, one of the writers I most admired, George Johnston, had died. He did so without finishing the autobiographical trilogy that began with *My Brother Jack* and *Clean Straw for Nothing*, though the uncompleted third volume, *A Cartload of Clay*, appeared posthumously.

George and his wife Charmian Clift embodied the doomed strain that runs through so much Australian cultural life. As a rocket expends most of its energy attaining orbit, they'd dissipated their creative energy in escaping to countries which promised more opportunities, only to find their individuality diluted by the adopted culture – a new and peculiarly Australian addition to Cyril Connolly's 'enemies of promise'.

George reported on World War II from China, and later wrote a *roman à clef* about that time, *The Far Face of the Moon*, between the lines of which I intuited that he'd slept with Hollywood star Paulette Goddard during her visit to that particular front line. He followed with crime stories like *Death Takes Small Bites* and a trilogy set in seventeenth-century China, written in collaboration with Charmian. Moving to Hydra in 1955 removed much of the remaining incentive to work, and while Charmian emerged as a writer with books like *Peel Me a Lotus* and *Mermaid Singing*, most of their creative energy was, literally, pissed or fucked away.

They returned to Australia in 1964 when *My Brother Jack* had become a best-seller and was about to be turned into a TV mini-series. George, always rake-thin, proceeded to die by inches from tuberculosis, though never without a cigarette in his hand, while Charmian just as deliberately rushed towards death clutching a glass. Everyone expected her to outlive him, but she cracked first. In 1969, washing down an overdose of pills with alcohol, she climbed into bed so that George, waking, would find her corpse beside him. He survived the wound of this exquisitely cruel death for only one more year.

I got to know them when I included one of George's Hydra stories, *Vale Pollini*, in an anthology. In person, he was an inspired spinner of yarns, never more so than when he described how, shivering through the fog-shrouded London winter of 1947, he'd received a call from the French Embassy. Could he come in and see the Trade Attaché?

'You're sure you don't mean the *Cultural* Attaché?' George asked.

No, it was M. Dubois of the Trade Desk who wanted to talk to him. And yes, it was George Johnston, the writer, he wanted to see.

M. Dubois had a sad story to tell. During the Nazi occupation, French *vignerons* continued to make wine. They now had millions of litres of the stuff, far more than Europe could drink. They were looking for alternative markets. Australia, perhaps?

'Australians do like a drink,' George conceded, 'but mainly beer. They don't go much on plonk . . . er, wine.'

'Ah, that is where you come in, M. Johnston,' the diplomat said. 'We wish to commission a series of articles about French wine for Australian newspapers and magazines. If this creates a demand, we could ship the wine to Australia in quantity – by tanker, perhaps.'

George hesitated. The plan sounded crazy to him. On the other hand . . .

'I'm no expert on French vintages,' he temporized.

But Dubois was ahead of him. They'd send him to France, all expenses paid, for a tasting tour. Would he be interested?

Savouring the moment more than twenty years later, George lit another fag. 'I thought back over my life,' he said. 'I'd done many contemptible things, but obviously somewhere, somehow, I'd performed a good deed. And this was my reward.'

The trip to France – what he could remember of it – was a boozer's dream. At every château through Burgundy, Champagne, the Loire and the Rhône, the *propriétaire*, usually a *duc* or *comte*, if not a *prince*, waited at the gate to greet him; this, after all, was the Australian who was going to make them rich.

Tastings took place before, during and after meals, and at every opportunity in between.

By the time he reached the great vineyards around Bordeaux, George's palate had gone west and he could barely remember where or who he was, let alone what he'd drunk. So it was with some alarm that, after a huge dinner awash with wine after wine, he followed his current host – probably Baron Robert de Rothschild, he thought – into the ancient *caves* cut deep in the clay of the Médoc.

After winding through corridors and tunnels so vast and complex they'd defeated even the ingenuity of the Nazis, they arrived at last in a tiny chamber where, awaiting them, was what George called 'the *oldest* old fart I'd ever seen'.

M. Petitjean, explained the baron, directed the wine-making in his father's time. Long retired, he'd come in tonight specially to see George, and had brought 'something interesting'.

The old man held up a bottle. Its shape differed from modern bottles: wider, more squat, with a longer neck. Dust obscured the frayed and faded label but George made out the figures '1812'. Napoleon still ruled most of Europe when this was bottled. Then, to his consternation, the old man eased out the cork, and poured a spoonful into a glass.

George regarded the straw-coloured fluid in astonishment. 'A *white* wine?'

The baron winced. Naturally not. This was the legendary 1812 red Bordeaux – the last bottle, as it happened; saved from Napoleon, the Commune and Hitler for George Johnston to drink. All the solids had settled out, leaving only this plasma.

For the first time, George noticed there was only one glass. 'But . . . you'll taste it with me?'

The baron's shrug blended appreciation of the generosity of George's offer with regret at the impossibility of acceptance. The honour of this historic *dégustation* belonged to their distinguished guest alone. They awaited his discriminating judgement.

'Well, I tasted it,' George told me, 'but my palate was so buggered, not only with the wine I'd drunk that week but the years of arak and jungle juice and saki and bad scotch, that it could have been lemonade. It simply didn't taste of anything.'

Petitjean and the baron were looking at him expectantly. Honour was at stake.

'My skills as a drinker had deserted me,' George recalled, 'but I thought my skills as a writer might save the day.'

'Gentlemen,' he said gravely, 'how shall I put it?' He held the glass up to the light. 'Perhaps, like me, you have attended the farewell concert of some great old baritone, now long past his best.'

The two men frowned. What had this to do with Bordeaux?

'This wine,' he went on, 'is like that baritone. The voice is gone – and yet, now and then, and faintly, one hears one great and perfect note.'

The baron translated for M. Petitjean. The old man took a step towards George and embraced him, tears in his eyes.

'I never felt so low in my life,' George said.

With too few subjects to interest me as a collector and all my books in storage, I found an outlet for my scavenging instincts in becoming a runner. My primary client was Nicholas Pounder, who, with his *de facto* brother-in-law Simon Taaffe, ran a tiny bookshop on the edge of King's Cross. Dropping by Nicholas's shop with my finds became a regular part of my week. Since I bought as much as I sold, most of the profits remained there, and the rest was blown on ink-black espressos and tile-hard *biscotti* ferried from the local cafés, or long lunches in the leafy outdoor restaurants of Double Bay.

The conversation of Nicholas and Simon was lively and informed, the wit acute, and the Cross provided enough grotesque passers-by and gossipy visitors to make each day more fascinating than the last. Solicitor Howard Hilton, recently disbarred, would drop by to enquire after the first edition of Doctor Samuel Johnson he'd ordered. Occasionally, some literary figure skulked in, desperate not to be recognized, only to storm out a few minutes later, furious that he hadn't been. 'You know who *that* was,' Nicholas would confide gleefully, inaugurating a good half-hour of literary scandal.

Occasionally, news arrived from England, mostly via visiting dealers making a once-a-decade swing through the antipodes. One of them, a collector and dealer based in Monaco, even brought news of Martin Stone.

'John Baxter?' he said to Nicholas. 'Is he here now? He used to finance Martin Stone's coke deals, you know. They both left London in rather a hurry. Martin's in Paris now, I believe.'

This wonderful but totally fictitious version of our relationship secretly delighted me, and I did everything to see that it circulated widely.

Though Nicholas emigrated from England as a boy, he'd been comprehensively Australianized by a spell as a messenger on the streets of Sydney, then some years on a commune near the northern New South Wales town of Nimbin, production centre for those reviving herbal compounds that did so much to fuel and finance the counterculture of the Sixties.

It was here that he earned his reputation as a goat-slaughterer. 'Yes, I was sent to Coventry by a whole shire for organizing a goat roast,' he recalls. 'Took the miserable beast out with a ball peen hammer. Snuck up from behind when he was nice and relaxed. I thought it was quite humane. I later threaded him on an angle-iron fencepost. I invited all the best musicians and singers (and one or two renegade cultivators of the devil's weed known locally as Wadeville Madness). We turned that golden carcass all day over the coals with its laurels of rosemary, the fat and olive oil sputtering and smoking as it dripped below.' His culinary enterprise wasn't appreciated. When he turned up at the local food co-op the next day, he was ostracized. 'Every soul turned their back on me. Utter silence.' From this position of universal obloquy, it was only a short step to the rare book business.

Belying his raunchy past, Nicholas retained a clean-limbed *Young Woodley* athleticism, and could, particularly with his glasses on and his long-unused English accent in place, convey the bookish hauteur of a Caius College don destined to publish the definitive study of the umlaut in Finno-Ugaric. This 'passing for posh' was Nicholas's favourite disguise, developed, as he once told a journalist – to the chagrin of his wife Jeanie – when he realized that screwing middle-class girls could be the entrée to a more comfortable lifestyle.

One of the pleasures of our friendship was seeing this meticulously created but eggshell-thin persona shattered. It was a toss-up which Nicholas would emerge blinking into the light. Sometimes it was the unsure Home Counties adolescent, voice teetering on the edge of a stammer. At other times, it was the manic sensualist, loping naked through the mulga, hair to his shoulders, stoned out of his skull.

Both manifested themselves in his first acquaintance with David Barton-Jay's *The Enema as an Erotic Art and Its History*. When I walked into the shop one morning in 1987, Nicholas was examining this work with glee. Privately published by the author in 1984, the large-format paperback was lavishly illustrated from a collection of photographs, books, magazines, advertisements, playing cards and equipment all related to anal erotica. *The Village Voice* had praised it as 'an art director's dream, from its subtle cover to its carefully chosen illustrations to its quality paper and well positioned text. This isn't a book to be read in one sitting. Impressive historical, sociological and psychological data is backed up by *belles lettres*, out-takes, photos, and true-life experiences. If Barton-Jay prevails, Americans will soon be chanting, "We have met the enema and . . ."'

The 'subtle cover' as I remember it, featured a deceptively simple photograph of a car pausing at an intersection in an American suburb. On closer inspection, what appeared on the road sign wasn't 'Halt' but a douche bag.

The book inspired Nicholas to heights of bawdry. How much better, he exclaimed, if it had been bound in that smelly, insidiously tactile orange rubber from which douche bags and hot-water bottles were made. He could give the commission to Susie Midgeley, who ran a company called Wet Jobs Round the House and made latex garments for the fetish trade. He himself had such a necktie . . .

The fantasies rolled on. It was a side to Nicholas's character I hadn't seen before, made all the more surprising when, a few days later, I read a piece in Leo Schofield's column for the *Sydney Morning Herald*, describing the book as actually bound in rubber – which was untrue, and as having been sold – which *was* true, to Sydney's best-known dominatrix, known professionally as 'Madame Lash'. The following weekend, both Nicholas and I attended a Canberra literary festival, where this literary coup was much discussed. Melvyn Bragg was the main celebrity guest, though I spent more time with the American novelist William Gaddis and his companion, Muriel Murphy. Gaddis figured in my adolescent literary memories because the 1962 English edition of his doorstop novel *The Recognitions*, along with the English first of Gore Vidal's *Messiah*, had been a recurring feature of Australian remainder tables throughout the Sixties. Macgibbon & Kee produced only 1,500 copies of his

885-page meditation on forgery, most of which appeared to have been shipped to Australia, the least likely market for such a book short of Greenland, where at least they could have burned them for fuel. To make it even less attractive, the copyright details on many copies had been effaced by a rubber stamp so heavily inked that it bled through the preliminary pages. Nobody knew what transgression this disguised, since nobody read the book anyway. In heaps, it lingered in book sales throughout the Sixties. I remember seeing it (and *Messiah*) in David Jones's department store priced at one penny, and no buyers even at that.

So it was with some satisfaction that I presented my copy, a brand saved from the burning, for Gaddis to sign, along with the equally enormous *J. R.*, and his newer, and thinner, *Carpenter's Gothic*.

Bragg, Gaddis and I were scheduled to share a panel on the subject of screenwriting, which was odd, since I'd never seen Gaddis's credit on anything.

'I'm not surprised,' Gaddis grated in the gravelly voice peculiar to reformed boozers, who always sound as if they need a drink just to clear the throat. 'I never wrote a movie in my life.'

'But the blurb copy on one of your books . . .'

'Aw, that,' he said dismissively. 'Between *The Recognitions* in 1962 and *J. R.* in 1975, I didn't publish anything. While I was in the army, I worked on a documentary movie about artillery. So the publisher put "screenwriter".'

This gave a bizarre spin to our panel. While Bragg and I alternated Hollywood anecdotes, Gaddis sat between us, mostly silent. It was like Abbott and Costello sharing the bill with Samuel Beckett.

At the end, of course, Gaddis stole the show.

'I only know one film person,' he said. 'The director Sidney Lumet. He told me a joke, which he says sums up precisely the nature of film-making.

'Two explorers in the African jungle are captured by a wild tribe. The chief confronts them, and says, "White man, I give you the choice. Death, or KeeKee."

'The first explorer, reasoning that nothing can be worse than death, elects for KeeKee – which turns out to be a protracted form of torture and mutilation.

'The second explorer is offered the same choice.

'"I choose death," he says with resignation.

'"Very well – death," grins the chief. "But first – KeeKee."'

Back in Sydney the following week, Simon and I were both in Nicholas's shop – the two of us chatting at the back – when a white chauffeur-driven Mark 5 Jaguar pulled up outside, and Barry Humphries, in a three-piece suit the colour of curdled cream and a furry fedora to match, strolled, cane in hand, into the shop.

As sacred monsters go, Australia has few as feral as John Barry Humphries. Before the braying grotesque of Dame Edna Everage gorged him whole, he had been an inspired satirist in a score of characters, not least his own, and an inventive comic writer who shared S. J. Perelman's glee in antique words and eccentric brand names. A biographical note for his 1966 show *Excuse I* claims he attended a small kindergarten in the suburb of Camberwell run by one Mrs Flint. 'It is to his traumatick experiences in her Canadian bungalow that he attributes his subsequent predilection for galleon firescreens, buffalo grass, and Fowler's Vacola apparatus . . . His hobbies include the collection of first editions of L. F. Wynne ffoulkes (author of *Poems of Life and Form*) and Mulvel Ousley (author of *Kitty and the Viscount*) . . . His 250-page volume, *Bizarre*, has just been published by Elek Books and the contents are drawn from his own collection of curiosa, painstakingly assembled over a period of twenty years.'

The unexpected arrival of this apparition silenced all of us. Simon and I were the first to recover. Falling into the characters of vendor and client, we started discussing the rising price of Patrick White first editions at the top of our voices.

'I read in the *Herald*,' Humphries drawled to Nicholas, 'that you had a rather interesting piece of erotica. Could I see it, please?'

Vibrating like a violin string, Nicholas explained that *The Enema* had been sold.

'Pity,' said Humphries. 'Could you get me another copy perhaps?'

'Might be difficult,' Nicholas murmured. 'Customs officers . . . limited edition . . . out of print . . .'

'Hmm, I see.' Humphries began to browse the shelves. 'Got any Firbank? Carl Van Vechten?'

Remembering that Nicholas's stock included a copy of the *Bizarre* anthology, I grabbed it and thrust it under Humphries' nose. 'Would you mind signing this?'

He did so with some surprise; normally he was asked to put his signature on programmes and playbills, and mostly in the Dame Edna persona. The Edwardian formality of his inscription – 'Acknowledged as his own work by the compiler and pseudonymous author, Barry Humphries, Sydney 1987' – fitted a man who could present a fifteen-minute TV lecture on the painting of Charles Conder with the aplomb of a career art historian. Unfortunately, he'd found, like numerous Australian artists before him, that there was more money in playing the fool.

*

Australia offered so many time-consuming projects – not least the writing, with Brian Hannant, of the film *Time Guardians*, which is worth a book in itself – that it wasn't until the mid-Eighties that I realized I had no place being there.

The old quotes with which I'd excoriated it as a teenager were replaced by new but no less jaded ones: a scrap from one of the monologues of American radio artist Ken Nordine from his *Word Jazz* album – 'we lived on tall tales of What Once Was, or What Might Have Been If. We lived on histories and hopes'; a comment by John Updike, one of my new enthusiasms, in his novel *Couples*, that we lived in a decade where one could 'navigate only by sex and stoicism and the stars'.

Sex, stoicism and stars were available in quantity in Australia – especially sex. This visit reintroduced me to the sheer physical pleasure of the place, the satisfaction of warmth and clean air. In Britain, heating was still a luxury, cunningly sold with advertisements of underwear carelessly draped over furniture in empty rooms. The implication was obvious – 'Install central heating and fuck in the warm.'

But all the flesh in the world didn't cushion me from the jabbing sense of being in the wrong place. We of the Sixties had been ocean people. Metaphorically, I spent that decade with other writers from a long tradition of Australian imaginative fiction, sitting on a headland staring out to sea, waiting for the Radiant Future or the Atomic Cloud or the Yellow Horde – whichever happened to turn up first. In one of my science-fiction stories, *Beach*, a tribe of white Australians survive lethargically on Manly Beach, their long-since-exhausted transistor radios mute in sand-scoured plastic bags, the Eskis that once held chilled beer now dry as sea caves. But they remain there because the suburbs behind them have been invaded by some nameless race of creatures, pale and bloodless.

Ironically, it wasn't the beach that turned out to be the really usable metaphor but the landscape on which we turned our backs: the desert and the plains. And the film-makers beat us to it. George Miller took those 'Mad Miles' of dead-straight road outside every country town, crossed them with a sense of the deadly inevitable from his own Greek heritage, added the maimed Oedipean hero of the same tradition and came up with 'Mad' Max Rockatansky, the road warrior, the wanderer of the wasteland.

Just how precisely Miller located the G-spot of Australian culture was dramatized for me in 1986 when a Sydney newspaper advertised a free flea market to be held in a shopping mall in the western suburbs. 'Just load up the car,' they said, 'park, open the boot and start selling.' Hoping for books, I went along. But aside from comics, children's stories and the ubiquitous *Reader's Digest Condensed*, there wasn't much. Well, why should there be? A new Australian literature was being written around me. The language was car accessories: fog lamps, stereos, roof racks, bonnet emblems from F. J. Holdens. And tools! Who would have thought the world held so many gadgets? If the American West began where the rainfall declined below twenty inches a year, the new Australia – post-literate, non-narrative, desert-directed – started where the books disappeared and the roads began. Mad Max's country. But not mine.

The vehicle of this *satori* was an old friend, Richard Keys, then with the Australian Film Commission, who invited me to act as an assessor in allocating a quarter of a million tax dollars for short films. As director Michael Caulfield, producer Kent Chadwick and I began sifting hundreds of applications in search of even a hint of promise, I remembered something London critic Derek Elley had said when we met on the street one day as he was heading for a programme of British experimental films. 'Another afternoon of onanistic celluloid,' he'd muttered with resignation.

The most memorable moment of the assessment process came at the end. When we'd started work a fortnight before, the two ladies in charge of allocating money to films by women asked us to consider some projects they hadn't had the funds to finance. Now, as we sat in the conference room, they strolled in to see what we'd decided. Their manner was cordial, even seductive. Not quite, 'Hi there, guys,' but close. This didn't survive our announcement that we'd backed none of their submissions.

The subsequent stream of abuse was astonishing to me at least: neither Michael nor Kent seemed as surprised. One took it with bowed head, shrugging it off as part of the price you paid. The other nodded, smiled and sympathized.

I left. A cardboard carton a metre square stood outside the conference room, brimming with the debris of the day's meetings and interviews. With all the force I could muster, I kicked it. Tea bags, coffee grounds, fruit rinds, cigarette butts and waste paper exploded satisfyingly along the corridor and up the walls. The lift doors opened and I stepped in. It was just as well I left Australia when I did. Otherwise, this would have happened long before, and probably with some bureaucrat rather than a carton of rubbish.

The divorce that followed seemed as much from the country as from Joyce, who, though American, liked it well enough to remain. Where I was to go was settled by Mo Kennedy-Martin, an old friend, and wife of Ken Wlaschin, long-time director of the London Film Festival and the National Film Theatre in London, but now living in Los Angeles. Hoping to link up with her brother Troy, who'd come to

Australia supposedly to write a screenplay but not been heard from since, she arrived in one of those soggy autumns that reminds you that it's still monsoon country.

She visited the Great Barrier Reef, and spent three days staring out of the window at torrential rainstorms. I drove her into the Blue Mountains. At Katoomba, we stood on the lookout above a Kangaroo Valley so fog-filled you couldn't see a metre beyond the fence.

'You've got to get out of this place,' she said. 'Come to California.'

'And do what?'

'Write books. Screenplays. Do journalism. I don't know. You can't stay here.'

I looked out into the grey-white void. California? Why the hell not?

CHAPTER FOURTEEN

There and Back Again

'Tip the world on its side and everything loose will
land in Los Angeles.'

Frank Lloyd Wright

LOS ANGELES PROVED TO BE AN IDEAL PLACE FROM
which to observe the most radical change in the rare-
book trade for forty years. By the end of the century,
it would be transformed as completely as it had been
by the emergence of chic London and New York
dealers in the Sixties.

To begin with, however, I was less interested in
buying books than in making a living. Installed in an
apartment, luxurious by Australian standards, in the
tree-shaded (and Armed Response-guarded) suburb
of Westwood, close to the campus of UCLA and only
a couple of kilometres from the Pacific at Santa

Monica, I started looking for ways to pay the rent.

Once again, the freemasonry of collecting proved invaluable. I made contact again with Forrest J. Ackerman, who'd moved his enormous fantasy collection into the mansion on Glendower once occupied by Jon Hall, star of *Arabian Nights* and *Pacific Island* romances in the Forties. Impressive as it was to piss in a bathroom with solid gold taps, I was nostalgic for his old place, where one groped to the bog through a jungle of hanging posters for rampaging insect movies like *Tarantula* and *Them!*

Through Forry, I was reintroduced to Bill Warren, whose two-volume work on science-fiction movies, *Keep Watching the Skies*, took my early book on the subject and multiplied it a hundred times in wit and scholarship. And one of Bill's closest friends, Bill Rotsler, engendered my first success as a Hollywood journalist.

A veteran science-fiction fan, cartoonist and occasional novelist, Rotsler enjoyed a second career in the Sixties as a 'glamour' photographer and soft-core film-maker. He was rare in being capable of a genuinely aesthetic transport in watching porn. This inspired his comprehensive, often scholarly 1973 book *Contemporary Erotic Cinema*, which pushed past the 'Wow! Oh baby!' clichés to contrast the bloodless pallor of *Deep Throat*'s Linda Lovelace with the authentically sensual body language of Marilyn Chambers, star of *Behind the Green Door* and *Insatiable*.

The Sixties had been Bill Rotsler's playground. Every bus into Los Angeles brought another hundred women who'd shorn their hair in a ritual rejection of their Midwestern inhibitions – he coined the phrase 'Midnight Haircut' – and come to California to 'discover themselves'. Many discovered Bill, who wasn't ashamed to boast that he contributed to the liberation of any number of them, either with his lens or, more intimately, later.

We'd corresponded over the years. Bill typed his letters on the back of discarded 10" x 8" glossy still photos from porn films, which gave them an arresting additional dimension. We first met in person at the 1979 world science-fiction convention in Brighton, where some jokester had the idea of seating Bill, myself and Jerry Pournelle together; three writers who had published meteorite-striking-the-earth novels. (With only a little more effort, he could have added Harry '*Skyfall*' Harrison, only a stone's throw away.)

In 1989, however, Bill's health was wrecked. As a war veteran, he fortunately qualified for free medical care, but, to eat, he invented fanciful erotic biographies for the porn magazines of the women who serviced LA phone-sex lines; almost the same job I did for *Squire* magazine twenty years before.* I

* In an even odder coincidence, Jon Stephen Fink, the brilliant student from Hollins, had also launched himself as a professional writer as an editor on *Adam Screen World*, one of the magazines for which Bill wrote.

spent hours in Bill's home, a weatherboard bungalow far out in the San Fernando Valley, lapped by sun-crisped brown lawn and painted the colour of milky tea. Framed nude photographs on the walls and cabinets filled with indexed cartoons and designs showed how he'd run his life when he was in good health. Now, the pictures were crooked, the cabinets overflowing. Drifts of X-rated movie mags sagged across the floor, piling up against boxes of video cassettes. Nobody had cleaned up in a decade; one walked on discarded pages, unanswered letters, cartoons, photographs. Bill hadn't then been hit by the strokes and heart attacks that killed him, but a spinal injury and chronic overweight kept him a semi-invalid. Even more debilitating, however, was his despair at failing potency. Surrounded by images of tanned and naked girls orgiastically embracing trees or exposing themselves to the blazing desert sun, he embodied Dylan Thomas's 'old ramrod, dying of women'.

Among his jobs, Bill designed the so-called 'Porn Oscars', the Heart-Ons, wooden hearts with a poker-work text presented every Valentine's Day by the Association of Adult Film Critics. As an elder statesman of the industry, he wangled me an invitation to the Association's get-together – the last, as it turned out – at Gazzari's rock club on Sunset Boulevard, also now defunct. My dazed and wondering report on this event, called 'The Playpen of the Damned', though sensitively renamed by *Australian Playboy* 'Night of a Thousand Orifices', was published by numerous magazines, and launched me as a showbiz journalist, the trade that kept me fairly comfortable for a year and a half in Los Angeles.

With money in my pocket, I started to range Los Angeles in search of books, both to collect and to sell. I discovered Harvey Jason's Mystery Pier Books, a tiny bungalow tucked away behind Sunset Strip, and occasionally poked my nose into the Heritage Bookshop, where even the air felt like it should cost five dollars a breath. In Santa Barbara, I ate Tex-Mex with dealer Maurice Neville and his wife overlooking the blue Pacific. After lunch, with the reticent Bob Dagg, then Neville's assistant but now a successful dealer in his own right, I toured the converted chapel in which Maurie stored his stock. In such ecclesiastical surroundings, and in Bob's monkish presence, one felt that to handle one of these beautifully maintained books was at least a venial sin: to open one surely courted damnation.

Mostly, however, book hunting in California was a dispiriting business. For every well-run shop with respectable stock, there were a dozen, usually the largest, which, had they been restaurants, would have long since been closed down as insanitary. The older books in such shops, desiccated over decades of summer air conditioning and winter heating, felt mummified. Many cracked when opened, showering a powder of glue and a cascade of pages.

Conditions were better in the sleepy towns scattered among the hundreds of square miles of irrigated vegetable farms to the north and east of Los Angeles. A few blocks of two-storey buildings, they reminded me of Australian outback towns, down to the defunct shops with their painted-over windows. Most such towns had bookshops of a sort, or antique 'marts' with a shelf of books. My Horace McCoy collection swelled with dust-wrappered copies of *Kiss Tomorrow Goodbye*, *Scalpel* and other obscurities. People sold first editions of crime novels, even Mickey Spillane's nastily nihilistic *I, the Jury*, for a few dollars, confident that nobody as *déclassé* as Spillane could possibly be valuable.

These tiny towns made one doubt the famous American genius for salesmanship. Half the shops were boarded up and the rest permanently closed for lunch. One wanted to shout, 'Who's minding the store?' – but who would have heard? Jan Morris reacted much the same as myself. Passing through a town in Texas and finding the Chamber of Commerce office and Visitors' Bureau still closed at four in the afternoon, she slipped a note under the door that read: 'I'm an industrialist thinking of opening a factory near here, but don't worry – I'll try the next town.'

In one such satellite of Los Angeles, the inattentive shopkeeper in an antique-cum-junk shop sold me for less than $20 two first editions of the notoriously uncommunicative poet Wallace Stevens, one inscribed, the other with a letter tipped in, expressing condolences on the owner's death. They'd belonged to a local man who supplied Stevens with his annual Thanksgiving and Christmas turkeys. *Anything can be anywhere* . . . The two Stevens books paid my bills for months.

The book market was changing as new players took an interest. Once, it had been rare for showbiz people to be interested in books, but the Eighties saw a stampede. Whoopi Goldberg was one such collector. She joined Tony Bill, actor James Spader, actor/director Danny deVito, director George Pan Cosmatos and scores of others in investing in the market.* Celebrity interest pushed up prices of the year's fashionable hits, even though, on past performance, it's not best-sellers that become collectors' items but books which accumulate a following over decades. Few recent books have been as sought after as the Harry Potter fantasies. 'We tried to buy a first of the first book, *Harry Potter and*

---

* The latest of Hollywood's major collectors is Sarah Michelle Gellar, alias Buffy the Vampire Slayer.

the Philosopher's Stone, from a collector here in Los Angeles,' says Harvey Jason. 'We offered him $30,000 and he laughed. I said, "What could you possibly want for it?" and he said, "Oh, $45,000. Maybe $43,000."'* When it was rumoured that quantities of the first printing of a quickly reprinted Harry Potter title were shipped to Australia first, dealers and collectors hot-footed it out there, returning with priceless copies for which they had paid no more than list price. The profit on just one of them would have more than paid for the trip.

The film industry began to include first editions in its Christmas round of internal gift-giving. People who once got a watch or a pair of platinum cufflinks received a signed Hemingway instead. Harvey Jason supplied first editions to the Academy of Motion Picture Arts and Sciences as gifts for Oscar presenters like Julia Roberts, who, by tradition, are not paid.

Some of this celebrity collecting was discriminating, most not. Nothing had changed fundamentally since Lana Turner had that first edition of *The Postman Always Rings Twice* preserved in something more like a handbag than a binding.

Movies and TV began to depict booksellers as figures of more glamour. In the film of Russell Hoban's *Turtle Diary*, Ben Kingsley played a

---

* A signed copy is currently on offer at $45,000.

bookseller who quixotically joins with children's author Glenda Jackson to kidnap sea turtles from London Zoo and release them into the ocean. After Hugh Grant played the bookseller who marries film star Julia Roberts in *Notting Hill*, top-level London dealer Simon Finch, launching a new shop in the same area, persuaded Grant to spend the opening day serving behind the counter. Reflecting the new direction of the trade, Finch stocked both first editions of J. D. Salinger and Fender electric guitars that once belonged to Jimi Hendrix.

This new interest in books as collectables and elements of home décor coincided with an explosion of classic literature in paperback. There was almost no book which some obscure press hadn't reprinted. Once the Internet made finding them a matter of a few keystrokes and a credit card number, people simply stopped buying second-hand books for reading or research. In Britain, *The Bookdealer* shrank to a third of its usual 200 pages, and its long-running American equivalent, *Antiquarian Bookman's Weekly*, closed at the end of 1999.

All over the world, the concept of 'passing trade' was revealed for the fantasy it was. People who walked into bookshops usually wanted a street guide, a dictionary, a toilet, or were sheltering from the rain. The rest were shoplifters.

Rick Gekoski used to devote one wall of his London shop to books priced between £10 and £100. 'Here's something interesting,' his accountant told him. 'Those books accounted for 90 per cent of our sales last year – but only 2 per cent of our income.' In other words, the big-ticket items paid the rent: the cheaper books were just a nuisance. Gekoski put the whole lot into auction, and now devotes his energies to scouring the world for books he can sell for tens of thousands of dollars.

All over the US, small bookstores started to die. With some, death was natural. In New York, the Gotham Book Mart turned the portrait of founder Frances Steloff to the wall, sold out to the Hassidic diamond merchants who already owned the rest of West 47th Street, and moved to off-street premises where clients could browse in comfort with no risk of being mugged.

Other shops didn't go gently. A corporation called Alibris bought up many, stripping the stock, selling off the very cheap items and the very expensive, and shipping the collectable cream to a warehouse in Nevada, from where the books were offered at top-of-the-market prices via the Internet, supported by a publicity campaign in the glossier magazines. Dealers remaining in business could still list their stock with Alibris, who would merchandise it at a 20 per cent commission. Not sinister, perhaps, but certainly soulless.

Suddenly, the old back-street bookseller in the ash-stained cardigan began to look less like a Neanderthal and more like a subject for Norman Rockwell.

When the shakeout was over, surviving book dealers found they were no longer in the business of selling books. They were another branch of the antiques market. The collectables industry, never slow to spot a trend, jumped onto this one. Companies like Franklin Mint, which had done so well with commemorative porcelain, medals, coins and plates, flooded the market with leather-bound first editions. They were followed by Easton Press, and others, less scrupulous, who replaced leather with its plastic imitator, Rexine, and Updike, Chatwin or Heller with reprints of detective or science fiction.

Not all these books were insignificant in collectors' terms. The 1984 printing of *The Witches of Eastwick* issued by Franklin Library's Signed First Editions Society, signed by John Updike and with a new introduction by him, is well worth having. And the Franklin 1987 signed edition (and true first) of *The Songlines* was stampeded when its author Bruce Chatwin died shortly after.

There are questions, of course. Maybe *The Witches of Eastwick* deserves the elaborate treatment given to it; marbled endpapers, all edges gilt, silk bookmark, gold-stamped full morocco binding with raised bands. But Mickey Spillane? Or William Gibson?

However much I admire and collect their work, this nineteenth-century treatment makes a travesty of it.

These editions can be claimed to be 'limited', but the actual number of copies to which they are limited is rarely, if ever, publicized. About twelve thousand copies seems a good guess, which is hardly 'limited'. Many of the new 'collectable book' presses also advertise their productions as good investments that will appreciate in value. How true is this? Not very. However, with the exception of *The Songlines*, which, even after fifteen years, only sells for around $150, almost any Franklin title can be found for $75 or less – and with very few takers even at that price. Which means that, if you wanted to sell, a bookseller, since the trade pays anything from a third to a half of its selling price, would give you $30 – assuming he wanted the book at all in such a clogged market.

The book most likely to appreciate in value is still the clean copy in a dust wrapper of the first edition as it first appeared on the shelves of the corner bookstore. Notwithstanding the Franklin Mint *Songlines*, a good copy in dust wrapper of the 1987 first edition from Jonathan Cape still sells, even unsigned, for $100, and the first American trade edition from Viking about the same. An inscribed copy of the Viking printing is on the market at $850. If that inscription was particularly private or significant, the price would double again. And if that copy came from the library of, for instance, Chatwin's sometime sexual partner Rudolph Nureyev, the price would be in the thousands. Rarity can be created, but not value. That has to be achieved. It gathers on a book like the patina on a bronze, over decades of diligence and care.

What saved the low end of the book trade was the Internet auction site eBay.com. Started in September 1995 by Pierre Omidyar in his San Jose living room, it was meant initially as a way for his wife, a collector of Pez plastic candy dispensers, to meet and trade with other enthusiasts. But eBay exploded as only ideas do whose time has come. By the turn of the millennium, it was the biggest and most successful selling site on the net, with millions of deals concluded every day.

EBay's genius was its simplicity. It turned that American institution, the swap-meet, into a website. Instead of hauling boxes of corroded bicycle accessories, paperbacks and general tat halfway across town, you posted them on eBay, where they fell under the eye not just of a few dozen people browsing that corner of a drive-in cinema but of millions. Collecting is a universal human urge, but not everyone has the means or the mobility to pursue it. EBay brought it into the home, and made buying and selling a matter of a few keystrokes. Suddenly, everyone seemed to be selling on-line. This was nowhere truer than in the world of books. On any given day, half a million books are on offer on eBay.

The new collectors coaxed out by eBay didn't, as a rule, want first editions. Mostly they looked for books about their enthusiasms – scouting, backgammon, genealogy, farm machinery, their state, their town, their family, themselves. All that general stock, discarded a few years before by booksellers as a bore and a drug on the market, became newly valuable overnight. The new passing trade wasn't human but electronic. Alibris, still buying up stores all over the world, played up to the tastes of these new buyers in their display advertising. Instead of value, they sold nostalgia. Reproducing the cover of a battered paperback of *On the Road* or Henry Kuttner's science-fiction novel *Mutant*, they captioned it 'Left on the beach January 1969. Rediscovered on Alibris 2002.'

Nowhere in the world of books is selling so much a matter of packaging as on the Internet. An attractive or amusing description, a couple of well-chosen images, an appeal to snobbery, exclusivity, fashion or the forbidden can turn a 10c purchase into a $100 sale. If *Knit Your Own Royal Family* is the perfect book title for the British market, then 'Sexy Paris art deco limited edition' will sell almost anything on eBay from a paperback of *Madame Bovary* to a box of red, white and blue condoms.

Loyal to the metaphor of all bookselling as a form of angling, I see this as analogous to fly-fishing. The bundle of feathers and thread that you float out over the surface is not the crunchy insect the fish believes it to be. But, as he gazes up through the shimmering water at these glittering, shifting objects, instinct takes over: he leaps, snaps, and is caught.

Making fun of eBay is almost too easy. Its percentage of rednecks and rogues is high, and many of its offers represent the triumph of hope over logic. (see Appendix III: eBay Gems) Yet, though its owners, anxious to push it up-market, would like to purge this element and turn eBay into the world's biggest on-line department store, I'd be sorry to see this happen. As long as we can get down on our knees in the dirt of a parking lot and rummage, even if that parking lot is electronic, we won't have lost the sense of surprise and delight in collecting, the conviction that anything can be anywhere.

Everyone should spend a year in Los Angeles, if only to discover the limits of their imagination. After twelve months I'd tried everything from garlic ice cream to colonic irrigation. I'd partied with porn stars, dined with millionaires, and been an extra in a Roger Corman production where, perhaps most bizarrely of all, on being introduced to Jon Davison, the producer of *Robocop*, he'd replied, 'Not *the* John Baxter?'

But there was more. One moonlit night in March 1989, I stood on Malibu Surfrider Beach with two or three hundred people. Flashlight beams skittered over the waves rippling in from the Pacific. Higher up, where the sand petered into scrub, the Topanga Symphony Orchestra, a pick-up group of thirty-five local musicians assembled around an ice-cream-white Yamaha piano, performed *Night of the Grunion*, which local composer Sandra Tsing-Lao (pronounced, of course, 'Sing Low') had dedicated to the real guests of tonight's party.

Suddenly people squealed as the water came alive with hundreds of tiny silver fish. About 25 cm long, they spasmed in the liquescent sand as the waves receded, straining erect on their tails, seized by a frenzy of procreation. Buckets in hand, the watchers darted among them, scooping them up in hundreds.

Grunion, *Leuresthes tenuis*, come ashore to spawn. They do so only on these beaches, and only during three hours after each of the three high tides following the highest. The females deposit between two and three thousand eggs each, which the males fertilize as they're laid. Those *Leuresthes* not caught by parties like ours, to be tossed in seasoned flour and fried in bacon fat, struggle back to the sea. Two weeks later, the waves of the next high tide carry their fertilized eggs out into the Pacific.

Now I'd seen the grunion run. What was left?

The answer, it turned out, was more astonishing than anything I could have imagined.

'Have you ever been hypnotized?' Susy asked me.

One of the diligent, driven and lonely women who really run Hollywood, Susy had given the best years of her life to a notoriously irascible Hollywood personality. Until his not-unexpected demise a few years before from coronary congestion, brandy, cocaine and the worst case of haemorrhoids known to medical science, she had done almost everything from line-producing his movies to sharing his bed – the latter on the infrequent occasions it wasn't occupied by a floating cast of starlets, hookers, and, very rarely, his long-suffering wife.

Love being what it is, however, his death left Susy bereft. She regarded it as just another cruel trick of a fate which, apparently systematically, had robbed her of anything that might even remotely pass as family. Her parents, aunts and uncles had succumbed to the Holocaust, leaving no other children. Her lover had been everything to her, and now he was gone too. His manifold cruelties, physical and mental, appeared insignificant compared with the emptiness not only of her future, but of whatever might come after death.

She expounded her despair to me through a series of lunches – not so much power as powerless.

'If only I thought we might be reunited, sometime,' she said. 'It would make it easier to go on.'

I tried to look sympathetic, while thinking that, if her lover ended up where he truly belonged, rejoining him would be no fun at all.

'You don't believe in that stuff surely.'

'No . . .' The subtext was almost audible. *But it would be better than nothing*.

Which is how I ended up accompanying Susy to a series of gurus, spirit guides, and seances all over suburban LA.

I won't say it was uninteresting. There were card readers, and a woman who asked us to draw trees, from which she divined our futures, and we attended a spiritualist church that met in a bungalow in Encino. After a few such excursions, Susy rang with her hypnotism enquiry.

'No,' I replied. 'I've never been hypnotized. Why?'

A man in City of Commerce, an outlying suburb halfway to Long Beach, apparently needed subjects for some sort of survey, but they had to agree to be hypnotized. She was up for it, but not before someone whom she knew and trusted had done it first.

Joe proved to be a personable young psychologist in one of the city's many mental institutions. His project, he explained, was to find people who had known Jesus.

'Born-again Christians?'

'Not exactly.'

Light dawned. 'What, you mean actually *knew* Him? In another life?'

'More or less.'

I tried to let him down as easily as possible. 'I'm sure you're sincere, but ... really ... I simply don't believe that stuff.'

'That's OK,' he said amiably. 'But as long as you're here, why don't we try it?'

I hesitated. One of Los Angeles's largest second-hand bookstores, the Book Baron, wasn't far away. If I left now ...

But a residual sense of duty to Susy nudged me into agreement. Which is how I found myself lying on a threadbare corduroy couch under a Spraycrete ceiling, staring at the hook that once secured a macramé plant holder, and listening to myself counting backwards from a hundred.

I was, it turned out, an all-too-suggestible subject, drifting into a trance before my countdown even reached sixty. *I could continue counting*, I told myself. *I just don't choose to do so. Not just now ...*

As we delved back into my childhood, all manner of startling material emerged. The following Saturday I returned. And the Saturday after that. The long drive through industrial suburbs and on elevated freeways above acre after acre of five-card-stud poker clubs and casinos came to be a ritual.

I discovered the roots of the fantasies that fuelled

my fiction, re-experienced the frenzies of a Catholic adolescence, even endured what looked and felt very like an encounter with a ghost. But at about nine years of age, the memories petered out. It seemed I'd never known Christ in an earlier life – or anybody else, for that matter. I hadn't even been Napoleon, which put me in the minority in Hollywood. At 'come as you *were*' costume parties, half the men dressed as Bonaparte and all the women as Cleopatra.

But Joe was philosophical; few people have such low expectations as a Californian mental-health worker. 'I appreciate the time you've spent, John,' he said on the afternoon of our last meeting. Drifting in the now-familiar hypnotic trance, I listened to him say, 'I'd like to give you a gift – a post-hypnotic one. Visualize the three things that have given you greatest pleasure over the years. As you describe each one, I'll squeeze your left wrist. And each time you squeeze that wrist in future, you'll re-experience the same pleasure.'

Under hypnosis, you do what you're told. And my responses astonished me.

Pleasure number one wasn't what you think. It was simply the satisfaction of sitting down at the computer keyboard each morning to write. Obviously, nothing mattered as much.

Pleasure number two, and related, was a song: 'Finishing the Hat' from Stephen Sondheim's *Sunday in the Park with George.* Painter Georges Seurat laments that the woman who'll wait for you to finish working isn't the woman you want to find waiting when you finish work. But, for consolation, you have the work. *'Look, I made a hat. Where there never was a hat.'*

By now, I was gripped by an utterly unexpected cathartic experience. I could hear my voice repeating, 'Who would have thought it would be a *song*? Who would have thought it would be a *song*?'

Which brought me to Pleasure number three.

It was a memory of ten years earlier – the 2nd of December 1979, to be exact. I was back in the flea market in Clignancourt, outside Paris, with Marie-Dominique, whom I'd met at Hollins College and with whom, some time later, I'd had a long, intermittent affair. It was cold, and we were eating *frites* with mustard out of a cone of white paper. I could taste the fat and salt, feel the cold ground through my shoes, watch the breeze ruffling the fox fur of her coat collar. So *this* was what Marcel Proust was talking about.

I drove back home in a daze. Why that song? Why Marie-Dominique? She was now a radio journalist in Paris, and though we still exchanged occasional letters and phone calls, we hadn't seen each other in years.

With my tape of *Sunday in the Park with George* playing, I rang her in France.

'What are you doing these days?' I asked.

'Working hard.' She sounded tired. It was Bicentennial year. Radio journalists were busy.

'You'll need a holiday. Come out to Los Angeles when you're done.'

A few months later, she did.

CHAPTER FIFTEEN

Guaranteed Anatomically Correct

Love – it's so simple, really.

Garance (Arletty) in Les Enfants du Paradis,
screenplay by Jacques Prévert

'WHAT IS YOUR PURPOSE IN VISITING FRANCE?' ASKED
Monsieur Ripois in the French Consulate in Los
Angeles.

'I'm working on a book.' Well, I would be.
Eventually.

'You understand you will not be permitted to take
paid employment in France?' he said.

'I don't intend to,' I said recklessly.

I had no idea how I'd support myself in France. The
fact that I spoke barely a word of French was a minor
detail. Things like that always are when you're in love.

It was, as the French say, a *coup de foudre* – a

thunderbolt. One minute, I was meeting Marie-Dominique off the plane at LAX. Dissolve, and we were in bed, where we stayed, it seemed to me, for a week.

At the start of week two, I began introducing her to Los Angeles. The direction of our future relationship was already evident, the current very definitely flowing towards Paris. One part of me, however, still believed that, with sufficiently skilled public relations, it might be possible to make her stay.

'Forget it,' my English friend Kelvin said.

I'd introduced Marie-Do to Kelvin and his girlfriend Barbara, because they seemed a living advertisement for cultural change. Among other things, Barbara's childhood as the daughter of a CIA spook in Brussels had fitted her out with a multi-lingual education which included perfect French.

We looked across to the opposite banquette of the Santa Monica jazz club where Marie-Do and Barbara were engaged in rapid-fire French conversation. Occasionally they'd glance at us and smile tolerantly, as if this was a livestock sale and we a couple of bulls they might or might not bid on.

'You know what they say,' Kelvin said smiling, enjoying my dilemma. 'You can take the girl out of Paris but you can't take Paris out of the girl.'

Undeterred, I embarked next day on my Special LA Tour.

We did old Los Angeles, the city of Charlie Chaplin and Raymond Chandler, gutted by developers and pierced by freeways but still fitfully alive after the trauma. We toured Silverlake, Edendale, and Bryant Park with its old graveyards showing the waves of settlement: Anglo-Saxon at the centre, Japanese after that, then Hispanic graves crowded close to the railings.

After that, we hit some of the city's stranger restaurants, like the Wallaby Darned at Long Beach that featured Australian cuisine, including a sad portion of Vegemite on every table. At the Mercado General in the *barrio*, we ate chicken in black chocolate *mole* sauce to the sound of four deafening mariachi bands, sharing long tables with the pool men, gardeners and handymen who kept Los Angeles clean, neat and green. Ours were the only white faces in sight.

'There is no Mexican food in Paris,' Marie-Do admitted. 'But have you ever been to the Tour d'Argent? The duck is wonderful. I live quite close.'

I hurried her on to Disneyland. My alternative commentary, honed over countless visits for incredulous foreigners, identified the sites of the Magic Kingdom's accidental deaths and occasional murders, the location of its luxury VIP members-only eating club, the roof-top security offices from which guards enjoyed turning their binoculars on the bedrooms in the Disneyland Motel. I recounted some legends: how, for instance, since anyone in a wheel-chair jumps the two-hour queues for attractions like George Lucas's Star Tours, an incognito Michael Jackson took Jackie Onassis on her first visit by pretending to be handicapped, while Jackie played his nurse.

'They are building EuroDisney in France,' Marie-Do said complacently. 'At Marne-la-Vallée. It's not too far from Paris.'

Hoping that scenery would succeed where glitz had failed, we set off up the coast. After Thanksgiving dinner of turkey and split-pea soup in Buellton, Cal, the World Split-Pea Soup Capital, we checked into the GoodTime Motel on the other side of the restaurant car park. Its scratchy, mended sheets, plastic bedspread, paper-thin walls and rickety side table, edge notched with cigarette burns, perfectly typified the cheap motel experience, and had an expectedly erotic effect.

But Marie-Do didn't need to tell me there were cheap hotels in France as well. I could remember my first one, a *Quartier Latin* flop on Rue de l'Harpe, with serpentine corridors carpeted in dried-blood red, a twanging bed, a bidet behind a screen, one bathroom to each floor and, downstairs, street guitarists and a café that roared until 3 a.m.

I knew when I was licked. At Mariposa Reina, on a curve of US National 1 highway that offered a ravishing view of the sapphire Pacific, I proposed. In Berkeley, across the bay from San Francisco proper, we ate an engagement breakfast at the House of Pancakes – buttermilk pancakes, maple syrup, bacon and sausage on the side and the Bottomless Cup of Coffee. A one-dollar silver ring from a street market stall made it official. The shop behind us was selling replicas of the genitals of bisexual porn-movie star Jeff Stryker. The copy on the astonishingly roomy boxes assured us the contents were moulded from flesh-like plastic and 'guaranteed anatomically correct'. (It's since been revealed that Stryker exaggerated by a full inch.) It was a very Californian courtship. But clearly it was at an end. All that was left for me to do was pack up the apartment and start learning French.

Monsieur Ripois didn't know anything about my emotional state, but maybe he suspected. 'You're resident here, Mr Baxter?'

I gave him my Green Card, entitling me to live anywhere in the USA and accept paid employment.

It's a truism to say the Green Card isn't green, but for millions of immigrants from South America and Asia that tiny plasticized ID with its awkward three-quarter-face portrait and thumb print spells green; a green light, green pastures, greenbacks.

Ripois took the card. For the first time, he looked impressed. He knew how hard it was to get one of these things. 'Hmmm.' He glanced over my shoulder at the backpackers gathering in the corridor beyond the glass door.

'There's only one kind of visa I can issue you,' he said. 'It's for five years . . .'

He watched closely to see if my eyes lit up. But Hollywood pitch meetings train one to remain impassive in the face of everything from criminal lunacy to cardiac arrest.

'. . . but you may only remain in France for two three-month periods in any one year. You understand? A total six months in any twelve.'

I nodded. 'Fine.' It meant I was in. And, having got into France, I could make my own arrangements. After all, how hard could it be?

Like the few French people I'd met in the American film business, Marie-Do spoke good, if sometimes fractured, English. But Anglophone ability wasn't, I quickly found, a national characteristic. Her mother, for instance, didn't speak English. Not a word.

I'd discovered this when I took a couple of phone calls while Marie-Do was in Chicago, visiting an old boyfriend. The voice on the line from Paris was slow, polite but, I sensed, deeply suspicious of my inability to explain why her daughter hadn't returned home when she'd said she would.

I told Marie Do about the call when I picked her up from LAX. 'She said something about . . .' I looked at the notes I'd taken down phonetically, '. . . Europe Urn? And someone called Terry?'

'Thierry is my boss,' she said, 'Europe Une is my radio station. I was supposed to be back for work last week. I should ring him. What did you tell her about us?'

'Nothing. How could I? It would have been easier if your plane had crashed. I could have explained in movie titles. *Préparez Vos Mouchoirs. Les Jeux Sont Faits.* Get Out Your Handkerchiefs. The Games Are Over.'

'*Son* Fay,' Marie-Do said absently. 'You don't pronounce the "t".'

One of the first things I'd learned about the French is that they correct your grammar. It's a national tic, like the way the Japanese bow. They even joke about it themselves. In Jean Renoir's movie *The Vanishing Corporal*, Jean-Pierre Cassel is being helped to get out of a German prison camp by the local dentist's daughter. Even as she outlines his escape route, he corrects her French.*

* There is also the joke about the English tourist in the French café.
Tourist: 'Waiter, there's a fly in my soup.'
Waiter: 'M'sieur?'
Tourist: 'In my soup. A fly. Un mouche.'
Waiter: '*Une* mouche, m'sieur. It's feminine.'
Tourist (peering): 'Blimey, you've got good eyesight.'

'I thought your mother was an expert on teaching French to foreigners,' I said. 'How come she doesn't know any English?'

'You don't need to know English to do that. Only French. She speaks very good French.'

'But *I* don't.'

'You will learn.' I wasn't sure about her tone. It could have been reassurance. But maybe it was an order.

Then I was into the whirlwind of leaving.

I gave a month's notice to Whitney, my landlord. Alice, his live-in lady, was Swedish. He'd met her overseas and brought her back with him, so he sympathized with my decision. (I never thought to ask Alice if *she* did.)

I emptied the apartment – not a problem in Los Angeles, where a year at the same address is a lifetime, and the garage sale is a more hallowed institution than the Supreme Court. Within a week, I was down to the rugs and an extraordinary quantity of books, which Kelvin and Barbara agreed resignedly to ship in my wake.

The farewells began. Expats like Kelvin accepted them as a fact of life. We'll meet again; don't know where, don't know when. Conventionally, Americans are casual about relationships, and the people of California, that state of change, more casual still. But

I was taken aback by the resentment of some friends. 'This what you do all the time, Baxter?' Bill Warren said accusingly. 'Move into a town, make friends, then *leave*?' He made it sound like a betrayal – which perhaps it was.

One goodbye was more subversively disturbing than the rest. It took place at City Café, a restaurant on La Brea in West Hollywood so archetypally LA that it should have been preserved in a vacuum at low temperature, like Walt Disney's remains and the Declaration of Independence.

City looked and sounded like a squash court. The menu, spurning fat and salt as if they were carcinogens, celebrated in their place the newly typical Californian flavours of bitter, acid and char. It was City Café's owner/chefs Mary Sue Milliken and Susan Feniger who introduced snail salad to America; no fat, no cholesterol, raised entirely on plant food, the snail was the perfect Californian meat.

City Café's mixed appetizers offered a morsel of tandoori chicken, a spoonful of cucumber in low-fat yogurt, some marinated eggplant and an asparagus spear or two, served with an air of stony virtue. Desserts were displayed in an illuminated cabinet like an autoclave, sunk into the wall. It ought by rights to have had a radiation trefoil or a Hazchem sign. 'Approach at your own risk.'

Our hosts were Alex, an Australian journalist

friend, and his lady Joanna, a minor rock star, passing through LA to shop for a new producer. Like most people in the music business, she had a feral look and wore clothes of a starkness that would have done justice to any house of correction. I didn't like to think of her in a bad temper.

Joanna looked from Marie-Do to me. 'So you got here two weeks ago,' she said to Marie-Do in a let's-get-this-straight tone.

'Yes.'

She turned to me. 'And now you're following her back to Paris?'

'Yes.'

Alex was contemplating his mesquite-broiled skinless chicken breast served on arugula with a dressing of balsamic vinegar as if unsure whether to eat it or simply let it sit as a fashion accessory.

'I think,' said Joanna, looking at him pointedly, 'that's *awfully* romantic.'

Romantic? People like Joanna didn't use words like 'romantic'. It made our decision sound Byronic; the sort of thing that only happens in high-life soaps like *Santa Barbara*. Maybe it was. I began to realize how bizarre my behaviour was. No work? No French? Who cares! It was Paris, after all. I waved for the waitress, gesturing to the empty bottle of chardonnay.

At various times, I tried to set up meetings with Susy so that she could meet Marie-Dominique, but she always found a pretext to avoid them.

The day before we left, she cancelled yet another one.

'I'm afraid it's now or never, Susy,' I said.

'Then it's never,' she replied shortly. We never spoke again.

There used to be a ride in Disneyland's Tomorrowland that promised the effect of being injected into the microscopic world. Locked in a metallized gondola, you were carried by a jolting conveyor belt to the mouth of a wide tunnel, then accelerated down into grey plastic twilight filled with whirling shapes.

Moving through Aérogare Charles de Gaulle at Roissy on this December evening felt like that ride. On previous visits, the serpentine parking access tunnels and plastic escalator tubes of Roissy had made me think of plumbing. This time, however, I was struck by an even more alarming image: it was like being digested.

The passport officer perfunctorily checked my visa and thumped down his stamp. We moved on to customs, pushing a trolley teetering with most of my worldly goods.

Marie-Dominique wasn't taking much notice of the formalities. She was waving and grinning through the glass doors at the crowd outside, and gesturing towards me as if I was an interesting souvenir she'd picked up.

Beyond the barrier, I caught a glimpse of a woman in her sixties, wearing tweeds and leather boots. She shared Marie-Dominique's eyes and imperious nose. This would be Madame, her mother.

Twenty minutes later, Madame's Fiat dodged expertly among traffic. American drivers tend to head for the outside lane and put the pedal to the metal. The European system was different; cars eddied and bobbed, jostling for a space. Their yellow headlights gave everything a submarine effect – in those days, France was the only country in Europe to demand them; it has since abandoned the practice in the name of European ecumenicalism. I felt like a grunion, surging towards the light of an uncertain future.

Marie-Dominique leaned over the front seat, carrying on a machine-gun conversation with her mother. My name surfaced a few times, like a twig in the flood. The rest, except for an occasional noun at the end of a sentence, was incomprehensible.

What I could see out of the window fed my growing sense of isolation. The flat green country must have been pretty before they put the airport there. The few surviving châteaux glimpsed through the thickening dusk beyond the freeway's concrete wall reminded me that this was the setting for

Histoire d'O. Réage muffled her heroine's screams with a gramophone. These days, the autoroute did a better job.

Marie-Do took time off from conversation to say, 'Mother asks would we like to go to dinner when we get home?'

'I don't know. Aren't you tired?'

'A little. But she invites us.'

I sensed some subtext to this remark. Did it matter who made the invitation? I was used to the easier Californian social structure where one simply said, 'Hey, wanna go eat?'

'Let's see,' I said evasively.

More rapid-fire French. Madame swung the Fiat towards an exit sign. A dozen destinations were listed, some in white on green, others in white on black, some in green on white. A couple of additional direction boards were wired to the post below. None of them said PARIS.

We dropped under a bridge and rocketed into a nightmarish three-way intersection overshadowed by two elevated motorways. Cars dodged and hooted as if in a fairground ride. Then we were out of it and onto a road jammed with yellow-glaring cars.

Marie-Do pointed out of the window. 'Look.'

Below us, the pewter-grey Seine glinted with yellow lights. Grey-black bridges hulked above it. Leafless trees, the ends of their branches knobbed like amputees' stumps, lined the banks. Cars clustered, parked on every open space, even the pavements. People moved silently, hands shoved in the pockets of anoraks or thick black overcoats. I didn't need to open the window to know it was deathly cold.

Nineteenth-century apartment buildings, terraced in long six-storey blocks, glided past in the gloom, dark and tall as old liners in a fog. At the many multiple intersections, they tapered to a point, clustering bow to bow, like some mid-Atlantic traffic jam.

I knew Paris from earlier visits, but on those occasions I had been a tourist. What looked romantically exotic as a place to spend a weekend became threatening when one thought of it as home. The city appeared alien after the discipline of Los Angeles. Shops let their stock spill out onto the pavement, and Parisians wove without complaint around piles of fruit and vegetables, clothes racks, displays of shoes and, of course, café tables. In the equivalent sections of LA, it was illegal to put so much as a garbage can on the sidewalk.

Above the shops, chinks of light through shutters showed that people lived there, occasionally silhouetting the feathery edge of a window box. Higher still, the distinctive roofs sloped back like foreheads, a line broken often by the dormers of attic apartments. And, above that, the night sky, sooty grey tinged with chemical yellow, like a TV set tuned to a dead channel.

Another bridge. 'Pont Neuf,' Marie-Do said.

On the other side of it, Madame nosed the car into an alley, which opened out into a triangle of sandy park not much larger than a couple of tennis courts, studded with bare trees and hemmed in on its two long sides by more six-storey apartments. We rumbled over cobbles and stopped in front of a restaurant. Inside, a few people studied menus. It looked pleasant enough, in an old-fashioned stone-and-wood way. A young man with a moustache was fussing behind the cash register near the door. Over the big front windows it said Le Caveau du Palais.

'I don't know if I can manage a big dinner,' I said.

'I told mother we were too tired.' Marie-Dominique opened the car door.

'Then what . . . ?'

She looked at me, then at the restaurant. 'Oh, no. No. We don't eat here. This is where I live.'

I climbed out into the cold. Between the restaurant and the bar next to it – closed – was a narrow door, its glass panels criss-crossed with metalwork. It looked medieval, but the numerical security lock next to it was modern. Marie-Dominique punched numbers – 'I'll have to write you the code' – and the door clicked. She shoved it open.

A hallway, dark; stone underfoot. A bank of

letterboxes, and a wooden staircase twisting up into the dark.

We hauled suitcases up the stairs, so narrow it was easiest just to lean against the curving wall and slide your shoulder upwards, dragging the bags. How on earth did you get furniture up here? On the second landing was a tall door. Locks turned with a clanking that sounded like dungeons. Inside, a tiny hall and the musty smell of a flat long closed. Across the ceiling ran rough-hewn wooden beams, the skeleton of the house, which, from the size of the staircase, must be at least a century old. (It was closer to three.) To my left was a glass dining table big enough to seat four. On the floor to the right, a futon with a patchwork coverlet. There were two small armchairs and a trunk with a lamp.

And that was it.

Off the tiny hall was a tiny bathroom, barely big enough for a basin and a short bath. Above the bath hung some sort of collapsible framework draped with towels. Next door was a minuscule toilet. From the brooms, vacuum cleaner, portable heater and shelves of toilet paper and detergent, it was clear it also doubled as a cupboard.

Was there a kitchen? I found it behind a pair of double doors salvaged from an antique wardrobe. This was appropriate, since it was just about wardrobe size. There was a fridge, cupboards and a sink, with two hotplates sunk into the counter beside it. Under these, where the oven should have been, was a washing machine.

I went back into the living/dining/bed room and sat down heavily. My Westwood apartment had two bedrooms, two bathrooms, a large kitchen with stove and oven, a wet bar, and a living/dining room longer than some golf holes. By Californian standards, this place was like a fairly well-furnished elevator.

Thanks to jet lag, we fell into bed before discussing how two people could live in this pocket-sized excuse for an apartment, let alone work there.

But I woke at 4 a.m., with that panic-stricken emptiness that goes with the hour. 'In the dark night of the soul,' Scott Fitzgerald has said, 'it is always four a.m.'

One rule I'd learned from living in England: when in doubt, make tea. I rolled off the futon and stumbled towards the kitchen.

Taped to the fridge was a cartoon. A woman was sitting up in bed and saying to her sleeping husband, 'I just remembered. That litre of UHT milk in the fridge goes out of date at midnight.' The sensitivity it showed to the contents of one's fridge wasn't borne out by what I found behind the door of this one. Except for a can of passionfruit pulp, the rind of a Camembert ossified to the consistency of porcelain, and a yogurt two months old, it was empty.

I made tea from a kettle that had probably won a design award but was hell to boil: heat was transmitted direct from the hotplate to the handle, and only then to the water inside. The streetlights from Place Dauphine cast a yellow glow through the curtains. Marie-Do, lovely in the moonlight, slept easily, with the unmussed serenity of a woman in a mattress commercial. Apparently my doubts weren't contagious.

I couldn't go back to sleep, but there wasn't enough light to read by. Nor did I want to start rummaging in my bag for a book. On a shelf in the tiny alcove of the hall I discovered a paperback with parallel text, English and French. I hauled a chair into the hall, opened the lavatory door, turned on the light and sat down with my sugar-less, milk-less tea and *Alice au Pays des Merveilles*. The familiar description of Alice following the tantalizing white rabbit and falling down a black hole suddenly had a personal relevance.

The autoroute west out of Paris crawls through the sprawling forest park of the Bois de Boulogne, follows the Périphérique along the Seine, then swings across the river at St-Cloud and rockets towards Versailles. We took it on Christmas Day, 1989.

I'd read in Simon Schama's study of the French Revolution, *Citizens*, that, during the Revolution, Parisian mobs routinely tramped the whole thirty kilometres to demonstrate at the Palace of Versailles, then the residence of King Louis and Marie-Antoinette. As we climbed the heights of St-Cloud and headed west, I paid silent tribute to their love of freedom, but mostly to their stamina.

How did those barefoot gangs of the untrousered feel as they neared the spiked fences and armed guards of the royal palace? Maybe the way I felt myself, facing my first Christmas dinner with Marie-Do's family at the country house of Madame.

Richebourg is a village sixty kilometres west of Paris. Except for one shop and a fourteenth-century church with a fanciful tower, there's not much to it. Madame's country place stood on the very outskirts, a centuries-old stone barn converted over the years into a comfortable house.

While Madame, Marie-Do and her sister Caroline assembled dinner in the kitchen, my future brother-in-law, Jean-Marie, a gigantic young man with black curly hair, a fearsome five-o'clock shadow, a crushing horny-handed grip and oil-stained nails, showed me round. Since he and Caroline had arrived on a Harley, I'd put him down as a mechanic who'd married above him. In fact he was a special counsel for the French Grain Control Board, though his real love is the antique motor cycles he restores.

Jean-Marie had about as much English as I had French, but we got along. His large hand slapped one of the rough chocolate-coloured beams that supported the mezzanine jutting out over the tiled dining room.

'*Ancien. Très ancien.*'

'Old,' I agreed.

We didn't deserve any prizes for this insight. This was exactly the sort of authentic French country house whose effect, TV programmes like *Changing Rooms* are always assuring us, can be achieved with some copper warming pans and a couple of hand-woven baskets. Faced with the reality of a stone fireplace huge enough to roast a pig, and gnarled beams hand-shaped by an adze and pegged together at the joins, the suggestion seemed even more improbable. The real recipe for this place would start: 'Take a house, marinate for two centuries . . .'

Outside it was icy cold, but clear, the stars diamond sharp. The garden, dotted with old, drooping peach and cherry trees, sloped away into the dark. A giant hedge separated the house from an almost identical one next door, which belonged to Madame's younger sister, Marie-Do's *tante* and *marraine* – godmother – Françoise. Lights showed through from Françoise's kitchen, where she was readying, I'd been told with much raising of eyebrows and rubbing of hands by Jean-Marie, *sa belle mousse au chocolat*.

Caroline came out of the kitchen wiping her hands on an apron and said, '*Jean-Marie. Nous sommes prêts.*'

Jean-Marie ducked outside and came back a few minutes later with the pannier from his Harley. Unwrapping half an issue of *France Soir*, he revealed a large glass preserving jar. Inside, immersed in golden fat and looking like something removed from a very ill alcoholic, was an entire goose liver. As carefully as a surgeon handling a beating heart, he extracted it, watched attentively by Caroline.

'*Cuiller*.'

With the spoon she handed him, he carefully scraped the liver clean. The goose fat went into a bowl, reserved for making meltingly crispy fried potatoes.

'*Torchon*.'

He wiped away the last residue of fat, leaving just a gleaming sheen.

'*Couteau*.'

The wooden handle of the knife had been weathered almost white, its blade worn razor-thin and concave with honing. Jean-Marie began cutting judicious portions, each fractionally more generous than a restaurant slice. The excess demonstrated that this was 'family'.

He'd just finished and the women were arranging his slices artistically on a plate, flanked by the small crunchy pickled *cornichons*, when Tante Françoise arrived.

Behind her was her husband, a frowning white-haired man in his seventies in a blue suit and tie. This was the redoubtable Jean-Paul. An eminent chemist and a world authority on industrial oils who'd transformed himself on retirement into a highly successful painter, he was famously irascible and reserved.

He shook hands, muttered a gloomy '*Bon soir, m'sieur*' and disappeared into the living room. I watched him carefully put on his glasses to examine the labels on the night's wine, lined up to breathe along the stone mantel above the huge open fire.

Françoise carried a bowl filled to the brim with brown mousse. The others looked at it admiringly.

'*Riche*,' I suggested.

Françoise raised her eyebrows and turned down the corners of her mouth. '*Ce n'est pas . . .*' Remembering I was a foreigner, she shifted down painfully into English. I was to get to know this effect, rather like a decathlon runner who's been pelting along on concrete suddenly slogging into deep sand.

'It is . . . hmph hmph . . . not so rich, I think. Just . . . rph hmph . . . the cream, the *chocolat*, some . . . er . . . cognac and . . . umph . . . *Comment ça se dit . . .*' She muttered through numbers; one of the hardest things in any language is learning to count. '*Un, deux, trois . . . vingt-cinq . . .* umph, twenty-five eggs?'

We sat down to *foie gras*, white *boudin* veal sausage with fried apple, roast guinea-fowl, potatoes cooked

Dauphinoise with cheese and cream, green beans, carrots, cheese and the mousse of twenty-five eggs. In Los Angeles, a meal so riddled with cholesterol, salt and alcohol plainly offended against some city ordinance. But we weren't in California any more. And it was, after all, family.

The *foie gras* was delicious, smeared luxuriously on slices of fresh crusty white *pain*, larger brother of the more common *baguette*, and washed down with 1984 Bordeaux from Madame's *cave*, which really was a cave, hollowed out of the rock on which the house was built.

But as the conversation stuttered round the table, I sensed it wasn't going very well. The women never stopped handing round plates, offering more *foie gras*, returning to the kitchen for salt and extra *cornichons*. Jean-Marie and the white-haired Jean-Paul exchanged a few phlegmatic words, then fell silent. From time to time, Jean-Paul would tilt the wine bottle away from him and peer at the label, as if its date might have changed miraculously into a vintage year. I began to see the problem. *I* was the problem.

Their attitude was understandable. Marie-Do had brought this stranger from the other side of the world and introduced him into the family. But who was I? Seducer? Fortune-hunter? Bigamist? Would I be an ornament to this tight little clan or an embarrassment, to be hushed up and apologized for, like cousin Nicolas, who periodically broke with his girl, smashed his apartment, climbed onto the roof and had to be locked up for his own safety? In one sense, this lavish supper had been laid on for one purpose only: to see me sing for it. I took a healthy swallow of Bordeaux.

'Ummm,' I said, starting to talk without really knowing what I was going to say. 'I have . . . um, *j'ai un ami, un écrivain . . .*'

In fractured French, with frequent translations from Marie-Do, and illustrated with gestures, noises, much waving of arms and badly acted impressions of French aristocracy and decrepit *sommeliers*, I recounted George Johnston's story of his 1947 wine tour and the adventure with the 1812 Bordeaux.

I reached the end feeling like I had just hauled a wardrobe up six flights of stairs. There was silence round the table. A half-eaten slice of bread with a morsel of *foie gras* was still on my plate, and the table in front of me was disordered where I'd employed wine glasses, knives and forks as props.

But everyone was smiling – Madame a little in bemusement, I thought. But smiling still. Caroline and Jean-Marie had obviously got the point. And Marie-Do looked flushed and cheerful.

Uncle Jean-Paul looked ominously round the table – and for the first time, smiled too.

'*Voici un grand raconteur,*' he said, pouring some more wine and raising the glass to me. Madame bolted, beaming, to the kitchen for the guinea-fowl. Everyone started to talk at once. Under the table, Marie-Do squeezed my hand.

On the last day of January, I woke to the rattling of our windows. Where one had been left open, the curtains billowed. It was icy in the room. I shoved the window closed, locked it and looked down into Place Dauphine.

Overnight, a wind had swept the ground clean. M. Gruyère opposite stuck his head out of a door, hands in the pockets of his coral and lime anorak, Gauloise wedged in the corner of his mouth. His little dog Snowy peered around his ankles, desperate need warring in his eyes with innate caution. He looked up plaintively, but Gruyère just stared at the slate-coloured sky. Nothing was getting him out in this gale.

Finally Snowy scampered across the street, found a spot in the shelter of a tree, performed a sketchy crap and, with only a perfunctory flick of one back foot in the direction of hygiene, fled back to shelter.

'There's a storm,' I said to Marie-Do.

'It'll go away,' she said sleepily. 'Come back to bed.'

But when we finally got up at 9 a.m., the wind hadn't gone away. If anything, it blew more strongly;

people were propelled across the square like scraps of newspaper, and there was a steady drone overhead.

According to the TV news, the wind had been blowing all night across most of northern and eastern France. Trees were down and buildings had lost their roofs. Until then, Marie-Do had been uninterested, but the mention of roofs and eastern France had her reaching for the phone. 'I wonder if mother is at Richebourg.'

Madame was in her Paris apartment. There was an animated conversation, with frequent excursions to the window for a weather check.

'There is nobody at Richebourg,' said Marie-Do. 'Mother worries that a tree might be blown down on the house. I said we would go and look.'

'You think it's safe?'

The TV showed a caravan crumpled in a ditch like a sodden cardboard box. A six-storey building under renovation was coming to pieces, sheets of corrugated iron scaling off like leaves, and industrial-strength PVC ripping like toilet paper.

'OK,' I said. 'Let's go. We might have time to look in at Versailles. There won't be too many tourists on a day like this.'

Once we got onto the Périphérique, the full force of the storm was evident. Trees thrashed, and torn twigs littered the road. Pleasure boats were jammed against the stone abutments of the Seine, and down by the Pont d'Iéna, where the *bateaux-mouches* – the tour boats – docked, men were struggling to slide the big plastic windows closed before the wind blew them out.

Once over the Seine at St-Cloud and into the beginnings of the country, the wind got worse. Trees had been levered from the ground like rotten teeth. The roads were almost empty, and the drivers we did see clutched their wheels and stared ahead with an attention totally uncharacteristic of the French.

Nobody else took the exit to Versailles. We skirted the huge park where, inside spiked railings, surrounded by lawns, forests and boating lakes, private theatres, fountains, pavilions and wooded avenues like something out of a painting by Poussin or Claude Lorraine, Louis XVI and his Austrian wife Marie-Antoinette had lived as if this was the only reality.

Nobody manned the main gate, but we found the *gardien* about fifty metres down the wide avenue. He'd taken shelter in a plastic box the size of a telephone booth, from which he stared out in astonishment – whether at two people crazy enough to be out in this chaos, or at the chaos itself, it was hard to tell. From the woods on either side, we heard a rushing crack.

'The trees are falling!' the old man yelled over the noise, with a sort of glee. 'Marie-Antoinette couldn't do it. Louis Quatorze couldn't do it. But they're coming down now!'

At the foot of the drive, the road ended at the edge of the lake. The gale rushed across the grounds like the revolution that had blown Louis, his wife and their court to decapitation in the Place de la Concorde. Under the scudding clouds we were alone but exhilarated, infected by the same madness.

On the other side of Versailles, a giant beech had hammered a car flat. A policeman directed us around the wreck.

At Richebourg, one of the poplars was down, and the garden was littered with broken branches, but the house was safe. We hid inside while the wind buffeted the house, not even bothering to take down the heavy wooden shutters. Twenty-eight people died in France that weekend, and many more in the rest of Europe. That night, in a wide bed tucked into an alcove overshadowed by walls of bookshelves, while the wind slammed against the shutters, our daughter Louise Virginie Caroline was conceived.

Well, Joanna was right. Paris was very romantic.

CHAPTER SIXTEEN

Shakespeare and Company, and Company

LISE: Paris has ways of making people forget.
GERRY: Paris? No, not this city. It's too real and too beautiful. It never lets you forget anything. It reaches in and opens you wide, and you stay that way. I know.

Leslie Caron and Gene Kelly in An American in Paris *(1951), screenplay by Alan Jay Lerner*

SIX MONTHS AFTER ARRIVING IN PARIS, I LUGGED TWO large bags of groceries up the stairs to our new home.

At the fifth floor, I paused at the door to the apartment where Sylvia Beach and her partner Adrienne Monnier had lived when Beach ran Shakespeare and Company. Both were long dead, and cheap Chinese knick-knacks were now sold in the little shop just down the street where Frank Harris and Scott

Fitzgerald, Hart Crane and William Carlos Williams, Hemingway, Pound and Joyce had once chatted and read. But there was no denying the plaque above the door indicating that, on that spot, Shakespeare and Company had once flourished and *Ulysses* had been published. Nobody could take that away.

The pause outside the Beach apartment wasn't entirely reverential. I needed to catch my breath. We lived on the sixth floor, and there was no room for a lift in the narrow stairwell with its sinuous balustrade worn to the patina of old bronze by two centuries of hands.

And what hands! Ezra Pound and Gertrude Stein and Samuel Beckett had climbed these stairs. Scott Fitzgerald had thrown up on them: the threadbare carpet didn't look like it had been shampooed since. Between the first and second floors, Hemingway, arriving with his private army in 1944 to 'liberate' Rue de l'Odéon – old Madame Dechaux on the ground floor could remember this clearly – had hugged Adrienne Monnier but, before bounding up to their apartment, demanded an assurance that Sylvia had not collaborated with the Germans.

Less than a kilometre separated Rue de l'Odéon from Place Dauphine, but in changing homes I had moved into a new world. For Marie-Dominique, the change was less radical, since this was the apartment where she had grown up. Far from taking the girl out of Paris, I had let her install me at the very heart of it.

Marie-Dominique hadn't been pregnant for very long before it became obvious that it would be a difficult pregnancy, most of which she would need to spend in bed. Later, the obstetrician admitted she'd estimated the chances of miscarriage at 75 per cent. Since there simply wasn't room in the studio on Place Dauphine, Madame, with enormous generosity, agreed to swap. She moved into our studio, spending weekends and most of the summer in Richebourg, while we occupied the large apartment on Rue de l'Odéon where she'd lived for years alone. By comparison with the studio, the new place was enormous. As well as a huge bedroom and bathroom and a roomy kitchen, a long living and dining room ran the length of the building, with a terrace offering a panorama of Paris roofs, with stately Notre-Dame lying amid them like an ecclesiastical liner at anchor.

For the first eight months, in between preparing soup, tea and cold compresses, making and taking phone calls in my gradually improving but still splintered French, and ushering doctors, nurses and anxious relatives in and out, I began to explore Paris's world of books.

Up until the time she could no longer get out of bed, Marie-Dominique occasionally joined me in a stroll along the *bouquinistes* whose green lock-up stalls lined the balustrades along the Seine. On one such excursion, as we inched along the narrow pavement of Rue St André des Arts *en route* to the river, an apparition limped towards us. Shoving himself forward on two aluminium crutches, he wore an ancient and greasy suit, and a battered felt hat pierced at the edge of the brim for the piece of string which had at one time attached it to his coat collar to stop it from blowing away. A crooked fag smoked in one corner of a toothless mouth.

'Martin!'

Marie-Dominique, having pressed herself against the wall to avoid any possibility of touching him, stared in disbelief as Martin Stone and I warmly shook hands. Did she want the father of her child to know such people? The answer was obvious on her face.

The crutches were Martin's souvenir of the French Bicentennial celebrations. Partying in a crowded Place de la Bastille, he and his girlfriend had climbed the two-metre-high plinth of the central column to join a group of dancers. As fireworks began to be thrown, he jumped off, shattering the bones of both heels, which had to be rebuilt with titanium. Obviously nothing had changed. Martin's motto continued to be 'Everything in excess'. As he limped off down the street after we'd exchanged addresses, I felt a little more at home in Paris.

*

Book hunting in France confronted me with a new set of problems. Superficially, everything appeared the same, and could continue to do so right up to the moment the shop owner thrust you into the street, slammed the door, and turned over the hanging sign inside to read 'Fermeture annuelle' – closed for holidays. It was simply not the same world. As James Thurber said in *My Secret Life*, inspired by the memoirs of Salvador Dali, 'Let me say at the outset that my secret life is to that of Salvador Dali as a ukelele in the attic is to a piano in a tree – and that's a piano with *breasts*.'

When Napoleon called England 'a nation of shopkeepers', he wasn't only sneering at their apparent lack of military style; he was expressing the general scorn of all right-thinking *Gaulois* for anyone who buys and sells for a living. The French like to think of themselves as essentially landed gentry or military. The historian who mentioned that, if you went back far enough, the whole nation descended from Charlemagne the Great, tapped such a spring of popular sympathy that he could have run for president. He confirmed what the waiter, the butcher, even the *bouquiniste*, all believe – that however diluted, the blood of emperors flows in their veins.

This puts a different complexion on the world of commerce in France. It explains, for instance, the less-than-cordial reaction of a café owner when a foreigner walks in, takes a table and waves for a menu. The café owner isn't in *business*. This place is his *home*, where he may, if it suits him, serve you a cup of coffee and a *croque-monsieur*. But only if it amuses him to do so. It helps to see the restaurant as the man's living room. On entering, you naturally greet your host – '*Bonjour, m'sieur*' – or, if his wife is there too, '*Bonjour, 'sieur, 'dame.*' If other people are present, you include them as well, with a general nod – fellow guests, whom you'll get to know in the course of the evening.

Britons find such casual intimacy unimaginably alien. In his *Diaries*, Alan Bennett cites 'a woman entering Marks & Spencer's and saying brightly, "Good morning!"' as 'evidence of madness'. But in France it's a cornerstone of commercial intercourse.

One never demands the menu; in someone's home, would you ask, 'What's for dinner?' In time, the *carte* will be produced. Dishes will be 'proposed' or 'suggested'. Once you've eaten, the bill will be paid, but discreetly, with any tip disguised, for fear it might imply that the waiter served you for any reason but the pleasure it gives him. It used to be called a '*pourboire*' – 'Have a drink for yourself, my friend' – but these days it's added automatically, the mutual embarrassment of money changing hands exiled to the tiny italics at the foot of the bill (*Service compris*).

All of which explains why entering a French

bookshop was nothing like going into Any Amount of Books on London's Charing Cross Road or Skyline Books on New York's 13th Street. It's no coincidence that a bookshop in France is a *librairie*, with all the scent of private ownership that the word implies, while a library is a *bibliothèque* – a soulless source of reading material. The French even have a slang term for a second-hand book – something that doesn't exist in English. They call it a *bouquin*, which can also mean an old goat, too tough to be worth cooking, or the well-chewed mouthpiece of a pipe. Someone who deals in them is a *bouquiniste*, a term that carries a sense of battered resilience.

Then what, you will ask yourself, is a descendant of the Holy Roman Emperor doing in a rat-hole behind the Gare d'Austerlitz, flogging paperback Agatha Christies? Obviously, it must be because it amuses him to trade your one-euro piece for a dog-eared translation of *Dix Petits Nègres*. You don't imagine he does this for a *living*, do you? The bearer of a distinguished name like his, in *trade*? His grandfather the *général* would have spitted you like a grouse.

So yes, you *did* have to say, 'Hello, Mr Bookseller,' when you entered the shop, and 'Hello, everyone,' if there were other customers present. Responses to this could vary. Every bookseller would respond, '*Bonjour*.' Some clients might do so too, though more

usually they just looked around and nodded –
because another part of French bookshop etiquette
holds that the client is not some book junkie either,
but himself a descendant of dukes or generals too,
admiring the library of his friend out of sheer
pleasure at the discrimination of his acquisitions.

Another element of French book-buying that took
some getting used to was the in-shop discussion.
Whatever *librairie* you entered, the owner was likely
to be in conversation with one or two of his clients,
though never about books. ('Why would we talk
about books? What do you think this is – a
bookshop?') If you became a regular at his shop . . . er,
that is, a frequent guest in his library, you might find
yourself included. The first time Elise Soler, who
manages the *librairie* opposite our home, asked me,
'Don't you find that true, M. Baxter?' I knew I was on
the way to becoming a *rat des librairies*. And the first
time she insulted me ('What do you know of *foie gras*?
Australians eat kangaroos!'), I'd arrived.

The aristocratic attitude to bookselling meant that
whole areas of Anglo-Saxon book-dealing expertise
simply didn't apply. In visiting a *librairie*, you were
paying a social call and admiring a collection. You
were expected to walk appreciatively along the
shelves, taking down books at random, admiring
the bindings, rubbing a hand over the worn
morocco, perhaps reading a few pages, nodding at a

well-turned phrase, even smiling. Browsing, yes, but *not as we know it*. To discourage any unseemly interest in purchase, many *librairies* didn't categorize their stock. ('How do *I* know if I have any books on golf? Look down the back. But before that, feel this edition of Lamartine. They don't make them like that any more, my friend.') Or sometimes the books *were* categorized, but under inscrutable headings. *Esotérisme*, for instance, could include anything from books on flying saucers to a photographic survey of what S. J. Perelman called 'anatomical deviations in showgirls'.

If you asked Caroline Tascon, when she managed Poussier du Temps, on the banks of the Seine, just next to Tour d'Argent, for anything but first editions of Proust, she would wave contemptuously to the rear of the shop. 'Look down there. I'm not interested in *varia*.' *Varia* included limited, numbered editions of John Steinbeck and a pile of theatre programmes from the Thirties, many featuring Josephine Baker. I refrained from gloating at my finds and Caroline refrained from showing how hopelessly I'd compromised myself by buying such *ordure*.

Ask a British bookseller if he has any foreign-language books, and he'll show you a few shelves, usually of dog-eared French primers. But enquire where he keeps the porn and he'll tell you he doesn't stock such trash. Put the same questions to a *bouquiniste* and he'd point with pride to a well-stocked shelf of *éditions osées* (shameful books). But an enquiry about books in English would, at best, get you a shrug, or at worst the sort of glare given to people who demand change to feed the parking meter.

That popular image of the writer scribbling in a Paris café, sustained by numerous cups of strong coffee and the occasional cognac, is a creation of Hollywood movies – the same ones in which the author strode across the hills in hiking boots and moleskin trousers, pausing to lean reflectively against an oak and jot down some rustic quatrains.

Ernest Hemingway wrote in cafés because it was too cold to work at home. The enthusiasm with which he described the company at La Coupole was nothing to his appreciation of the charcoal braziers provided by its obliging management. French authors spent, and continue to spend, large parts of their spare time in cafés, but mainly to meet their friends. They don't *write* there. Writing is not a craft one practises in public, any more than dentistry. If you see anyone writing in a Parisian café, he or she is a tourist.

Nor do French writers normally sign books – not in public, at least. In private, they are fanatics for it. Pick up any slim volume of verse and it's likely to be passionately inscribed. But to sign books in public, and for strangers ... well, one's ancestors would groan in their tombs.

The public reading and signing session, so much a part of the Anglo-Saxon book scene, barely exists in France. Nor do French writers generally exhibit themselves with the enthusiasm of those in Britain, the United States, Australia. The fact that writers like Philippe Sollers seem never to be off the television underlines just how infrequently the others show themselves.

When you sign a book in France, it's usually a stealthy business. The first time I had a book published in Paris, the publicist asked me to come by and 'sign a few copies'. She conducted me into the bowels of the building, where three other writers were scribbling on the flyleaves of hundreds of books. I was handed a list of critics and journalists and told to inscribe copies to all of them personally. I'd only met a few of them, but I did as I was told – usually the best rule in France.

My chore was negligible compared with the lady opposite, who had compiled *Paris Pas Cher*, a popular annual guide to cheap everything. She'd already inscribed hundreds, she told me. She'd started out with her husband and co-editor, but he'd collapsed with writer's cramp and been hauled to the nearest café for a reviving cognac.

The authors of a book about the French

educational system were signing at the other end of the room. They made us look like amateurs. 'What's the name of that chap who runs the Education Authority in Bordeaux?' one asked. 'You remember, we had dinner with him last year.'

'Jacques something. Cendrars. Jacques Cendrars. Wife was . . . Odile.'

'We talked about boats, I remember. I'll put "Happy voyages".'

It was a lesson in how little the literary world has to do with literature. 'A boy's gotta hustle his book,' said Truman Capote.

Most of these copies signed in publishers' basements end up in shops like the one opposite us in Rue de l'Odéon. I'd seen them there; drifts of shiny new books at 50 per cent off, and all inscribed to local literary figures. There was a certain defiance, even arrogance in the way Françoise Giroud or Régis Debray dumped these books, obviously unread – and often understandably so. I once bought a pile of science-fiction comic-book albums by the French doyen of such artists, Philip Druillet, all inscribed, in some cases with original sketches, to Jeanne Moreau – not a lady, one would have thought, of the ray-gun persuasion. Selling them was the old snobbery, in a new form – 'What do I, once Minister of Culture,' (or 'intimate of Che Guevara' or 'movie star') 'want with your tedious production?'

Lesser lights don't have that much brass, which leads to a particularly irritating practice almost unique to France. Some people go to the trouble of removing their names from the dedication, either by scribbling over it with felt pen, or physically snipping it out, leaving a hole in the page. A man whom gay poet James Kirkup had favoured with some inscribed – presumably very *warmly* inscribed – editions ripped out the incriminating pages altogether; the love that dare not speak its name obviously doesn't like seeing it written either. Elise Soler got cross when I turned up my nose at these mutilated items. 'But it's the same book,' she said. To me, it was like someone offering me their handkerchief and saying, 'I only used it once.'

Of all the dedication copies I accumulated in Paris, none gave me so much pleasure as those which Dominique Aury, alias Pauline Réage, signed for me.

Chatting to the shop assistant in the bookshop diagonally opposite our apartment, I discovered that she knew Aury, who, after a good deal of negotiation, agreed to let Marie-Dominique film her for a possible documentary about *Histoire d'O*.

Though, at ninety, her memory was none too good, she found plenty to say about the book. Paulhan inspired it, she explained, when he claimed that no woman could ever write a truly erotic novel. She decided to try her hand, both as a literary challenge and in the hope that it would rekindle their long-standing affair. Since Paulhan couldn't drive, Aury chauffeured him around Paris, and, as she finished each episode, she read it aloud to him, usually in the car, parked in some discreet lay-by or in the secluded Bois de Boulogne.

Marie-Dominique also asked her the most obvious question of all. Had she ever experimented with the rituals described in the book – the whippings, brandings, multiple sex with anonymous partners?

'I would have quite liked to have tried sex with many lovers,' Aury said wistfully. 'But Jean was too jealous. And he, I think, would have enjoyed submitting me to the whips and chains. But I didn't care for that. And so we never did.' At the end of the interview, she inscribed two copies of the French first edition – as both Aury and Réage. But not under her real name, which was Anne Desclos; the woman who'd lived with secrets died with them as well.

Paris had plenty of English-language bookshops and libraries. They had always acted as informal contact points for visitors, augmented by a few long-time Anglophone residents who'd cemented themselves into the social structure. I got to know all the shops, from Tea and Tattered Pages, a combined bookshop and tea room where you could eat a grilled cheese sandwich and gloat over the dust-wrappered copy of *The Naked Lunch* which the owner, reckoning that no paperback is worth more than 25 francs, had just sold you for about a thousandth of its value; to the American Library, a bastion of American culture in the shadow of the Eiffel Tower that combined a superior reference and lending library with a programme of readings by visiting and local writers. At the American Library I once again ran into William Jay Smith, whom I hadn't seen since Hollins, and who, since his retirement, lived half the year in Paris. I also met Diane Johnson, Mavis Gallant, Jerome Charyn and other writers who, in general, preferred to think of themselves not as expats but simply people who made Paris their home.

Odile Hallier's Village Voice bookshop on Rue Princesse, just a few minutes' walk from the Odéon, belonged to the same tradition. Odile hosted regular readings and signing sessions, but otherwise ran the shop with no concessions to supposed Parisian charm or eccentricity – unless it was to employ noted eroticist and scholar of anti-Semitism Michael Neal behind the *caisse*. The Village Voice could as well have been in Greenwich Village or Knightsbridge as Paris, and Odile was quietly offended when Diane Johnson included in her novel *Le Divorce* a scene in a bookshop called the Town Cryer where an argument about Vietnam during a reading leads to a near-riot.

Odile's strategy was finally the most effective for an English-language bookshop. The others, on the principle that, if a spoonful is good the whole bottle is better, deluged you in cordiality. For a while, an Australian couple ran a shop called Cannibal Pierce, named for the convict who escaped from a Tasmanian prison and survived by eating his friends. Profiled in one of the English-language giveaway magazines that open and close like oysters in Paris, the woman announced she was researching cross-legged masturbation, about which she proposed to write a book.

Other shops, not quite so welcoming, contented themselves with offering coffee or tea, but even there they went too far. George Whitman, the unkempt émigré octogenarian who co-opted the name 'Shakespeare and Company' after Sylvia Beach's death and opened a shop under that name, used to brew both coffee and soup – it was hard to tell the difference – on a gas ring next to the cash desk. It took a fire which nearly destroyed the place to stop him.

George, along with sometime theatre producer and underground publisher Jim Haynes, was on the must-meet list of every American literary pilgrim to Paris. Their celebrity was no accident. Where Mavis Gallant and Diane Johnson, like Samuel Beckett before them, aimed to blend into the background,

Whitman and Haynes, both skilled self-publicists, turned their foreignness to advantage, hanging out their signboards as professional expatriates.

Haynes, co-founder of Scotland's Traverse Theatre and one-time editor of *Suck*, the paper that once, notoriously, featured a full-page photograph of Germaine Greer, nude, with her ankles tucked behind her ears, held weekly soirées at his spacious book-lined apartment, charging 70 francs for a basic buffet supper and the chance to mingle with other lost souls. With a little light teaching on the side, these events paid the bills, kept him in the public eye, and ensured his celebrity long after more talented contemporaries were forgotten.

Whitman's pose was more elaborate. Buying up a prime piece of the river frontage almost directly opposite Notre-Dame, he'd turned it into a setting for his crusty-old-bugger performance as Paris's pre-eminent literary exile. The shop became a famous crash-pad, with half a dozen sway-backed beds installed in the book room on the first floor. A backpacker could trade a few nights on one of these for some light janitorial work or serving in the shop.

On Sunday, George hosted afternoon 'teas', where visitors could 'meet the legend'. He also produced postcards identifying the shop, which stood near the point from which all distances were measured in France, as 'Kilometre zero' for literature as well, the point from which all literary journeys should be calculated. A large rubber stamp with the same message was slammed onto every book sold. If you protested, he was quite likely to refuse to sell you the book at all: 'People *ask* to have that put on their books,' he'd snarl. 'It makes it a collector's item.' Periodically, the stamp would be stolen, either as a souvenir or to protect books from defacement, but another always turned up a few days later.

George's Shakespeare and Company flourished during the Sixties, when Paris became even more jammed than ever with Americans, some trying to 'find themselves', others hoping to stay lost. Beat poets like Gary Snyder and Gregory Corso worked for him at odd times, sleeping on the floor of his 'Rare Book Room', a tiny annex next door to where he kept the better stock. They and their visiting friends such as Allen Ginsberg gave readings there. Others just thought they had. Resourcefully, George swept up photographs, quotes from letters and annotations in his Visitors' Book into an anthology which further promoted the legend.

And Martin Stone? Inevitably, of course, his charm worked its spell on Marie-Dominique as it has on everyone who has known him. It helped that, in a complicated deal with a Seattle book collector, he acquired a gleaming set of teeth. These inspired him to buy a better hat, a few more suits and, in particular, a pair of narrow crocodile shoes that became his trademark. Watching him confidently host a restaurant dinner party for Barbara Bray, Beckett's translator, I could agree with his girlfriend Lynne: 'On a good day, Martin can be quite dapper, really.'

Our adventures in book buying continued, sometimes in company, sometimes alone; a succession of increasingly complex deals and deals-within-deals; more midnight meetings on street corners, more trips to remote parts of France, more tottering up stairs with shoulder bags, boxes, crates of books. More surprises in musty cellars and dusty apartments, with deals done as the removals men stood impatiently in the hall; more things learned about the intricate world of books where there was always more to learn. Truly this was a subject, as Jo von Sternberg said, that I could not exhaust.

By my third year, the sixth-floor apartment was starting to overflow. Fortunately, my sister-in-law owned the unoccupied, indeed derelict three-room apartment above ours. After taking one look at its spectacular view over the roofs of the 6th *arrondissement* we bought it and converted it into offices and a library, which is where, with the sun rising behind Notre-Dame, I am writing this.

What series of extraordinary events had brought me to a city, indeed a street and a building that embodied everything I loved and admired about books and literature? One could make a case that reading Joyce's *Portrait of the Artist as a Young Man* and Fitzgerald's *The Great Gatsby* in Junee and finding that copy of *transition* in Roanoke provided signposts of a sort, but there were even more indications pointing me towards a career as a pen-pusher in the New South Wales Government Railways – probably now called Ozrail. I might just as well have become, like some of my old science-fiction friends, a part-time writer or full-time alcoholic. Or, like Ron Smith, died before my time.

Fitzgerald wrote at the end of *Gatsby* that we are all 'boats against the current, borne back ceaselessly into the past'. I never felt that. If any writer summed up how I felt, it was the traveller Freya Stark, who, in a passage from one of her early books remembered how, at the age of three, she had set out down the road with a penny in her pocket and 'a sense of all experience racing towards me like a wave'.

That December, I shipped from Australia and England the books I'd had in storage there for years. After three months the crates arrived at the foot of our staircase. Twelve hours and two tonnes later, and for the first time in my life, every book I owned was close at hand. There were no words for how that felt. Except maybe those Hemingway gave to Nick Adams in *Big Two-Hearted River*, the memoir of fishing in Michigan which he'd written only a few blocks away:

> Now things were done. There had been this to do. It had been a hard trip. He was very tired. That was done. He had made his camp. He was settled. Nothing could touch him. It was a good place to camp. He was there, in the good place. He was in his home where he had made it.

Acknowledgements

Extract from 'The Man Who Collected Poe' by Robert Bloch, from *Famous Fantastic Mysteries*, July 1951; cited in *The Man Who Called Himself Poe*, ed. Sam Moskowitz, Gollancz, 1969.

Extract from *The Dumas Club* by Arturo Pérez-Reverte, published by Harvill Panther; reprinted by permission of The Random House Group Ltd.

Extract from an essay by William Gibson in *You Can Find Inspiration in Everything* by Paul Smith; reprinted by permission of Violette Editions.

Extract from *Notting Hill* by Richard Curtis. Reproduced by permission of Hodder & Stoughton Limited.

Extract from an article by Iain Sinclair, 'Heroes and Villains', published in the *Independent Magazine*, 4 March 1995.

Lines from *The Plains* by Gerald Murnane, published by Nostrilia Press, Melbourne, 1982.

Extract from 'The Devil, George and Rosie' by John Collier, first published in *The Devil and Such*, Nonesuch Press, 1934.

Extract from *The Big Sleep* by Raymond Chandler, published by Penguin Books, London, 1948.

Extract from André Gide's introduction to Antoine de St. Exupéry's *Night Flight*, published by Century, London, 1932.

Extract from editorial by Forrest J. Ackerman in *Super Science Stories*, No. 1, 1940.

Extract from 'Dürer, Innsbruck, 1495' by Ern Malley from the collection *The Darkening Ecliptic*, published by R. Alistair McAlpine, London, 1974.

Extract from 'The Astronomer' from *Pigeon Feathers and Other Stories* by John Updike, published by Alfred A. Knopf, NY, 1965, and Penguin, London, 1965.

Extract from *The Moviegoer* by Walker Percy, published by Alfred A. Knopf, 1961.

Extract from *Abbey's Road* by Edward Abbey, first published by Dutton, 1979.

Extract from *In Search of Wonder* by Damon Knight, published by Advent Press, Chicago, 1956.

Extract from *New Found Land* by Tom Stoppard, 1975, reproduced by permission of Faber & Faber Ltd.

Extract from *Venice in the Fog* by William Jay Smith, published by Unicorn Press, Greensboro, NC, 1975.

Extract from *Pilgrim at Tinker Creek* by Annie

APPENDIX I

Lists

RATHER THAN CHASING A SPECIFIC WRITER OR particular genre, some collectors like to fill a list. It can be all the winners of a particular prize: the Pulitzer or the Booker for literature, the Hugos and Nebulas awarded for science fiction, the crime world's Edgars and Silver Daggers. Others prefer lists proposed by literary authorities of the best books of a genre or era.

The most popular list with collectors is *100 Key Books of the Modern Movement*, compiled by British editor and critic Cyril Connolly. It's rivalled only by *Queen's Quorum*, the choice made by crime writers Frederic Dannay and Manfred B. Lee, alias 'Ellery Queen', of the greatest novels of detection and mystery. (As detective historian Howard Haycraft added another nineteen 'cornerstones' in 1948, the list is sometimes known as *Haycraft/Queen Quorum* or

Cornerstones. It's also been updated since, so I've included both the original and revised versions.)

In 1984, Anthony Burgess decided to bring Connolly up to date as well by proposing the ninety-nine best novels published in English between 1939 and 1984. His choices aren't collected as assiduously, but their popularity will grow as Connolly and Queen titles become rarer. Likewise, the value of Booker winners is increasing visibly, so I've included them as well.

Collecting a list can be maddening. Everyone is after the same titles, some of which were obscure to start with and have now effectively disappeared from the market. On the other hand, a bookseller who wouldn't underprice a first edition of *Ulysses* might miss Arnold Bennett's 1905 *The Loot of Cities* or George Moore's *Memoirs of My Dead Life*, neither of which would be worth much were they not in *Queen's Quorum* and *Modern Movement* respectively.

To collect either Connolly or Queen seriously, you should have the following books about the lists themselves. They tell you what the titles are about, and give lots of bibliographical information on the various printings:

Cyril Connolly, *100 Key Books of the Modern Movement from England, France and America, 1880–1950* (Allison & Busby, London, 1986)

Ellery Queen with Howard Haycraft and others, *Queen's Quorum: A History of the Detective–Crime Short Story etc. with Supplements through 1967* (Biblio & Tannen, New York, 1969)

If Connolly, Queen, Burgess or the Bookers don't catch your imagination, winners of the Pulitzer Prize and National Book Award, Edgar and Silver Dagger recipients, as well as lists of winners in science fiction, children's books and many more genres, appear in Allen and Patricia Ahearn, *Book Collecting: A Comprehensive Guide* (Putnam, New York, 1995) – which is where I got some of the following.

Cyril Connolly's *The Modern Movement*

1881: Henry James, THE PORTRAIT OF A LADY
1881: Gustave Flaubert, BOUVARD ET PÉCUCHET
1883: Villiers de l'Isle-Adam, CONTES CRUELS
1884: Joris Karl Huysmans, À REBOURS
1885: Guy de Maupassant, BEL AMI
1886: Arthur Rimbaud, LES ILLUMINATIONS
1887: Charles Baudelaire, OEUVRES POSTHUMES
1887: Stéphane Mallarmé, LES POÉSIES
1887–96: Edmond and Jules de Goncourt,
JOURNAL DE GONCOURT
1891: Joris Karl Huysmans, LÀ-BAS
1896: Alfred Jarry, UBU ROI

1899: Henry James, THE AWKWARD AGE
1902: André Gide, L'IMMORALISTE
1902: Joseph Conrad, YOUTH: A NARRATIVE AND
TWO OTHER STORIES
1903: Henry James, THE AMBASSADORS
1906: George Moore, MEMOIRS OF MY DEAD LIFE
1907: Joseph Conrad, THE SECRET AGENT
1907: J. M. Synge, THE PLAYBOY OF THE WESTERN WORLD
1907: E. M. Forster, THE LONGEST JOURNEY
1911: Norman Douglas, SIREN LAND
1913: D. H. Lawrence, SONS AND LOVERS
1913: Guillaume Apollinaire, ALCOOLS: POÈMES, 1898–1913
1913: Marcel Proust, DU CÔTÉ DE CHEZ SWANN
1914: William Butler Yeats, RESPONSIBILITIES
1914: Thomas Hardy, SATIRES OF CIRCUMSTANCE
1915: Ford Madox Ford, THE GOOD SOLDIER
1916: Ezra Pound, LUSTRA
1917: James Joyce, A PORTRAIT OF THE ARTIST
AS A YOUNG MAN
1917: Norman Douglas, SOUTH WIND
1917: T. S. Eliot, PRUFROCK AND OTHER OBSERVATIONS
1917: Paul Valéry, LA JEUNE PARQUE
1918: Percy Wyndham Lewis, TARR
1918: Guillaume Apollinaire, CALLIGRAMMES
1918: Gerard Manley Hopkins, POEMS
1918: Arthur Waley, A HUNDRED AND SEVENTY CHINESE POEMS
1918: Lytton Strachey, EMINENT VICTORIANS
1920: Wilfred Owen, POEMS
1921: D. H. Lawrence, SEA AND SARDINIA
1921: Aldous Huxley, CROME YELLOW

1922: Katherine Mansfield, THE GARDEN PARTY
AND OTHER STORIES
1922: William Butler Yeats, LATER POEMS
1922: James Joyce, ULYSSES
1923: Raymond Radiguet, LE DIABLE AU CORPS
1923: Ronald Firbank, THE FLOWER BENEATH THE FOOT
1923: Wallace Stevens, HARMONIUM
1923: E. E. Cummings, TULIPS AND CHIMNEYS
1924: E. M. Forster, A PASSAGE TO INDIA
1924: Ernest Hemingway, IN OUR TIME
1925: F. Scott Fitzgerald, THE GREAT GATSBY
1925: Ezra Pound, A DRAFT OF XVI CANTOS
1926: Ernest Hemingway, THE SUN ALSO RISES
1926: André Gide, SI LE GRAIN NE MEURT
1926: William Somerset Maugham, THE CASUARINA TREE
1927: Virginia Woolf, TO THE LIGHTHOUSE
1928: André Breton, NADJA
1928: William Butler Yeats, THE TOWER
1928: D. H. Lawrence, LADY CHATTERLEY'S LOVER
1928: Evelyn Waugh, DECLINE AND FALL
1928: Edith Sitwell, COLLECTED POEMS
1929: Henry Green, LIVING
1929: Ernest Hemingway, A FAREWELL TO ARMS
1929: Robert Graves, GOODBYE TO ALL THAT
1929: Jean Cocteau, LES ENFANTS TERRIBLES
1929: Ivy Compton-Burnett, BROTHERS AND SISTERS
1930: Hart Crane, THE BRIDGE
1930: T. S. Eliot, ASH WEDNESDAY
1931: Antoine de Saint-Exupéry, VOL DE NUIT
1931: William Faulkner, SANCTUARY

1931: Virginia Woolf, THE WAVES

1931: Edmund Wilson, AXEL'S CASTLE

1932: T. S. Eliot, SELECTED ESSAYS

1932: W. H. Auden, THE ORATORS

1932: Louis-Ferdinand Céline, VOYAGE AU BOUT DE LA NUIT

1932: Aldous Huxley, BRAVE NEW WORLD

1933: Nathanael West, MISS LONELYHEARTS

1933: André Malraux, LA CONDITION HUMAINE

1934: Dylan Thomas, EIGHTEEN POEMS

1934: F. Scott Fitzgerald, TENDER IS THE NIGHT

1934: Henry James, THE ART OF THE NOVEL

1935: Marianne Moore, SELECTED POEMS

1936–9: Henry de Montherlant, LES JEUNES FILLES

1936: Henri Michaux, VOYAGE EN GRANDE GARABAGNE

1938: Jean-Paul Sartre, LA NAUSÉE

1939: Louis MacNeice, AUTUMN JOURNAL

1939: Christopher Isherwood, GOODBYE TO BERLIN

1939: James Joyce, FINNEGANS WAKE

1940: Graham Greene, THE POWER AND THE GLORY

1940: Arthur Koestler, DARKNESS AT NOON

1940: W. H. Auden, ANOTHER TIME

1942: Stephen Spender, RUINS AND VISIONS

1942: Albert Camus, L'ÉTRANGER

1944: T. S. Eliot, FOUR QUARTETS

1945: George Orwell, ANIMAL FARM

1946: Dylan Thomas, DEATHS AND ENTRANCES

1947: Albert Camus, LA PESTE

1948: John Betjeman, SELECTED POEMS

1948: Ezra Pound, THE PISAN CANTOS

1949: George Orwell, NINETEEN EIGHTY-FOUR

Haycraft/Queen Cornerstones, 1748–1948

1892: Israel Zangwill, THE BIG BOW MYSTERY

1894: Mark Twain, THE TRAGEDY OF PUDD'NHEAD WILSON

1894: Arthur Morrison, MARTIN HEWITT, INVESTIGATOR

1894: A. Conan Doyle, THE MEMOIRS OF SHERLOCK HOLMES

1895: M. P. Shiel, PRINCE ZALESKI

1897: Bram Stoker, DRACULA

1899: E. W. Hornung, THE AMATEUR CRACKSMAN

1902: A. Conan Doyle, THE HOUND OF THE BASKERVILLES

1903: Erskine Childers, THE RIDDLE OF THE SANDS

1905: A. Conan Doyle, THE RETURN OF SHERLOCK HOLMES

1905: Jacques Futrelle, THE THINKING MACHINE

1906: Godfrey R. Benson, TRACKS IN THE SNOW

1906: Robert Barr, THE TRIUMPHS OF EUGÈNE VALMONT

1907: Maurice Leblanc, ARSÈNE LUPIN,
GENTLEMAN-CAMBRIOLEUR

1907: Gaston Leroux, LE MYSTÈRE DE LA CHAMBRE JAUNE

1907: R. Austin Freeman, THE RED THUMB MARK

1908: Mary Roberts Rinehart, THE CIRCULAR STAIRCASE

1908: O. Henry, THE GENTLE GRAFTER

1908: G. K. Chesterton, THE MAN WHO WAS THURSDAY

1908–9: Gaston Leroux, LE PARFUM DE LA DAME EN NOIR

1909: R. Austin Freeman, JOHN THORNDYKE'S CASES

1909: Cleveland Moffett, THROUGH THE WALL

1909: Baroness Orczy, THE OLD MAN IN THE CORNER

1909: Carolyn Wells, THE CLUE

1910: Maurice Leblanc, '813'

1910: A. E. W. Mason, AT THE VILLA ROSE

1910: William MacHarg & Edwin Balmer, THE ACHIEVEMENTS
OF LUTHER TRANT

1911: R. Austin Freeman, THE EYE OF OSIRIS

1911: G. K. Chesterton, THE INNOCENCE OF FATHER BROWN
1912: R. Austin Freeman, THE SINGING BONE
1912: Arthur B. Reeve, THE SILENT BULLET
1913: Mrs Belloc Lowndes, THE LODGER
1913: Sax Rohmer, THE MYSTERY OF DR FU-MANCHU
1913: E. C. Bentley, TRENT'S LAST CASE
1914: Ernest Bramah, MAX CARRADOS
1914: Louis Joseph Vance, THE LONE WOLF
1915: A. Conan Doyle, THE VALLEY OF FEAR
1915: John Buchan, THE THIRTY-NINE STEPS
1916: Thomas Burke, LIMEHOUSE NIGHTS
1917: A. Conan Doyle, HIS LAST BOW
1918: Melville Davisson Post, UNCLE ABNER
1918: J. S. Fletcher, THE MIDDLE TEMPLE MURDER
1920: Agatha Christie, THE MYSTERIOUS AFFAIR AT STYLES
1920: Freeman Wills Crofts, THE CASK
1920: H. C. Bailey, CALL MR FORTUNE
1920: 'Sapper' (Cyril McNeile), BULL-DOG DRUMMOND
1920: Arthur Train, TUTT AND MR TUTT
1921: Eden Phillpotts, THE GREY ROOM
1922: Maurice Leblanc, LES HUITS COUPS DE L'HORLOGE
1922: A. A. Milne, THE RED HOUSE MYSTERY
1923: G. D. H. Cole, THE BROOKLYN MURDERS
1923: Dorothy L. Sayers, WHOSE BODY?
1924: A. E. W. Mason, THE HOUSE OF THE ARROW
1924: Freeman Wills Crofts, INSPECTOR FRENCH'S
GREATEST CASE
1924: Philip Macdonald, THE RASP
1925: Edgar Wallace, THE MIND OF MR J. G. REEDER
1925: John Rhode, THE PADDINGTON MYSTERY

1925: Earl Derr Biggers, THE HOUSE WITHOUT A KEY
1925: Theodore Dreiser, AN AMERICAN TRAGEDY
1925: Liam O'Flaherty, THE INFORMER
1925: Ronald A. Knox, THE VIADUCT MURDER
1926: Agatha Christie, THE MURDER OF ROGER ACKROYD
1926: S. S. Van Dine, THE BENSON MURDER CASE
(Or alternate: THE CANARY MURDER CASE, 1927)
1926: C. S. Forester, PAYMENT DEFERRED
1927: A. Conan Doyle, THE CASE-BOOK OF SHERLOCK HOLMES
1927: S. S. Van Dine (see alternate, 1926)
1927: Frances Noyes Hart, THE BELLAMY TRIAL
1928: John Rhode, THE MURDERS IN PRAED STREET
1928: W. Somerset Maugham, ASHENDEN
1929: Anthony Berkeley, THE POISONED CHOCOLATES CASE
1929: Ellery Queen, THE ROMAN HAT MYSTERY
1929: Rufus King, MURDER BY THE CLOCK
1929: W. R. Burnett, LITTLE CAESAR
1929: T. S. Stribling, CLUES OF THE CARIBBEES
1929: Harvey J. O'Higgins, DETECTIVE DUFF UNRAVELS IT
1929: Migeon G. Eberhart, THE PATIENT IN ROOM 18
1930: Dorothy L. Sayers & Robert Eustace, THE DOCUMENTS
IN THE CASE
1930: Frederick Irving Anders, BOOK OF MURDER
1930: Dashiell Hammett, THE MALTESE FALCON
1930: David Frome, THE HAMMERSMITH MURDERS
1931: Dashiell Hammett, THE GLASS KEY
1931: Stuart Palmer, THE PENGUIN POOL MURDER
1931: Francis Beeding, DEATH WALKS IN EASTREPPS
1931: Glen Trevor (James Hilton), MURDER AT SCHOOL
1931: Damon Runyon, GUYS AND DOLLS

1931: Phoebe Atwood Taylor, THE CAPE COD MYSTERY
1932: H. C. Bailey, THE RED CASTLE
1932: Francis Iles, BEFORE THE FACT
1932: Barnaby Ross, THE TRAGEDY OF X
1932: Barnaby Ross, THE TRAGEDY OF Y
1932: R. A. J. Walling, THE FATAL FIVE MINUTES
1932: Clemence Dane & Helen Sipson, RE-ENTER SIR JOHN
1933: Erle Stanley Gardner, THE CASE OF THE VELVET CLAWS
1933: Erle Stanley Gardner, THE CASE OF THE SULKY GIRL
1934: Dorothy L. Sayers, THE NINE TAILORS
1934: Margery Allingham, DEATH OF A GHOST
1934: James M. Cain, THE POSTMAN ALWAYS RINGS TWICE
1934: Rex Stout, FER-DE-LANCE
1935: Rex Stout, THE LEAGUE OF FRIGHTENED MEN
1935: Richard Hull, THE MURDER OF MY AUNT
1935: John P. Marquand, NO HERO
1937: Anthony Berkeley, TRIAL AND ERROR
1938: Philip Macdonald, THE NURSEMAID WHO DISAPPEARED
1938: John Dickson Carr, THE CROOKED HINGE
1938: John Dickson Carr, THE JUDAS WINDOW
1938: Nicholas Blake, THE BEAST MUST DIE
1938: Michael Innes, LAMENT FOR A MAKER
1938: Clayton Rawson, DEATH FROM A TOP HAT
1938: Graham Greene, BRIGHTON ROCK
1938: Daphne Du Maurier, REBECCA
1938: Mabel Seeley, THE LISTENING HOUSE
1939: Ngaio Marsh, OVERTURE TO DEATH
1939: Eric Ambler, A COFFIN FOR DIMITRIOS
1939: Raymond Chandler, THE BIG SLEEP
1939: Georges Simenon, THE PATIENCE OF MAIGRET

1940: Raymond Chandler, FAREWELL, MY LOVELY
1940: Raymond Postgate, VERDICT OF TWELVE
1940: Frances & Richard Lockridge, THE NORTHS
MEET MURDER
1940: Dorothy B. Hughes, THE SO BLUE MARBLE
(Or alternate: IN A LONELY PLACE, 1947)
1940: Cornell Woolrich, THE BRIDE WORE BLACK
1940: Manning Coles, DRINK TO YESTERDAY
1941: Manning Coles, A TOAST TO TOMORROW
1941: H. F. Heard, A TASTE FOR HONEY
1941: Craig Rice, TRIAL BY FURY
(Or alternate: HOME SWEET HOMICIDE, 1944)
1942: Ellery Queen, CALAMITY TOWN
1942: William Irish, PHANTOM LADY
1942: H. H. Holmes, ROCKET TO THE MORGUE
1942: James Gould Cozzens, THE JUST AND THE UNJUST
1944: Dashiell Hammett, THE ADVENTURES OF SAM SPADE
1944: Hilda Lawrence, BLOOD UPON THE SNOW
1944: Craig Rice (see alternate, 1941)
1946: Helen Eustis, THE HORIZONTAL MAN
1946: Charlotte Armstrong, THE UNSUSPECTED
1946: Lillian De La Torre, DR SAM JOHNSON, DETECTOR
1946: Edmund Crispin, THE MOVING TOYSHOP
(Or alternate: LOVE LIES BLEEDING, 1948)
1947: Dorothy B. Hughes (see alternate, 1940)
1947: Edgar Lustgarten, ONE MORE UNFORTUNATE
1947: Roy Vickers, THE DEPARTMENT OF DEAD ENDS
1948: Edmund Crispin (see alternate, 1946)
1948: Josephine Tey, THE FRANCHISE AFFAIR
1948: William Faulkner, INTRUDER IN THE DUST

Queen's Quorum

1898: M. McDonnell Bodkin, PAUL BECK, THE RULE OF THUMB
DETECTIVE

1898: Rodriquest Ottolengui, FINAL PROOF

1899: Nicholas Carter, THE DETECTIVE'S PRETTY NEIGHBOR

1899: L. T. Meade & Robert Eustace, THE BROTHERHOOD
OF KINGS

1900: Herbert Cadett, THE ADVENTURES OF A JOURNALIST

1901: Richard Harding Davis, IN THE FOG

1902: Clifford Ashdown, THE ADVENTURES OF
ROMNEY PRINGLE

1902: Bret Harte, CONDENSED NOVELS

1903: Percival Pollard, LINGO DAN

1905: B. Fletcher Robinson, THE CHRONICLES OF
ADDINGTON PEACE

1905: Arnold Bennett, THE LOOT OF CITIES

1906: Robert Barr, THE TRIUMPHS OF EUGÈNE VALMONT

1906: Alfred Henry Lewis, CONFESSIONS OF A DETECTIVE

1907: Maurice Leblanc, THE EXPLOITS OF ARSÈNE LUPIN

1907: Jacques Futrelle, THE THINKING MACHINE

1908: George Randolph Chester, GET-RICH-QUICK WALLINGFORD

1908: O. Henry, THE GENTLE GRAFTER

1909: Baroness Orczy, THE OLD MAN IN THE CORNER

1909: R. Austin Freeman, JOHN THORNDYKE'S CASES

1909: J. S. Fletcher, THE ADVENTURES OF ARCHER DAWE
(SLEUTH-HOUND)

1910: Balduin Groller, DETECTIVE DAGOBERT'S DEEDS
AND ADVENTURES

1910: T. W. Hanshew, THE MAN OF THE FORTY FACES

1910: William MacHarg & Edwin Balmer, THE ACHIEVEMENTS
OF LUTHER TRANT

1911: G. K. Chesterton, THE INNOCENCE OF FATHER BROWN
1911: Samuel Hopkins Adams, AVERAGE JONES
1912: Arthur B. Reeve, THE SILENT BULLET
1912: (Gelett Burgess), THE MASTER OF MYSTERIES
1912: Victor L. Whitechurch, THRILLING STORIES
OF THE RAILWAY
1912: R. Austin Freeman, THE SINGING BONE
1913: William Hope Hodgson, CARNACKI THE GHOST-FINDER
1913: Anna Katharine Green, MASTERPIECES OF MYSTERY
1913: Hesketh Prichard, NOVEMBER JOE
1914: Ernest Bramah, MAX CARRADOS
1914: Arthur Sherburne Hardy, DIANE AND HER FRIENDS
1916: Thomas Burke, LIMEHOUSE NIGHTS
1917: A. E. W. Mason, THE FOUR CORNERS OF THE WORLD
1918: Melville Davisson Post, UNCLE ABNER
1918: Ellis Parker Butler, PHILO GUBB
1919: John Russell, THE RED MARK
1920: William Le Queux, MYSTERIES OF A GREAT CITY
1920: Sax Rohmer, THE DREAM-DETECTIVE
1920: J. Storer Clouston, CARRINGTON'S CASES
1920: Vincent Starrett, THE UNIQUE HAMLET
1920: Arthur Train, TUTT AND MR TUTT
1920: H. C. Bailey, CALL MR FORTUNE
1922: Maurice Leblanc, THE EIGHT STROKES OF THE CLOCK
1923: Octavus Roy Cohen, JIM HANVEY, DETECTIVE
1924: Agatha Christie, POIROT INVESTIGATES
1925: Edgar Wallace, THE MIND OF MR J. G. REEDER
1926: Louis Golding, LUIGI OF CATANZARO
(Or alternate: PALE BLUE NIGHTGOWN, 1936)
1927: Anthony Wynne, SINNERS GO SECRETLY

1927: Susan Glaspell, A JURY OF HER PEERS
1928: Dorothy L. Sayers, LORD PETER VIEWS THE BODY
1928: G. D. H. & M. I. Cole, SUPERINTENDENT
WILSON'S HOLIDAY
1928: W. Somerset Maugham, ASHENDEN
1929: Percival Wilde, ROGUES IN CLOVER
1929: T. S. Stribling, CLUES OF THE CARIBBEES
1929: Harvey J. O'Higgins, DETECTIVE DUFF UNRAVELS IT
1930: Frederick Irving Anderson, BOOK OF MURDER
1931: F. Tennyson Jesse, THE SOLANGE STORIES
1931: Damon Runyon, GUYS AND DOLLS
1932: Georges Simenon, THE THIRTEEN CULPRITS
1933: Leslie Charteris, THE BRIGHTER BUCCANEER
1933: Henry Wade, POLICEMAN'S LOT
1934: Mignon G. Eberhart, THE CASES OF SUSAN DARE
1934: Irvin S. Cobb, FAITH, HOPE AND CHARITY
1934: Ellery Queen, THE ADVENTURES OF ELLERY QUEEN
1936: C. Daly King, THE CURIOUS MR TARRANT
1936: Louis Golding, (see alternate, 1926)
1938: E. C. Bentley, TRENT INTERVENES
1939: Margery Allingham, MR CAMPION AND OTHERS
1940: Carter Dickson, THE DEPARTMENT OF
QUEER COMPLAINTS
1940: William MacHarg, THE AFFAIRS OF O'MALLEY
1942: H. Bustos Domecq, SIX PROBLEMS FOR
DON ISIDRO PARODI
1944: William Irish, AFTER-DINNER STORY
1944: Dashiell Hammett, THE ADVENTURES OF SAM SPADE
1944: Raymond Chandler, FIVE MURDERERS
1946: Lillian De La Torre, DR SAM JOHNSON, DETECTOR

1946: Rafael Sabatini, TURBULENT TALES
1946: Antonio Helú, THE COMPULSION TO MURDER
1947: Stuart Palmer, THE RIDDLES OF HILDEGARDE WITHERS
1947: Roy Vicker, THE DEPARTMENT OF DEAD ENDS
1949: William Faulkner, KNIGHT'S GAMBIT
1950: Lawrence G. Blochman, DIAGNOSIS: HOMICIDE
1951: John Collier, FANCIES AND GOODNIGHTS
1952: Philip MacDonald, SOMETHING TO HIDE
1952: Lord Dunsany, THE LITTLE TALES OF SMETHERS
1953: Edmund Crispin, BEWARE OF THE TRAINS
1953: Roald Dahl, SOMEONE LIKE YOU
1954: Michael Innes, APPLEBY TALKING
1956: Stanley Ellin, MYSTERY STORIES
1956: Evan Hunter, THE JUNGLE KIDS
1957: Charlotte Armstrong, THE ALBATROSS
1958: Craig Rice, THE NAME IS MALONE
1958: Rufus King, MALICE IN WONDERLAND
1959: Georges Simenon, THE SHORT CASES OF
INSPECTOR MAIGRET
1961: Patrick Quentin, THE ORDEAL OF MRS SNOW
1963: Stuart Palmer & Craig Rice, PEOPLE VS.
WITHERS & MALONE
1965: Helen McCloy, SURPRISE, SURPRISE!
1966: Robert L. Fish, THE INCREDIBLE SHLOCK HOLMES
1967: Miriam Allen De Ford, THE THEME IS MURDER
1967: Michael Gilbert, GAME WITHOUT RULES
1967: Harry Kemelman, THE NINE-MILE WALK

The Booker Prize

The Booker Prize is awarded annually for the best literature in
the British Commonwealth of Nations.

1969: P. H. Newby, SOMETHING TO ANSWER FOR

1970: Bernice Rubens, THE ELECTED MEMBER

1971: V. S. Naipaul, IN A FREE STATE

1972: John Berger, G

1973: J. G. Farrell, THE SIEGE OF KRISHNAPUR

1974: Stanley Middleton, HOLIDAY/Nadine Gordimer,
THE CONSERVATIONIST

1975: Ruth Prawer Jhabvala, HEAT AND DUST

1976: David Storey, SAVILLE

1977: Paul Scott, STAYING ON

1978: Iris Murdoch, THE SEA, THE SEA

1979: Penelope Fitzgerald, OFFSHORE

1980: William Golding, RITES OF PASSAGE

1981: Salman Rushdie, MIDNIGHT'S CHILDREN

1982: Thomas Keneally, SCHINDLER'S ARK

1983: J. M. Coetzee, LIFE AND TIMES OF MICHAEL K

1984: Anita Brookner, HOTEL DU LAC

1985: Keri Hulme, THE BONE PEOPLE

1986: Kingsley Amis, THE OLD DEVILS

1987: Penelope Lively, MOON TIGER

1988: Peter Carey, OSCAR AND LUCINDA

1989: Kazuo Ishiguro, THE REMAINS OF THE DAY

1990: A. S. Byatt, POSSESSION

1991: Ben Okri, THE FAMISHED ROAD

1992: Michael Ondaatje, THE ENGLISH PATIENT/
Barry Unsworth, SACRED HUNGER

1993: Roddy Doyle, PADDY CLARK HA, HA, HA
1994: James Kelman, HOW LATE IT WAS, HOW LATE
1995: Pat Barker, THE GHOST ROAD
1996: Graham Swift, LAST ORDERS
1997: Arundhati Roy, THE GOD OF SMALL THINGS
1998: Ian McEwan, AMSTERDAM
1999: J. M. Coetzee, DISGRACE
2000: Margaret Atwood, THE BLIND ASSASSIN
2001: Peter Carey, TRUE HISTORY OF THE KELLY GANG

Anthony Burgess's Ninety-nine Novels

1939: Henry Green, PARTY GOING
1939: Aldous Huxley, AFTER MANY A SUMMER
1939: James Joyce, FINNEGANS WAKE
1939: Flann O'Brian, AT SWIM-TWO-BIRDS
1940: Graham Greene, THE POWER AND THE GLORY
1940: Ernest Hemingway, FOR WHOM THE BELL TOLLS
1940–70: C. P. Snow, STRANGERS AND BROTHERS
1941: Rex Warner, THE AERODROME
1944: Joyce Cary, THE HORSE'S MOUTH
1944: Somerset Maugham, THE RAZOR'S EDGE
1945: Evelyn Waugh, BRIDESHEAD REVISITED
1946: Mervyn Peake, TITUS GROAN
1947: Saul Bellow, THE VICTIM
1947: Malcolm Lowry, UNDER THE VOLCANO
1948: Graham Greene, THE HEART OF THE MATTER
1948: Aldous Huxley, APE AND ESSENCE
1948: Norman Mailer, THE NAKED AND THE DEAD

1948: Nevil Shute, NO HIGHWAY

1949: Elizabeth Bowen, THE HEAT OF THE DAY

1949: George Orwell, NINETEEN EIGHTY-FOUR

1949: William Sansom, THE BODY

1950: William Cooper, SCENES FROM PROVINCIAL LIFE

1950: Budd Schulberg, THE DISENCHANTED

1951: Anthony Powell, A DANCE TO THE MUSIC OF TIME

1951: J. D. Salinger, THE CATCHER IN THE RYE

1951–69: Henry Williamson, A CHRONICLE OF
ANCIENT SUNLIGHT

1951: Herman Wouk, THE CAINE MUTINY

1952: Ralph Ellison, INVISIBLE MAN

1952: Ernest Hemingway, THE OLD MAN AND THE SEA

1952: Mary McCarthy, THE GROVES OF ACADEME

1952: Flannery O'Connor, WISE BLOOD

1952–61: Evelyn Waugh, SWORD OF HONOUR

1953: Raymond Chandler, THE LONG GOODBYE

1954: Kingsley Amis, LUCKY JIM

1957: John Braine, ROOM AT THE TOP

1957–60: Lawrence Durrell, THE ALEXANDRIA QUARTET

1957–60: Colin MacInnes, THE LONDON NOVELS

1957: Bernard Malamud, THE ASSISTANT

1958: Iris Murdoch, THE BELL

1958: Alan Sillitoe, SATURDAY NIGHT AND SUNDAY MORNING

1958: T. H. White, THE ONCE AND FUTURE KING

1959: William Faulkner, THE MANSION

1959: Ian Fleming, GOLDFINGER

1960: L. P. Hartley, FACIAL JUSTICE

1960–5: Olivia Manning, THE BALKAN TRILOGY

1961: Ivy Compton-Burnett, THE MIGHTY AND THEIR FALL

1961: Joseph Heller, CATCH-22
1961: Richard Hughes, THE FOX IN THE ATTIC
1961: Patrick White, RIDERS IN THE CHARIOT
1961: Angus Wilson, THE OLD MEN AT THE ZOO
1962: James Baldwin, ANOTHER COUNTRY
1962: Pamela Hansford Johnson, AN ERROR OF JUDGEMENT
1962: Aldous Huxley, ISLAND
1962: Doris Lessing, THE GOLDEN NOTEBOOK
1962: Vladimir Nabokov, PALE FIRE
1963: Muriel Spark, THE GIRLS OF SLENDER MEANS
1964: William Golding, THE SPIRE
1964: Wilson Harris, HEARTLAND
1964: Christopher Isherwood, A SINGLE MAN
1964: Vladimir Nabokov, THE DEFENCE
1964: Angus Wilson, LATE CALL
1965: John O'Hara, THE LOCKWOOD CONCERN
1965: Muriel Spark, THE MANDELBAUM GATE
1966: Chinua Achebe, A MAN OF THE PEOPLE
1966: Kingsley Amis, THE ANTI-DEATH LEAGUE
1966: John Barth, GILES GOAT-BOY
1966: Nadine Gordimer, THE LATE BOURGEOIS WORLD
1966: Walker Percy, THE LAST GENTLEMAN
1967: R. K. Narayan, THE VENDOR OF SWEETS
1968: J. B. Priestley, THE IMAGE MEN
1968: Mordecai Richler, COCKSURE
1968: Keith Roberts, PAVANE
1969: John Fowles, THE FRENCH LIEUTENANT'S WOMAN
1969: Philip Roth, PORTNOY'S COMPLAINT
1970: Len Deighton, BOMBER
1973: Michael Frayn, SWEET DREAMS

1973: Thomas Pynchon, GRAVITY'S RAINBOW

1975: Saul Bellow, HUMBOLDT'S GIFT

1975: Malcolm Bradbury, THE HISTORY MAN

1976: Brian Moore, THE DOCTOR'S WIFE

1976: Robert Nye, FALSTAFF

1977: Erica Jong, HOW TO SAVE YOUR OWN LIFE

1977: James Plunkett, FAREWELL COMPANIONS

1977: Paul Scott, STAYING ON

1978: John Updike, THE COUP

1979: J. G. Ballard, THE UNLIMITED DREAM COMPANY

1979: Bernard Malamud, DUBIN'S LIVES

1979: V. S. Naipaul, A BEND IN THE RIVER

1979: William Styron, SOPHIE'S CHOICE

1980: Brian Aldiss, LIFE IN THE WEST

1980: Russell Hoban, RIDDLEY WALKER

1980: David Lodge, HOW FAR CAN YOU GO?

1980: John Kennedy Toole, A CONFEDERACY OF DUNCES

1981: Alasdair Gray, LANARK

1981: Paul Theroux, THE MOSQUITO COAST

1981: Gore Vidal, CREATION

1982: Robertson Davies, THE REBEL ANGELS

1983: Norman Mailer, ANCIENT EVENINGS

APPENDIX II

'If Your House was on Fire . . .'
An Informal Poll

IN HIS BOOK *I LIKE WHAT I KNOW: A VISUAL BIOGRAPHY*, THE
actor Vincent Price wrote: 'Everyone with possessions
plays the game of what you'd save in case of fire. New
Year's Eve, 1958, we had the chance of playing it for real
with a canyon brush fire that sent a hundred-foot wall of
flame within two hundred yards of our house. After we
had evacuated everything we could and finally were given
the welcome signal that everything was under control, I
emptied my pockets. Items: one nine-dollar jar of caviar,
one traffic ticket – and a two-and-a-half by two-and-a-half
inch oil, on ivory, by Goya.'

I asked some writers, collectors and friends with literary
leanings what book they would grab from their shelves if
their house was on fire and they could save only one.

These were the requirements:

(1) It must be a published book. No family albums,
address books, chequebooks, current manuscripts, etc.

(2) It should be irreplaceable – for reasons of rarity, sentimental value, inscription, binding.

(3) If possible, I wanted to know the edition and condition of the copy – not in detail, just, for example, 'The 1955 Putnam edition. It doesn't have a dust wrapper.'

It wasn't necessary to give reasons for the choice, though most contributors elected to do so.

Here are some of their responses. A few strayed outside the rules, but I didn't exclude them on that account.

Sue Baker
UKHQ buyer for Hammicks
Bates, H.E. **SUGAR FOR THE HORSE** (Michael Joseph, 1957)
'After falling in love with his Uncle Silas stories and especially the Edward Ardizzone illustrations, I found that there were many more stories available in this book which I have never seen available or reprinted. I had to have it traced, and eventually it was tracked down in South Africa, and over thirty-five years ago I found the price particularly painful on my minuscule wages. The book is without the dust jacket, fly spotted and water marked but it is one of my treasures. I shall reread it immediately.'

J.G. Ballard
Author (*The Drowned World*, *Crash*, *Empire of the Sun*)
Hemingway, Ernest **THE VIKING PORTABLE HEMINGWAY** (Viking Press, New York, 1944)
'This was the first adult book ever given to me, in 1945,

soon after leaving my Japanese internment camp near Shanghai. Superb introduction by Malcolm Cowley, which touches me as deeply now as it did my teenage self.'

Mark Barty-King
Chairman, Transworld Publishers

Wavell, A.P. (ed.) **OTHER MEN'S FLOWERS** (Jonathan Cape, 1944)

'My 1950 copy of *Other Men's Flowers*. This is an anthology of poetry collected by A. P. Wavell (Field Marshall Viscount Wavell) and first published by Jonathan Cape in 1944. Very much a boy's/young man's book, it's a little heavy on Kipling and Browning, but it has stood the test of time and never been out of print to my knowledge. Part of its charm are Wavell's soldierly introductions and notes to each section.

'My copy, which never had a jacket and is somewhat frayed as a result, was given to me as a reading prize in my last year at prep school, and is inscribed accordingly. It was, I think, the very first time I received a prize for doing what I loved to do!'

Anne Billson
Novelist (*Suckers*, *Stiff Lips*) and film critic (*The Thing*)

Searle, Ronald, and Willans, Geoffrey **DOWN WITH SKOOL** (Max Parrish, London, 1953)

Second edition with no dust jacket.

'I stole it from my brother many years ago. It is black with a white stain on the back (I dread to think what this might be, but it's somehow rather appropriate) and has a rather fabby Searle endpaper consisting of Molesworth's doodles of Spitfires, skulls and crossbones etc.

'These four books are my *vade mecum*. They contain pithy words of wisdom for every conceivable occasion. An alarming amount of Molesworthilia has lodged inexorably in my head and I used regularly to work quotes into my film column for the *Sunday Telegraph*, though the spelling mistakes were invariably corrected by diligent subs. But how better to describe Kenneth Branagh's *Hamlet* than as an "unweeded syllable"?

'I give you also "History started badly and hav been geting steadily worse"; "The whole business is unspeakably sordid"; "But Molesworth wot is the point of it?"; "You hav caught me, sir, like a treen in a disabled space ship"; "The french are slack" etc etc or rather ect ect: I could go on . . .'

Ray Bradbury
Author (*Fahrenheit 451, Something Wicked This Way Comes*) and scenarist (*Moby Dick*)
Shaw, George Bernard **PREFACES BY BERNARD SHAW** (Constable, London, 1934)
'Because he was the smartest playwright of the twentieth century, and the best playwright, and the prefaces to his plays were just as fascinating as the plays, and in some cases even better. A fantastic man, and a huge influence on my life.'

(Author's note: I was disappointed in a way that Ray

didn't choose the legendary limited edition of *Fahrenheit 451*, his story about a repressive future where all books are burned, and named for the temperature at which paper catches fire. When it published the first edition in 1953, Ballantine also produced 200 signed and numbered copies bound in Johns-Manville Quintera, a form of asbestos. It is therefore one of the few books likely to survive a fire – as well as being a rare example of a book dangerous to one's health. A first hardcover edition of *Fahrenheit 451* signed by Bradbury is worth $5,500. For a copy of the asbestos cover (none of which has come on the market in years) multiply by ten.)

Liz Calder
Publisher, Bloomsbury

'It has to be a tattered old copy of **ANNE OF GREEN GABLES** which my mother started reading to me and which I tore from her grip so as to read it myself . . . my first . . . it had the most beautiful colour plates which I used to pore over for hours and it gave me so many ideas of how I would like to be . . . a kind of combination of Anne and Diana, I suppose. It's a Harrap edition. No jacket but a frayed brownish cloth binding.'

Tim Curnow
Literary agent

Herbert, Xavier **POOR FELLOW MY COUNTRY** (William Collins, London, 1975)
Copy No. 9 of a limited edition of 150 copies, quarter

leatherbound, gold blocked title on spine plus slipcase and inscribed as follows: 'For Dear Tim, out of whose wiles it became a published book – and perhaps never would have otherwise, Xavier, at Curtis Brown, Paddington, Sydney, December 10, 1975.'

'This was the first major book deal I handled as a young literary agent and the 1463-page novel was published in England, the USA, translated into Italian, Japanese and Chinese and is still in print today. Just before my retirement the last major film deal I negotiated was for this novel – an option to Fox Searchlight Pictures in Los Angeles. For the author and the work I felt I made a difference and will treasure it as the most significant memento of a career in books. Also, it was a copy Xavier decided to give to me off his own bat as, generally, I did not ask clients to sign their book for me. If they wanted to themselves, that's fine.'

Harlan Ellison
Author (*Angry Candy*, *Shatterday*) and editor (*Dangerous Visions*)

Prokosch, Frederic, **THE SEVEN WHO FLED** (Harper & Sons, New York, 1937)
First edition. Inscribed by the author to Lady Emerald Cunard.

'It's one of my favourite books of all the thousands of books I've read, but also because it is a book to which I return again and again to be revivified by the excellence, the gorgeousness, the passion of the writing. That one book has probably taught me more about how to write than any other book I've read.'

John Foyster
Critic, science-fiction historian

'It is so much more pleasant to think about what book
one might at some future time rescue in case of fire
than to reflect upon what did happen thirty-five years
ago, when my house *did* burn, with my library inside.

'For a start, fires often occur when the occupants are
not at home. So it is not so much a matter of deciding
what book to choose as it is of looking at the sorry pile
that others have rescued. Only in the owner's eye is it a
sorry pile; what the firefighters have done is rush into
the only room not already engulfed in flames and
picked up what could be reached and taken as
mementos for the absentee occupants.

'Of course you know that your own choices would
have been so much more appropriate! But no one could
have known that that bottle on the shelf was the bottle
of VAT 69 that Sarah Vaughan, unaided, had
consumed back in late '65. And no one else could know
which books matter most.

'Should the book be "unique" – one of a kind because
of some characteristic acquired after leaving the
publisher? Or should it be "important" to you?

'Books, as word-containers, can often be replaced; if
not with the same edition, then at least another edition.
One of the many books that vanished thirty-five years
ago from my collection, **HOW TO READ ENGLISH
POETRY** by R. H. Blyth, is not easy to replace.

'Blyth is rather better known for his collections of haiku that, like **HOW TO READ ENGLISH POETRY**, were published by Hokuseido Press. This little book goes in the other direction, bringing English poetry to Japanese-born readers, and it goes without saying that rather than providing deep thoughts about literary theory, this is a manual on how to utter poetry in English. In his preface Blyth gives his motivation for writing the book explicitly, "I have an idea that the entrance examination to Heaven is a reading aloud of poetry," and this is his crammer.

'I tried to replace the book for many years, with not the slightest sign of success, although almost all of Blyth's other books are easy to find.

'When second-hand booksellers began listing their stocks on the Internet I thought I would succeed, but I could not see a copy anywhere. But almost everything else ever published became easy to find; when I sent a list of Lafcadio Hearn items to a Hearn collector friend, I added a note indicating that I was glad he had such easy access to Hearn items while I could not find just one book, Blyth's **HOW TO READ ENGLISH POETRY**. A week later a small brown parcel arrived, containing a copy of the first and probably the only edition of **HOW TO READ ENGLISH POETRY**. "I picked it up in a university book sale," said Bob.

'So this will be the first book I pick up in case of fire – having failed to do so at an earlier opportunity. After all, if I study it thoughtfully I might succeed at Heaven's entrance examination.'

Patrick Janson-Smith

Joint Managing Director, Transworld Publishers

Poe, Edgar Allan, **SELECTED POEMS,** selected by J. Potter Briscoe, FRSL (Gay & Hancock, London, 1910)

'A slim, small-format (approx. 2" x 4") edition (no dust wrapper), in well-thumbed but otherwise reasonable condition (just a stain – a cup mark? – on the front cover). I bought it in the late 60s for the princely sum of 3/6d (17.5p) and I used to carry it around in my jacket pocket on walks up from South Kensington, where I then lived, to Hyde Park and Kensington Gardens, taking it out and reading from it aloud when the fancy took me – *"We loved with a love that was more than love, I and my ANNABEL LEE ..."*; *"Once upon a midnight dreary, which I pondered weak and weary, over many a quaint and curious volume of forgotten lore ..."* – oh, how romantic it was and oh, how I adored the feel and the smell of that little book. I have it still, and I love it still; of no intrinsic value, but one of my most treasured possessions.'

Charrière, Henri, **PAPILLON**, translated by Patrick O'Brian (Hart Davis, London, 1970)

First edition, with dust wrapper designed by Stephen Abis, price 36s (£1.80).

Inscription, dated 18/5/70: *'Patrick – merci jeune Patrick de ton opinion de mon livre – merci d'être venu. Vive ta jeunesse et ta joie dans la vie. Papillon.'*

Jonathan Lloyd
Literary agent

'For family and no doubt financial reasons, it would have to be **OLIVER TWIST**. This is in three volumes published by Richard Bentley, New Burlington Street, 1838. The spines: Oliver Twist BOZ. Title page: Oliver Twist by Charles Dickens, author of The Pickwick Papers in three volumes.

'At the end of the book there is an ad for other titles, published price 6s, "and it will thus be placed within the means of the great body of English readers". The works which form the Standard Library being the copyright of Mr Bentley!

'These volumes were left to my wife, Marion, by her father Peter Dickens who was the great, great grandson of Charles. We have no evidence that they were in the original possession of the author but we like to think so! If only Dickens were still in copyright! I'd like to think he would have enjoyed having a literary agent.'

Jane Mays
Literary editor, *Daily Mail*

'A heavily annotated (in schoolgirl hand) and now somewhat foxed copy of **POETRY OF THE THIRTIES**, introduced and edited by Robin Skelton (Penguin, 1967, reprint, 5/-). This was an A-level text taught by an inspired English mistress in the 1960s which introduced me to the wonders – and anxieties – of Auden, MacNeice, Spender, Ewart, Empson et al and unlocked a lifelong enthusiasm for poetry old and new.'

Edmund Naughton
Author (*McCabe*, *The Maximum Game*)
'**A CIRCLE OF ACID**. The manuscript of a novel I wrote about twenty years ago. It was never published. The theme is incest. As the French say, "Better in the same town, better in the same street, better in the same house, better in the same family."'

Kim Newman
Fantasy author (*Bad Dreams*, *The Night Mayor*) and film historian (*Nightmare Movies*)
'After much thought, I'm afraid the embarrassing answer is that I'd probably take one of my own books – the bound proof or first edition of **ANNO DRACULA** (Simon & Schuster, 1992) or the hard-to-find first edition of **NIGHTMARE MOVIES**. The true first is from Proteus; came out in 1985, a week before the publisher went bust, sold out instantly, royalties sucked into void. It's rare, but the completely revised and much-expanded Bloomsbury edition is the preferred text. The reason is that thanks to insurance I could afford to replace almost everything I own, but I'd feel a real clot laying out serious money for something of mine.'

Charles Edward Pogue
Screenwriter (*The Fly*, *Dragonheart*, *D.O.A.*)
'With six thousand books, it's tough to choose. I suspect

it would be one of my two British first editions of **SHE** by H. Rider Haggard. It's in great condition with only a slight shelf cock to it. It's probably not the most valuable book in my collection (there is, for instance, a first edition **TARZAN OF THE APES** with Edgar Rice Burroughs' autograph tipped in), but it is my favourite book of all time, a book I re-read periodically, and a book that speaks to me on a very primal level. Haggard stirs deep waters. I have probably thirty other editions of this one title in my collection.'

Michael Prodger
Deputy Literary Editor, *Sunday Telegraph*
'**THE BOOK OF BLOKES** by William Nicholson, published by Faber & Faber in 1929 and priced 2/6d, is utterly inconsequential and utterly charming. It comprises twenty-nine caricature male heads in crayon – many formed from a single line without the pencil ever lifting from the paper – which were originally drawn as bedtime treats for Nicholson's daughter Liza. My presentation copy has a cracked spine and is inscribed "For Jimmy from William N July 1933". But the only printed words in this little book are the dedication – "To Max (Beerbohm, of course)".'

Yvonne Rousseau
Author and critic (*The Murders at Hanging Rock*)
'With the flames at my door – no chance to rescue more than one book – I would rush for a slim volume bound

in wine-coloured (pinot noir or burgundy) leatherette, its spine amateurishly mended with cloth tape in a dried-blood shade. It is the 1954 edition of Francis Turner Palgrave's **THE GOLDEN TREASURY** (1861) – "the best songs and lyrical poems in the English language" – enlarged and introduced by C. Day Lewis. The half-title page is inscribed in emphatic Indian ink: "Leongatha High School/Poetry Prize/ – 1957 – / Yvonne Rousseau".

'Twelve years old in 1957, I was shocked and incredulous when the success of my energetic poem "The Brumby" was announced at the school Speech Night, at the end of my first year of secondary school. The sixth-form winner of the companion short-story prize, announced at the same time, had only just finished collecting a sports award, and was therefore back on stage to receive her literary prize almost instantly. This left everybody waiting for me to rise from my seat and traverse the seemingly endless aisles of the Leongatha Memorial Hall. General laughter ensued, when my anxious alacrity created the impression of a small skinny person single-mindedly avid for her loot.

'Safely hidden from the public gaze again, I found in this volume hours of enthralment, year after year: Algernon Charles Swinburne's "As a god self-slain on his own strange altar, / Death lies dead"; William Blake's "Tyger! Tyger! burning bright / In the forests of the night"; Roy Campbell's "Harnessed with level rays in golden reins, / The zebras draw the dawn across the plains"; Thomas Hood's "One more Unfortunate / Weary of breath, / Rashly importunate, / Gone to her death!"; Emily Brontë's "Cold in the earth, and fifteen wild Decembers / From those brown hills have melted into spring –"; Edith Sitwell's "the amber dust that was a rose / Or nymph in swan-smooth waters"; and Walter de la Mare's uncanny assurance that "all things thou wouldst praise / Beauty took from those who loved them / In other days". In addition, thanks to the "Glossary of Poetic Terms", I could genuinely savour James Thurber's portrait (in "A New Natural History") of "A Trochee (left) encountering a Spondee".

'This edition is not the currently available Palgrave's – which I could not bear to buy, even at bargain price, during recent months of craving when my own edition was temporarily mislaid. But the physical copy itself is the thing: imbued (if for me alone) with recollections of Keatsian solace, in my youthful silently fierce rebellion against 1950s rural Australia. My **TREASURY** conclusively demonstrated another world and other imaginations – such as, indeed, joyously welcomed me at the University of Melbourne, where I matriculated in 1963 with the financial aid of a Commonwealth Scholarship. Equally deeply, however, this leatherette-bound copy is imbued with my youthful aspirations to poetry: treasured in memory, though never to be realized.

'By 1961, when a poem of mine won the annual Senior Commonwealth Literary Award offered by the

Australian Broadcasting Commission's radio club, the Argonauts – I felt that I had already lost my way in poetry. The award was not to blame: at least one subsequent winner (Michael Dransfield, in 1963 and 1964) matured (though too briefly) into an adult poet. By contrast, I continued secretively dithering (in a poetic sense) at university, where the poets among my lecturers and tutors included Vincent Buckley (subsequently commemorated by the Vincent Buckley Poetry Prize, alternating between Australian and Irish poets). Commenting in 1964 on a too-impressionistic examination paper of mine, Buckley allowed that, nevertheless, my observations about William Blake had inspired him to wonder whether I, too, practised the art of poetry. With a wild hope of salvation by professional guidance, I began to explain that I used to write poems when I was younger ... "Oh!" Vincent Buckley interrupted, dismissively (and I continue to accept his dismissal of my poetic vocation): "Which of us doesn't write poems when we are young?" I am sorry, however, that I was not equipped at that time to counter with G. K. Chesterton's damnation of his friend George Bernard Shaw: "Mr Shaw is (I suspect) the only man on earth who has never written any poetry."'

Walter Satterthwait
Crime novelist (*Miss Lizzie*, *Wilde West*, *Masquerade*)
'I'd save my old copy of **LOLITA**. It's a battered fifth impression of the Putnam edition, without a dust jacket, and it has no real intrinsic value. But when I

first read it at the age of fourteen, it changed my life by showing me that writing could be something more than simple storytelling.'

Iain Sinclair
Novelist (*White Chappell, Scarlet Tracings*, *Radon Daughters*), poet and bookseller

'You know that such a choice is impossible. I'd either, arms full, go down with the flaming hulk, or walk away in relief, the burden of curation (ownership, jealousy, library of the city and the mind) laid aside.

'One book I might slip into my pocket – since it arrived by accident – is **FATHERS AND SONS**. Translated from the Russian, with the approval of the author, by Eugene Schuyler, Ph.D. (n.d., Ward Lock and Co., London, New York and Melbourne), 248 pp. Dark blue cloth, lettered in gilt. Hinges starting. Some light foxing. A decent copy which has obviously been read.

'The first edition in English was published in 1867. This appears to be an undistinguished latecomer. There is an ownership signature on the front fixed endpaper. "Jessie Chambers, May, 1910". The book once belonged to the Jessie Chambers who was the model for Miriam in D. H. Lawrence's *Sons and Lovers* ("Fathers and Sons . . . "Sons and Lovers"). This copy was presented to Jessie Chambers by Lawrence. See *D. H. Lawrence: A Personal Record* by E.T. (1935) page 121. (The quote from Jessie's memoir does send a shiver down the spine. "He liked Turgenev immensely, and gave me his copy of *Fathers and Sons*, and impressed on me that I must read *Rudin* . . . When he sent me a book he would occasionally copy out a verse, or even a whole poem . . .")

'I happened to be in Nottingham when the cache of Lawrence/Chambers material came to light and was given, pretty much at random, this book, for helping in humping the tea-chests across the road to the bookshop.

'What I like is the everyday nature of the volume, the kind of book you could pick up anywhere, and its secret history. It would go alongside a pocket edition of Henry James's *Daisy Miller*, which turned out to be heavily annotated by the author. And an uncommon book of poetry by W. S. Graham with several lines rewritten in trial versions which have never appeared elsewhere.'

William Jay Smith
Poet (*Venice in the Fog*, *The Traveler's Tree*) and memoirist (*Army Brat*)

Stevens, Wallace, **PARTS OF A WORLD** (Knopf, New York, 1942. First edition)

'My copy, in which I had written my name when I bought it, has no dust jacket, and the binding and many of the pages show the effects of long exposure to dampness. When I went in July 1942 as a young naval officer to serve at the air station on Palmyra Island, a thousand miles south-west of Honolulu, this is one of the only books I took with me and I read it through many times during my four months on the tiny atoll. For me it had all the wit and gusto of the French symbolist poets, particularly Jules Laforgue, whom I had been reading. I took to heart the admonition at the conclusion of the first poem: "Piece the world together boys, but not with your hands." I began to put together the parts of *my* world in a series of poems that in 1945 won a prize from *Poetry* magazine. Two years later they appeared in my first book, a copy of which I sent to Wallace Stevens, and they met with his warm approval. I possess other first editions of Stevens, volumes that are in better condition and would bring higher prices, but the worth of this one to me is beyond measure.'

Colin Steele
Librarian, Australian National University
Gunn, Mrs Aeneas, **WE OF THE NEVER NEVER**
(Robertson & Mullens, Melbourne, 1954)
Signed limited edition.
'I was tossing up between my Sir Donald Bradman signed autobiography, and my early Terry Pratchett with rude words about a librarian, but having just visited the Northern Territory and Elsey Station and living in Elsey Street, I decided on this classic of Australian literature. First published in 1908, it tells the story of the newly married Jeannie Gunn and her travels with her husband to a remote cattle station (Elsey Station) in the Northern Territory in 1902. The venture claimed the life of her husband after a year. Gunn returned to Victoria to write this epic story of human endurance, spirit, comradeship and the relationship with the Aborigines in a geographically

isolated environment. I live in Elsey Street, Canberra, named after the Elsey Station, and a visit to the reconstructed settlement this year brought home the epic struggles of the early pioneers. The signature of Jeannie Gunn adds to associations of this item.'

Lucy Sussex
Novelist (*The Scarlet Rider*, *My Lady Tongue and Other Tales*)
Various, **THE BIBLE IN MINIATURE** (E. Newbury, London, 1780)
'It is literally tiny, 3 x 4.5 centimetres, less than an inch thick, but beautifully bound in red morocco with elaborate gold tooling. Maybe it was for a Georgian babyhouse, as I can't imagine anyone reading it. It lives in my own dollhouse, which once belonged to the Horlicks family (yea, verily, the night starvation mob). Why I would save it – it is probably irreplaceable, a thing of beauty in its small self. I could put it in my pocket and climb down a fireladder. And also, as I discovered when employed by the C18th imprints project, E. Newbury was Elizabeth, a widow, operating her late husband's printing business from the corner of St Paul's churchyard. That pleases me.'

Jessie Tilley
Publisher
King, Stephen, **WORLDLY REMAINS, CYCLE OF THE WEREWOLF, THE LAND OF ENCHANTMENT** (Christopher Zavisa, New York, 1983)

Trade hardcover edition. Dust cover. Illustrations by Berni Wrightson. Personalized autograph from Wrightson.

'This book was a gift from my family one Christmas. Whatever its current value, as a sentimental offering, I admit I've been unable to part with it through the years, though I've been offered considerable sums. And now with Berni's signature, I think it's here to stay.'

Robert Violette
Publisher (*The Words of Gilbert and George*, *Louise Bourgeois*, *Let Us Now Praise Famous Men*)

Dickens, Charles, **AMERICAN NOTES** and **PICTURES FROM ITALY** (Chapman & Hall Limited, London, and Henry Frowde, n.d.)

With six illustrations by Maurice Greiffenhagen. One of twenty-two unnumbered volumes in the Fireside Edition of the *Complete Works of Charles Dickens*. 192 pages. Crown 8vo, limited edition. Half-bound green Persian leather with green cloth sides, Japanese endpapers, gilt top, gold-and-green head- and tailbands. Gilt tooling on front, back and spine. Leather on spine slightly faded. Good condition. Original published price: 5s.

'Pathological as I am about what I publish, I just couldn't see myself risking life and limb to retrieve any book, unless I possessed a Caxton-printed folio, a unique last-remaining *Surrealist Manifesto*, or something truly irreplaceable, where I'd be doing humanity a service (unlikely). Most of my books, even the out-of-print artists' books (*Warhol Index*, etc.) are available on the secondary market. It would be a crying shame to see them burn, but they are not unique. I have two full drawers of signed and inscribed editions, but those again wouldn't be worth risking my neck for. Even the ones with personal notes from the late and great. But, still wanting to play the game, and assuming it would be on my way OUT of, not back into, a fire, I'd grab the Dickens.

'Chapter IV ("An American Railroad. Lowell and Its Factory System"; pp. 72-85) concerns Dickens' 1842 visit to Lowell, Massachusetts, my home town. Though established only twenty-one years before Dickens' tour of America, Lowell was already famous for its textile mills and their proprietors' progressive attitudes towards manufacture and employment. Notable passage: "Lowell is a large, populous, thriving place. Those indications of its youth which first attract the eye, give it a quaintness and oddity of character which, to a visitor from the old country, is amusing enough." (A true enough description too, perhaps, of Lowell's infamous artist-progeny James McNeil Whistler and, much later, Jack Kerouac.) Seventh anniversary present from my wife, Sandy Violette, inscribed in pencil on front endpaper: "To Bob, After seven years I still love you! Sx 10.10.95". And now? Still married, only Sandy's even more incredulous.'

Bill Warren
Film historian (*Keep Watching the Skies*, *The Evil Dead Companion*)

Heinlein, Robert A., **STRANGER IN A STRANGE LAND** (Putnam/Book of the Month Club, New York, 1961) Vg in dw. Inscribed by Heinlein.

'Towards the end of his life, Heinlein, whose life was saved by a blood transfusion, used only to sign books if the owner could produce a recent blood donation certificate, and then only at conventions where a blood drive was going on. When he signed this book for me, in 1961, it was well before the surgery.

'When I met with (book dealer) Barry Levin to help a friend sell the Gnome Press and other such books her father left her, out of curiosity I asked him about the signed book club *Stranger*. Very amusing reaction: "Well, it's a Book Club edition, so it's worthless. But wait, that's a *long* Heinlein inscription; very rare. So it's worth something. No, wait, it's a Book Club edition – but it's signed – but it's a Book Club edition . . ." He finally gave up trying to evaluate it.'

David Williamson
Playwright (*Don's Party*, *Sanctuary*, *Dead White Males*) and screenwriter (*Gallipoli*, *The Last Bastion*)

'The book I'd probably grab is a simple paperback, **GET SHORTY**, signed by Elmore Leonard when I met him in Adelaide. I think he's the prince of crime writers and he was such a pleasant guy to talk to.'

Mel Yarker
UKHQ buyer for Borders

'My choice has to be my signed copy of Salman

Rushdie's **MIDNIGHT'S CHILDREN**. It's the twentieth-century equivalent to a signed copy of *David Copperfield*.'

And a postscript from playwright Hans-Peter Litscher: 'A friend of mine got a phone call from a friend of his, a book collector, who told him in total panic that his house was on fire. My friend first thought that this was a joke but when he heard several fire trucks and their sirens, he ran over to his friend's house. All the book collector's friends were busy running in and out of the burning house, taking each time as many books as they could grab. There was only one person who did not participate in the whole operation: the book collector himself. He was standing in his apartment and hesitating what to do because he could not make his mind up which books he should take and which therefore he would leave behind him.'

APPENDIX III

eBay Gems

THE LAUNCHING OF THE INTERNET AUCTION SITE EBAY.COM IN 1995 opened the door to new buyers and sellers from all over the world who could suddenly trade in a commodity which, for generations, had been regarded as too arcane for the punter in the street.

These newcomers brought a fresh vitality to book collecting – an energy that was not always matched with an understanding of what made a book or paper item collectable, nor with a sure grasp of spelling and grammar.

The following were culled from eBay entries. Spelling, punctuation, etc., are as posted.

....

1837 Directory of Leeds, England – AWESOME!!

....

Autographed programme Jumper's London's National Theatre (1972) signed by Diana Rigg, Michael Hordern, Anna Carteret, Tom Stoppard. When I asked Mr Stoppard what the play was about he said "It's about making money." Contains photos and interview with Stoppard.

....

~Dr Jekyl & Mr Hyde~ Conversation Piece! Dr Jekyl and Mr Hyde Kidnapped by Robert Louis Stevenson Palmoral Edition MCMXXX.

This book definitely shows signs of wear. The cover corner edges are curled. Spline is softened and worn. Binding inside the front caver is damaged: paper has tear approximately 1 1/5" long starting at the bottom of the page. Cloth under binding paper is intact and visible. The front cover has several indents in it.

While this doesn't impair the reading, there is also a hole straight through the book. It doesn't show in the scan, but it starts on the outside of the front cover and goes through to the outside of the back cover. The hole appears to be some kind of bore hole similar to what you could find in a wormy apple. Maybe Book Worms are real?

....

Ernest Heimining A farewell to Arms. 314 Pgs. Item #337700480
Description: A Farewell to Arms. By Ernest Heminingway-1957–314 Pgs. Good Condition.

....

Old German Pocket size translator for different languages. Hardcover book, the cover paper is peeled off so I do not have a title. Owner has written translations inside front cover. On the first inside page I can read Philedelphia, im September 1849,

413

Uuguft Clafer, lebrer und Weberfeze der englifchen Eprache. The title of the first page reads: Nurze, leichtfakliche Grammatil. 285 pages. If I had to guess I would say that this book belonged to someone who came to America from Germany . . .

....

A 1-OF-A-KIND! 'Leaves of Life' by Elizabeth Baigert, c. 1969, Published by Vantage Press, First Edition, signed 'To Alma A. Rohe, "Best Wishes" Elizabeth Braigert'. 64 pages – 81 poems. I've included a page of poems – not the worst, believe me. I've also included the bio on the back of the DJ. I especially enjoyed the part about her hobbies. The DJ has a small bit of wear on the spine top and some marks on the back, but is in very good condition. The covers and interior pages are in excellent condition; unfortunately, better than the poems. (The yellow tinges are my scanner, not the book.)

These are honestly among the worst poems I've seen. This book can bring hours of enjoyment, reading to yourself or to your friends – guaranteed groans of pleasure!! Maybe a gift for someone you dislike?? Seriously, it's hard to believe you'll ever see another one.

....

This book is in fair condition for it's age. Copyright A. C. McClurg & CO. 1918. There's a few stains on a couple of the pages. Including some yellowing from age I would assume. Last page number is 348 with unknown pages missing. Spine is becoming loose, would assume that is how the unknown pages fell out. Book definately shows it's age. Please bid accordingly!

....

This old book titled 'Fern Leaves' from Fanny's Portfolio Second series was copyrighted in 1853 and published in 1854. There are 400 pages. A name was written inside the front cover dated May 1857, almost looks as if it was written with a quill pen. The cover is embossed and title is in gold which is almost all faded away. The blank pages inside the front & rear covers are yellowed but the pages of the book are still white. The covers are not warped but the pages seem to be, yet there are no signs of water or water marks. The binding and pages are solid and intact. Hard to believe when the book is 146 years old. My wife said it doesn't smell like some old books do. My smeller doesn't work so I rely on her.

....

ALEX HALEY SINGED 1st Ed. - 'ROOTS' - HB w/DJ

....

WILD HORES by Dick Francis Item #281358840

....

Definitely a masterpiece – and unique to boot. The Yale Shakespeare, The Complete Works, Bound Upside Down, Editors Wilbur L. Cross & Tucker Brooke. This book is great. It is hard bound in nice off-white cloth covers. This book was published under the direction of the Department of English, Yale University. The uniqueness of this book is that it is bound upside down. If you open what should be the front cover, it opens to page 1517 which is upside down. This is definitely a collector's piece.

....

Renoir, My Father, By His Daughter Jean,L@@K! Item
#281698737

....

'The Adam and Eve Guide to Sexual Pleasure' by Pat Littlewood,
book was never opened. 'California Nanny' by Victoria Parker, book
is unread. 'Power Positions' mini-magazine featuring several
shots of men and women engaged in sex in like new condition ...

....

... It was published in 1980 by Bruccoli Clark Publishers,
Bloomfield Hills, Michigan. Binding: Natural Buckram (a
gorgeous, rough cloth), with the author's signature stamped in
guilt.

....

First, I am not sure this is a first edition, so please, do not beat up
on me. This is The Art and Thought of Thomas Hardy, On A
Darkling Plain by Harvey Curtis Webster. Inside the front cover,
on the dust jacket is a price of $3.50. This book is published by
The University of Chicago Press and has green boards with gold
lettering ... Now, for the strange thing. Inside the front cover on
the first clean page is the inscription in blue ink: 'To Bob Hagel –
My favourite book, <u>though I like other things too</u>, by George
Liberace'

....

I really know nothing about this book I am selling it for my
mother it is a paperback a rather large paperback and it says
Vicking on it.

....

Item 181447475. RARE 1821 FRENCH LETTERS Full Leather Vol. 2

....

I am not sure of the value of this old book, so I will give you all of the info I possibly can and let you decide if it's of value! This is a hardcover of Noel Coward's play 'Cavalcade'. On the bottom of the title page, it says 'Garden City, New York, Doubleday, Doran & Company, Inc. MCMXXXIII'. I have determined that the Roman Numerals equal 1933 (perhaps this is the date of printing?)

....

This is a very unique blank book. It is made of cork and is in excellent condition. The cover and all of the pages are made of cork. This would probably make a great scrapbook or anything else you could think of to do with it.

....

This is a black and white photo signed by artist HENRY MOORE. Moore, an English artist, is best known for his sculpture of 'The Thinker'.

....

Buyer is to include $4.00 for s\h. Video will ship with a sense of vigour and certitude with a money order, or with a vague sense of torpor and anomie with a personal check. Thanks!

....